The Healing Craft

Dedicated to: Sandy Brock, Cate Dalton, Lhianna Sidhe, Charmaine, Susa Morgan Black, Avilynn Pwyll, the International Order of the Red Pentacle, and all the other witches on the wards.

The Healing Craft

Healing Practices For Witches
and Pagans

Janet and Stewart Farrar
and Gavin Bone, RGN

With line illustrations by Glenn Tyler

Phoenix Publishing

By the same authors:
The Pagan Path

By Janet & Stewart Farrar:
The Witches' Goddess
The Witches' God
Spells, And How They Work
Eight Sabbats for Witches
The Witches' Way
The Witches' Bible

By Stewart Farrar:
What Witches Do

PHOENIX PUBLISHING, INC.
P.O. Box 3829
Blaine, Washington USA 98231
www.phoenixpublishing.com

Distributed in the U.K. by
ROBERT HALE LTD.
45-47 Clerkenwell Green
London EC1R 0HT

ISBN 0-919345-18-2

Cover design by Creative Circus

Printed in the U.S.A.

Contents

Illustrations

Introduction

Why a book on healing, specifically for witches and pagans? There are many publications already on the market dealing with herbalism from a Wiccan viewpoint, but there are none that deal with the subject of healing in its entirety. In fact, there are very few books at all that deal with spiritual healing and how to use the chakras and the aura therapeutically.

We believe it is impossible to divorce the practice of healing, in its myriad of forms, from its origins in shamanistic and premono-theistic cultures. Chapter 1 elaborates on this idea. Logically, this connection with healing must apply to the current renaissance of paganism and witchcraft. Today's interest in alternative or complementary therapies is prompting an influx of books on individual aspects of the subject. Many of these therapies are very old, and were known to the village witch and cunning man. This book ties these practices together, providing an overview of healing from pagan holistic eyes.

Today's pagans show a heightened awareness for the current ecological crisis, but apart from the HIV and AIDS problem, many are unaware of the growing crisis in the world of medicine. The effectiveness of antibiotics against the threat of epidemics is receding. In the United States, diseases of yesteryear, such as bubonic plague, are rearing their ugly heads again. Antibiotic-resistant "super bugs" such as *staphylococcus aureus* are on the increase, due mainly to the overuse of antibiotics in the past few decades. Although most of these bacteria and viruses are not life threatening, many epidemiologists are worried that before long there will be lethal hybrids with tuberculosis, cholera and smallpox.

At first, the relationship between the medical and the ecological crisis may not be apparent, but from a spiritual and holistic viewpoint they both stem from man's separation from nature. Pagans are aware of this and realize that the unification of mind and body allows greater resistance to disease and increases the ability to care for Mother Earth more effectively. If individuals are unbalanced,

7

regardless of whether they are stressed physically or mentally, they will become myopic and unable to see beyond their own immediate physical needs as we point out in chapter 2.

Pagans and Wiccans are realists, and see the importance of working in cooperation with modern medical science. They also realize the great strides that modern medicine has made in making the human condition more bearable. Doctors and nurses go through years of rigorous training before they can practice the healing arts, and their professions have rigorous codes of ethics. Chapter 3 considers the ethics involved in healing, whether medical, nursing or spiritual.

Understanding how the human body works is vital to anyone involved in healing, whether spiritual or medical, so chapter 4 deals with the basics of human anatomy and physiology, while chapter 5 looks at the current psychological theories on the workings of the mind and how these can be applied by the healer.

To completely explain how the body and mind work would take several volumes; we have drawn a simple outline of the physical and mental functions for the reader to follow. The same also applies to all the therapies and healing practices we have included in this book. We recommend further reading on these subjects to anyone seriously interested in practicing healing (see bibliography).

Chapter 6 is one of the most interesting from a healer's point of view. In this we look at the different theories on the makeup of the individual's psychic and spiritual body. This chapter deals with the body's energy centers and how they are interpreted by different cultures, from the Hindu chakra system to the Cabala. We also cover the structure of the human aura, and how both the aura and the energy centers relate to the physical body and the mind.

The remaining chapters deal with specific techniques, from chakric healing to herbalism. We have included many methods which are traditional to western paganism, and some that are not. In chapter 11, Holistic Massage, we also discuss the use of aromatherapy. One of the tenets of modern Wicca has always been "If it works, use it!" Many pagans and Wiccans have adopted New Age healing therapies such as these, but unlike many involved in the New Age movement, the pagans tend to be more realistic about the capabilities and limitations of their use. In the end, the most important thing is to heal the individual and not to become pedantic about the origins of healing techniques.

Our intention was to create a book useful to pagans on a practical and intellectual level, but we hope it will find a place with all involved in the healing arts. There is a growing interest in complementary or alternative medicine, not only with the general public, but also among doctors and nurses. Gavin has found himself using aromatherapy and massage while working as a registered nurse, and personal experience has shown that many in the medical and nursing professions have a serious interest in the practical use of alternative therapies. In one establishment, lavender oil has successfully replaced the benzodiazepine-based night sedation among some of the patients. This resulted in savings on pharmaceutical bills, and more importantly, the eradication of the harmful side effects of the drugs that the lavender replaced.

We would like to make it clear that the primary source of material for this book has been Gavin. As a qualified staff nurse, he has medical and psychiatric experience to which he has added the other aspects covered here. Janet and Stewart's contributions have been editorial and research, plus their own quarter-century of Wiccan experience.

Janet & Stewart Farrar
and Gavin Bone
Ireland, 1999

1

The History of Healing Within Paganism
and Witchcraft

From a historical perspective, it is impossible to separate the beginnings of medicine from the pagan healing practices of our ancestors. This is evident to anyone who has read the Hippocratic oath, the oath of ethics taken on entering the medical profession (see page 38).

The first written records on the use of herbs and magic for healing come from the Middle Eastern cultures, but there is little doubt among historians that the practice of herbalism, often combined with magical rites, goes back to our paleolithic ancestors. This is borne out by studies of modern hunter-gatherer tribes, such as the Kalahari Bushmen, and from archaeological discoveries in Iraq. These point to Neanderthal man using marshmallow, groundsel and yarrow as far back as 60,000 years ago.

Gathered round a campfire and surrounded by darkness, our ancestors would have seen the world very differently from how we see it today. The darkness would have hidden malign spirits, who sought to harm members of the tribe. Illness and disease would have been seen as the manifestation of these attacks. In a hunter-gatherer tribe, continually on the move, it would have been the women's role to collect fruit, nuts and vegetables, while the men hunted the plains.

If one of the tribe was ill, one woman would have been responsible for collecting the right herbs during the food-gathering expeditions. She would have gained experience of which herbs to use by watching what animals ate when they were ill and what effect this had, and from what she had been taught by her predecessor, most likely her mother. Because of her knowledge, she would also have been responsible for looking after the needs of women during childbirth, and would have known the right herbs to use to ease the pains of pregnancy. In a very real sense she can be considered as the first witch, with her knowledge of herbs and the women's mystery of birth.

Because evil spirits attacked at night, the herbal remedy would have been administered at twilight, with a ritual to banish any malign entity. The tribal medicine- or spirit-man would then ritually dance around the campfire, to the awe and expectation of the rest of the tribe, symbolically grappling and wrestling with the spirit until it submitted to his will, leaving the ill person in peace. Such practices as these continue today, unchanged over the millennia. Many Native Americans still follow them, as do the peoples of the South American rain forests and the East Indies. They are generally categorized as forms of shamanism––the use of self-induced trance states. The modern practices of Voudon, Santeria and Macumba all include shamanistic forms of healing.

The earliest recorded use of herbs originates from the Sumerians, who inhabited the areas of the Euphrates and Tigris rivers about 4,000 B.C. Clay tablets listed the use of various herbs, including opium and liquorice as well as sulfur. Most information about medical practices in ancient pagan culture comes from discoveries in Egypt.

One of these, the Ebers Papyrus, housed in the Leipzig library, was found in 1873. It is believed to date from the sixteenth century B.C., and lists over 800 recipes, which include the use of aloe, hemp, castor oil and mandragora. It explains how to prepare them as decoctions, wines, and infusions, as well as pills and salves. There is also evidence within the papyrus that the Egyptians were using antibiotic remedies; one of these consisted of moldy bread (penicillin) on an open wound to prevent infection.

What most archaeologists consider to be the most interesting papyrus was found by Edwin Smith. It is dated as being over 3,600 years old, and is more than 16 feet in length. It lists over 48 surgical operations, and includes a comprehensive study of anatomy and physiology, which points to the Egyptians being aware of the role of the central nervous system in limb control. They were also familiar with the circulatory system, and talked of the heart "speaking in every limb."

Herodotus, the Greek scholar, noted that the Egyptian people were one of the healthiest he had come across. They were well aware of the importance of maintaining good health, particularly with relation to their diet; there was no evidence of cancer, and dental decay did not appear until the last few centuries of Egyptian history. In one papyrus it is somewhat ironically noted:

"Most of what we eat is superfluous. Thus we only live off a quarter of all we swallow; doctors live off the other three-quarters."

We know that the Egyptians considered medicine so important that they were willing to mount expeditions to discover new remedies. Queen Hatshepsut, the renowned woman Pharaoh, was financing such expeditions about the same time that the Ebers Papyrus was written. Many high-born individuals were buried with medicine chests for their future life.

Apart from herbalism, there is also evidence that they were aware of energy healing. Statues found by archaeologists show the use of one hand on the stomach and one on the back: the classic pose of the spiritual healer. There is little evidence to support this hypothesis, but if true it is likely that they had a developed system similar to the Hindu chakras. Most herbal and physical treatments in ancient Egypt were reinforced with charms, incantations and libations to Isis, Thoth or Imhotep, their specific healing deities (see page 126, chapter 8). The view that disease was caused by malign spirits had changed little since the Stone Age, and the priest maintained his role as the principle healer.

The question is: what happened to all this medical knowledge? European civilization was not to reach the same level of sophistication until the seventeenth century, and the extent of Egyptian knowledge did not become evident until the great archeological excavations of the nineteenth century. Most was lost with the fall of the Egyptian Empire, and with the destruction of the Great Library of Alexandria.

What did survive had been adopted by the blossoming Greek civilization through the work of scholars. According to Herodotus, the Greeks learned many of their religious customs and associated healing arts directly from the Egyptians. As evidence he cites the existence of temples of Egyptian deities in Greece; Isis had a magnificent temple at Pithorea, and Serapis one at Athens. But more importantly, alongside Plato, Socrates and Euphrides, he states that it was the mystical figure of Orpheus, who lived approximately 1,500 B.C., who was responsible for bringing the wisdom of Egyptian healing and magic to the Greeks.

The Greeks have a long history of using the magical arts for healing purposes. As with the Egyptians, medicine and healing was one of the major preoccupations of their priestly caste. These priesthoods were modeled very much after the Egyptians, being kept in the hands of one family or group of men and women, and practiced in the temples. Many of their temples were dedicated to Aesculapius, the god of healing, who like Imhotep was probably once a human healer who became deified. His symbol of the snake entwined around a staff is still commonly used today (see Fig. 1). The shrines of Aesculapius were a mixture of temple, hospital and health resort. Some patients stayed at them for years seeking cures from the resident priesthood. Methods of diagnosis varied, and before Hippocrates, the priests relied heavily on divinatory methods, which included soothsaying and dream interpretation––the well-known "temple sleep."

Temple sleep or *incubatio* was a common practice among the Greek priesthood. The preliminaries for this form of diagnosis and

Figure 1: Staff of the Greek god Aesculapius.

cure consisted of a full religious rite, involving the use of several specific charms, carried out over several days of fasting and bathing. After the sacrifice of a sacred animal, the patient would be brought by the priests to a special sanctuary, and made to lie down on the hide of the sacrificed animal to sleep. While the patient slept, the priest would invoke Aesculapius and enter the room accompanied by his priestesses and the sacred snake. He would then wake the patient and interpret his dreams.

From records found at Epidaurus we know that this method was sometimes successful; a man with paralyzed fingers dreamed he was playing dice, and the god jumped on his fingers and straightened them; and a woman who was blind in one eye recovered her sight after dreaming that the god had cut open her eye and poured ointment into it. But how did these miraculous cures work? As these rites were carried out in secret, it is very likely that part of the process was to use a mild narcotic drug on the patient before the priest performed surgery. If so, the Greeks can be credited with the first use of an anesthetic.

Still known as the father of modern medicine, it was Hippocrates who was to move the practice of healing into the modern era. In about 400 B.C. he stated that medicine was a science and an art, and began the process of moving healing away from the realms of mysticism. He regarded Apollo as the principal deity of medicine, rather than Aesculapius.

This change in deity by Hippocrates not only shows the change in views on healing practices, but also the change in Greek society as a whole, which was moving into a patriarchal, linear-logical age, aptly represented by the solar deity Apollo. Medicine began to move away from the ancient belief in disease being caused by malign entities, and Hippocrates began to extol the belief that illness was caused by an imbalance in the body.

Hippocrates held a holistic approach which saw the body as consisting of four humors, represented by the four elements of Earth, Air, Fire and Water. He saw the cardinal juices of yellow bile, phlegm, black bile and blood as being governed, respectively, by these four elements. When the natural balance of these juices was upset, illness resulted. To return the body back to health it was necessary to rid the body of the excess humors, and such practices as bloodletting, purging and sweating were to remain in use according to Hippocrates' direction up until the seventeenth century.

14

Hippocrates listed some 300 to 400 plants in his Hippocratic collection, most having purgative, diuretic, or emetic effects in line with his philosophy of the four humors. He also placed great emphasis on diet, lifestyle and exercise (something no doubt adopted from the Egyptians). But he is most famous for his underlying principle of medicine that "the important thing is to do no harm," laid down in the Hippocratic oath which is still declared by the medical profession today (see page 38, chapter 3).

The Romans were quick, not only to adopt the medical principles of the Greeks, but also to enlist the help of them personally in the field of healing. As early as 292 B.C., the Romans summoned the god Aesculapius on the advice of the Sybilline books to help stop a plague which had been ravaging Rome. It is said that the symbol of the god, the snake, was brought from the temple at Epidaurus and swam ashore onto an island in the Tiber. The plague stopped a short time after, and in gratitude the Romans built the first temple to Aesculapius on the island. They were quick to adopt many of the healing traditions of the Greeks, including the use of *incubatio*, charms and incantations.

Before learning from the Greeks, the Romans had already realized the importance of hygiene in preventing disease. The Romans remain famous for their baths, and two of their greatest achievements were the use of aqueducts to transfer clean drinking water and the construction of subterranean sewage systems. The Romans even set up shrines to Cloacina, the goddess of sewers and drains, to ensure their correct functioning, and to the Greek goddess Hygeia to help maintain good health.

By the first century A.D., the Romans had developed medicine into three distinct approaches: diet, pharmacy and surgery. Diet and rest were used on most illnesses, but failing that, excess humors were removed by surgery---normally some method of drawing blood. Many herbal remedies, as prescribed by Hippocrates, were also used, the favorite of the Romans being the use of honey and wines.

It was while in service with the Roman army that Discorides, who was to be hailed as the most influential author on herbalism, was to write his famous *De Materia Medica* in the first century A.D. This pharmaceutical guide dealt with more than 600 plants, 35 animal products and 90 minerals used in medicine. Its influence was so great that illustrated manuscripts of the work were to circulate for over 1,600 years throughout the West and the Middle East, and as late as 1544 it was produced in book form.

While many of the followers of Hippocrates, such as Discorides, had concentrated on the use of herbs, it was Galen who was to push forward the work of the physician. Born in Greece in 130 A.D., he had decided at the age of 16 that he would bring precision to the study of medicine. He spent the following years of his life studying at Alexandria, the center of medicine of the age. He served as a physician to a gladiator school after returning to his home of Pergamum, no doubt gaining valuable practical experience in surgery and anatomy. He went to Rome in 161 A.D., and was quickly accepted as one of the best physicians of his day.

Galen is acknowledged by the modern medical community as the founder of experimental medicine, but during his own lifetime he was criticized for his continued use of Hippocrates' theory of the four humors. His personal medical philosophy was the same as that of most Wiccans: "If it works, use it." This belief was to be adopted by his followers. It is from his work that the divergent medical theories of allopathic (cure a disease by its opposite) and homeopathic (like cures like) treatments were to develop.

With the spread of the Roman Empire across most of the known world, the healing practices of the Egyptians and the Greeks were to spread too. Romano-Celtic Europe developed a fusion of Middle Eastern and pre-Roman healing practices unique to the area. Before the Roman conquests, the medicinal practices of both the Germanic and the Celtic tribes differed very little from those of their Paleolithic ancestors. Magical healing practices, including libations at shrines to healing deities, differed little from the rites of the Egyptians or the early Greeks.

Healing had become a prime concern of the Druids, to the point where it was considered one of the major mysteries. Its secrets were jealously guarded by the Druidic colleges which taught them. Julius Caesar saw the Druids as a threat to the expanding empire; only they had the power to unite a potentially powerful Celtic civilization. When the Roman army invaded Gaul and Britain, the Druids were systematically destroyed, and some of their medical knowledge perished with them.

However, we do know a little about the Druids' medical practices, such as their therapeutic use of willow bark and mistletoe. Willow bark when scraped produces a pulp containing acetylsalicylic acid—the painkiller we know of today as aspirin. They regarded mistletoe as one of their most sacred plants because of the miraculous way it appeared on oak trees. Medicinally they considered it to be a panacea, and because of this, its reputation for being able to cure a range of illnesses from tuberculosis to cancer continued in folk tradition well after the Druids disappeared. Recent tests have shown that some of these beliefs are true. In experiments on cancerous tumors, mistletoe was found to cause remission in 50 percent of the cases, mainly because it acted in the same way as modern chemotherapy—by destroying the growth toxically.

Most of the herbal knowledge and healing practices of the Celts merged with those of the invaders, producing a blend of Egyptian, Greek and European practices. What had previously been healing shrines for the resident Celtic tribes became adopted by the Roman conquerors. Wells renowned for their healing properties, and dedicated to a Celtic goddess, soon found themselves dedicated to a Roman deity. Even after Christianity pushed paganism from Europe, the importance of wells as healing shrines continued, but under new ownership. Wells dedicated to the Madonna, Saint Bridget (the goddess Bríd) and Our Lady are common in Britain and Ireland; female saints replaced the Celtic goddess who was once worshipped there. Committed Christians continue to visit these holy wells to seek cures, and still leave offerings, just as their pagan predecessors did (for more on wells, see chapter 7).

With the collapse of the Roman Empire and the onset of what we now call the Dark Ages, the pagan Germanic tribes began to migrate into Christian Celtic Europe, destroying the Romano-Celtic civilization which had flourished in peace since the first century A.D. The Anglo-Saxons invaded and settled in Britain, and the tribes which were later to become the marauding Vikings migrated to Scandinavia. The Hippocrates-inspired methods of healing which had been adopted across the face of Europe were forced to withdraw back to Christian Rome, and healing practices returned to their shamanic roots until Europe was eventually re-Christianized.

As the Anglo-Saxons left no written records, what we do know of their healing practices comes from later monastic writings. Typical of those remedies recorded in the cloisters is the *Lacnunga Script*, now housed in the British Museum. This manuscript, although dated as late as the tenth century, indicates clearly the healing

17

practices of the Anglo-Saxons. It instructs on the use of a herbal remedy, a spell or rune, and the use of a specific ritual. It is obvious from the lateness of the manuscript that such pagan practices had become impossible for Christianity to destroy. The beginnings of English witchcraft date from this time, and there can be little doubt that its healing traditions emerged from this period.

The Christian church was forced to adopt many of the Anglo-Saxon pagan traditions, just as it had adopted the shrines of the Romano-Celts. Typical of this is the Nine Herbs Charm, which dates from the same period as the *Lacnunga Script*. Although Christianized, its pagan roots are obvious, mentioning the god of sorcery Woden and the use of runes to cure illness (line 31). The number nine is also mentioned several times in the script, this being a sacred number in Northern European paganism.

The Nine Herbs Charm

Forget not, Mugwort, what thou didst reveal,
What thou didst prepare at Regenmeld,
Thou hast strength against three and against thirty,
Thou hast strength against poison and against infection,
Thou hast strength against the foe who fares throughout the land.

And thou, Plantain, mother of herbs,
Open from the East, mighty within,
Over thee chariots creaked, over thee queens rode,
Over thee brides made outcry, over thee bulls gnashed their teeth.
All these thou didst withstand and resist;
So mayest thou withstand poison and infection,
And the foe who fares through the land.

This herb is called Stigme; it grew on a stone,
It resists poison, it fights pain.
It is called harsh, it fights against poison.
This is the herb that strove against the snake;
This has strength against poison, this has strength against infection,
This has strength against the foe who fares through the land.

Now, Cock's-spur Grass, conquer the greater poisons, though thou art the lesser;
Thou, the mightier, vanquish the lesser until he is cured of both.

Remember, Mayweed, what thou didst reveal,

What thou didst bring to pass at Alorford:
That he never yielded his life because of infection,
After Mayweed was dressed for his food.

This is the herb which is Wergulu;
The seal sent this over the back of the ocean
To heal the hurt of other poison.

These nine sprouts against nine poisons.
A snake came crawling, it bit a man
Then Woden took nine glory-twigs,
Smote the serpent so that it flew into nine parts.
There apple brought this to pass against poison,
That she nevermore would enter her house.

Thyme and Fennel, a pair great in power,
The Wise Lord, holy in heaven,
Wrought these herbs while he hung on the cross;
He placed and put them in the seven worlds
To aid all, poor and rich.
It stands against pain, resists venom,
It has power against three and against thirty,
Against a fiend's hand and against sudden trick,
Against witchcraft of vile creatures.

Now these herbs avail against nine evil spirits,
Against nine poisons and against nine infectious diseases,
Against the red poison, against the running poison,
Against the white poison, against the blue poison,
Against the yellow poison, against the green poison,
Against the black poison, against the dark poison,
Against the brown poison, against the crimson poison,
Against snake-blister, against water-blister,
Against thorn-blister, against thistle-blister,
Against ice-blister, against poison-blister,
If any poison comes flying from the East or any comes from
The North, or any from the West upon the people.

Christ stood over disease of every kind.
I alone know running water, and the nine serpents heed it;
May all pastures now spring up with herbs,
The seas, all salt water, be destroyed,
When I blow this poison from thee.

During the Dark Ages healing among the common people remained very much the domain of the village wiseman or wisewoman----the village witch. Most villages had their craftsmen, such as the blacksmith and the miller. Like them, healers were considered craftsmen or craftswomen and a necessity to the running of a village. As the religious focus of the village, they were responsible for its spiritual upkeep; they were priest, priestess, herbalist, spellworker and midwife. Like the other craftspeople within the settlement, they were paid by barter and trade, and no doubt treated with a great deal of respect by the other villagers.

The traditional healer's art was hereditary, being handed down from generation to generation; this had changed very little since the Stone Age. By the Middle Ages their art had been influenced from many sources; knowledge of Greek and Egyptian medicine had been passed on to the Celts from the Romans. In England, the conquered Celts passed on this and the wisdom of the Druids to the Anglo-Saxons, producing a unique tradition of healing.

During the early Middle Ages the politically aware Church of Rome concerned itself mainly with converting the rulers of the existing kingdoms. Most courts in Anglo-Saxon England and in Europe had their own sorcerers and magicians, who were unacceptable to Christianity, but a necessity to the court as healers. They had learned their skills in apprenticeships and by traveling the countryside in search of cures from the village healers. Under Christianity they became the court physicians and astrologers, and continued to practice their arcane arts in secrecy.

Unlike the village healers, this was a purely male-dominated profession, due mainly to the influence of Christianity. These practitioners began to move healing away from spirituality to the realm of science, influenced by the works of Hippocrates and Galen, and armed with the herbals of Discorides.

By the beginning of the eighth century the spiritual practices of the village witches had been seriously curtailed by the influence of the Church, which had now turned its attention to converting the whole population of Europe. Although their healing practices were now being challenged by the Christian religious orders, the Church could not deny their importance to society. Villagers practicing what the Church considered white magic were generally eyed with suspicion but left alone. The Church slowly attempted to gain control of medicine, with healing being considered an extension of the Church's mandate within Europe.

Sickness and disease were seen by the Church as proof of sin; a view widely different to that of the older pagan tradition which saw disease as a manifestation of an outside entity, an evil spirit. This view had not changed for thousands of years. Although the Christian healing orders used herbalism, they enforced repentance alongside it, considering this to be the main cure, therefore forcing those who were ill to be converted to Christianity. The Church began to try to discredit the healing practices of the village witch and of anyone who did not agree with the Christian scholars.

By the thirteenth century, wholesale persecution of anyone suspected of satanic witchery was widespread throughout Europe. Village witches were forced to become secretive about their healing methods for fear of being tortured and executed. If Margaret Murray is correct in her book *The Witch Cult In Western Europe*, the healing practices of this period had been handed down from generation to generation in certain families. Although this may be true, her other more romantic assumption that the witchcraft cult survived intact is unlikely. Herbalism as a practice could have survived easily enough, but there is little evidence for the survival of more arcane forms of healing apart from a few healing charms and spells.

Some of these survived by the adoption of Christian symbolism: a cure for snakebite was to drink holy water in which a snail had been washed; one cure against the evil eye was to cut a loaf of bread into a cross and then eat around it. Even the old practices of herb collecting were forced to succumb to Christianity: one collector of herbal remedies stated that it was useful to repeat the Lord's Prayer and the names of the four evangelists when collecting and administering herbs. The practice of invoking over herbs can be traced back to the Egyptians and beyond.

The use of energy healing----the laying on of hands----probably did not survive in Western Europe outside of the Church. The Anglican Church still uses this practice during ordination, in the same way as Wiccan high priests and high priestesses use it during initiation: to pass on magical lineage. There is little doubt this was an original pagan practice, and even the Church cannot deny it. Unlike herbalism, the use of this magical technique for healing would have been seen as proof of witchery or heresy and probably soon faded from memory.

Evidence of the survival of herbalism dating back to the Middle

Ages is ample. The best example comes from the eighteenth century with the discovery of digitalis, a drug still in widespread use today for cardiac complaints. A doctor in the Midlands of England, William Withering, heard that a village wisewoman was having success with foxglove tea. She was treating patients suffering from swollen ankles and water retention (classic symptoms of cardiac failure) with an incredible success rate. His curiosity got the better of him and he started to experiment with the plant, with the same amount of success. Treatment with foxglove in this area of England can be traced back to well before the coming of Christianity, and confirms that healing has been handed down from generation to generation for a long time.

While the fortunes of the village wiseman and wisewoman were declining, the new profession of physician was flourishing and developing into the medical profession we know today. Unlike the village practitioners, this was a male-dominated profession, mainly due to the influence of the Greeks and the Church. Many of these practitioners, often with the support of the monarchy, continued their roles as court magicians in secrecy. The new medical profession found that it was to its advantage to support the Church and the establishment against the village healer; by doing this it gained lucratively, and satisfied the misogynist pleasure of the Church with the dominance of men in the field of childbirth and the suppression of the female mysteries.

By the Middle Ages physicians had already replaced midwives in the courts of the monarchies of Europe, and were now replacing them in the higher social classes. By the eighteenth century only the poor employed the traditional midwife, and this profession was not to gain true credibility again until the twentieth century.

Mysticism continued to play an important part in the medical profession until the seventeenth century, and astrology was widely accepted as a recognized form of diagnosis. The use of the zodiac and planets to codify parts of the body, herbs, and pharmaceutical preparations was used by the medical profession as late as the eighteenth century. Typical examples of the use of astrological correspondences include the famous woodcuts attributing the zodiac to areas of the body (see Fig. 17). Even *Culpeper's Complete Herbal,* which uses planetary and zodiacal correspondences, was still considered one of the most important works on the subject until as late as the beginning of the nineteenth century by many doctors. Many of the herbs were associated with astrological symbols for very simple reasons. For example, the marigold is attributed to the sun simply because of its appearance. Others were related because of their physical action on the body; for example, a herb related to easing the pains of labor would be attributed to Cancer. Complementary therapists, as well as many of today's pagans, continue to use astrological correspondences.

The Victorian era saw an upsurge of interest both in the occult and in pagan ancestry. The Celts were portrayed as noble savages; neo-Druidical orders were formed, with the revival of the Summer Solstice rites at Stonehenge; and the myth of Ragnarok was explored in depth by scholars. The great digs in Egypt began to reveal the true healing abilities of the ancient priesthoods of the Middle East, but oddly enough the healing practices of our forefathers were explored in very little depth by those involved in this occult/pagan renaissance.

However, the use of homeopathic medicines, based on Galen's theory of like cures like, did come into vogue. Even Queen Victoria had her own royal homeopathist, and the Royal Family still uses the technique. Many of the alternative healing practices related to the spiritual dimension which were developed at the end of the nineteenth century can be attributed to two separate groups: the forerunners of our modern Spiritualist movement, and Madame Blatavsky's Theosophy movement. Both organizations began to explore the spiritual nature of the physical body.

The Spiritualist movement revived the laying on of hands as a form of healing, influenced both by Egyptian and by contemporary Christianity; this was soon adopted by a curious public, and the incorrect term "faith healing" was soon being used. The Theosophists were heavily influenced by material emerging from the British occupation of India----particularly the translations of the Vedas. The chakra system began to emerge as an accepted model for the energy centers of the human body among both Theosophists and occultists.

In *The Chakras----A Monograph*, written by the Theosophist C. M. Leadbeater in 1927, a similarity between the chakras and the caduceus of Mercury or Hermes is noted. This has led Gavin to speculate that the roots of the modern chakra system were known to pre-Christian European culture. The belief in the physical body having energy centers is common throughout the world----Christian

Europe being the exception. It is likely that such a system was known to the pagan priesthoods of Europe and the Middle East before the coming of Christianity.

One piece of evidence for this relates to the myth of Aesculapius (see page 124). It is generally accepted among many scholars that Aesculapius was the deification of one of the great physicians of the early European period. In the myth, the Greek god of medicine learns his art from the centaur Chiron. One view is that the centaur is a memory of the first encounters the Greeks had with nomads on horseback; until then the Greeks had no knowledge of horse riding. It is possible that Aesculapius and others from this early European period learned medicine and its theories from the tribes moving from the East to West.

In one myth the god is presented with the caduceus; the staff entwined with twin snakes, traditionally associated with the god Hermes (see Fig. 2). The caduceus has the same symbolism as in the chakras, where energy passes from center to center (see Fig. 13). Is the caduceus a memory of being taught a rudimentary system of energy centers? A system which developed and advanced in India into the chakra system we know of today? If this theory is correct,

Figure 2: Caduceus of the Greek god Hermes.

then it is highly likely that this system was known throughout Indo-European culture (which includes both the Celts and the Germanic tribes) and was lost with the advent of Christianity.

Regardless of this theory, since their adoption by Western occultism in the early half of the twentieth century, the chakras have become an accepted form for using energy centers among many pagans and Wiccans.

The 1960s saw a surge of interest in alternative healing practices, both in witchcraft and in the growing New Age movement. Interest in witchcraft had increased steadily since the witchcraft laws where repealed in 1951, and by the beginning of the 1970s many of those interested in this ancient form of worship began to realize its link with traditional pagan healing practices. The practice of using healing spells, charms and herbs was revived within Wicca (the name given to modern witchcraft)----areas on which Gerald Gardner, the founding father of Wicca, had not put much emphasis. Herbalism was the first of many techniques which modern witches and pagans have claimed as their own, and this is evident by the number of publications available on herbalism, written solely for pagans by pagans.

Because of the years of persecution by the Church and the authorities, many priest/priestess healers have found themselves having to research and reconstruct the forms of healing used within paganism. Some have adopted practices which stem from Spiritualism and Theosophy and the New Age movement----most of these are of pagan origin.

It is important to note that the way the pagan movement practices its healing techniques differs from the New Age movement mainly in philosophy and ethics. Paganism tends to be more holistic in its approach, balancing all the factors involved without excluding the physical, spiritual, mental or etheric (see page 29). Many New Age practitioners tend to over emphasize the spiritual and etheric, resulting in an imbalance within the individual.

The modern pagan movement, after initial growing pains and false starts, is beginning to find its direction. The realization by many pagans and witches that healing is an essential aspect of pagan philosophy has contributed greatly to this. New Age alternative healing practices are currently fashionable with the general public, but only paganism's heritage can act as a firm foundation for the survival of such holistic healing therapies.

2

The Philosophy and Practice of Healing

What is healing, and why heal? These two questions have to be addressed by anyone who is intending to take up healing seriously.

In prehistory, healing developed within early human culture for one reason----it was essential for the survival of the whole tribe. The greater the number of healthy people in the tribe, the more likely the tribe would survive. Humans are social animals; that is one reason for their success. As the hunter-gatherer tribe evolved the need for healing became even more important as the tribe members developed specialized skills: one man adept at tracking, another at trapping prey, and one who knew how to create fire; a woman with the knowledge to prepare herbs, and one who knew how to cure hides for clothing, and so on.

This specialization of skills which developed within mankind is one of the main reasons humanity has developed to where it is now; the most intelligent, the most creative and without doubt, the most destructive animal species on planet Earth. But there was one drawback to specialization, one which threatened the survival of a small group of humans in earlier times: if one person died, his skills died with him. Compassion and the desire to heal our fellow human beings, which had already developed before this specialization, now became an essential survival skill.

With this said, we can still claim that the driving force to heal another individual is love. Compassion for your fellow human beings is essential for anyone involved in the healing arts; without it, the momentum to heal dries up quickly. Orthodox Christianity has always claimed that man has a monopoly on compassion, the logic behind this statement being that man is separate from the rest of the animal kingdom by having a soul. This is something paganism has always disagreed with, believing that all living entities have a soul of some description.

As well, other animals do have compassion for one another, most noticeably within groups similar to early tribal man----intelligent mammals who hunt or gather in family groups. Compassion and caring does not seem to exist to the same degree within herbivorous herd animals such as sheep, where survival depends on sheer numbers.

Compassion and love for fellow members of the species is particularly noticeable among dolphins and porpoises, which are intelligent mammals that hunt for their food in a group or pod. They are known for their compassion to one another, bringing sick members of their pod food, protecting them from predators such as sharks, and helping them to the surface when they need air. In fact they are one of the few animals which will help species other than their own when in need, and stories about them rescuing humans at risk from drowning or from sharks have been numerous from classical times until today. This development of compassion and caring within dolphins has developed for the same reason as it has in humans----a reflex necessary for survival.

Some may feel that referring to compassion and love as a survival reflex is a cynical viewpoint. No doubt many would disagree with us, using the argument that man is separate from the animal kingdom and that love is a divine gift, and not a development of evolution. But this argument denies that man is part of nature; it is a refusal to accept the true significance of an individual's actions. In the history of Christianity in Europe, the existence of compassion as a survival reflex is noticeable. The primary reason the Church developed many of its existing healing orders and institutions was as a support for the medieval feudal system, of which it was an integral part. Lords and aristocrats could afford private medical attention, but the poor serf could not; and without his health, no work would be done, no crops would be grown and the social system would collapse. Government departments today still publish figures of how many days are lost in a year due to illness, and what effect this has socially and economically.

In their gaia hypothesis, Dr. James Lovelock and Dr. Sydney Epton postulated that the Earth and all of its living inhabitants act together to form a living organism. Their theory was published in the 1975 book *Gaia: A New Look at Life on Earth*, which stated the following two basic propositions:

1. Life exists only because material conditions on Earth happen to be just right for its existence.

2. Life defines the material conditions needed for its survival and it makes sure that they persist.

All species are dependent on each other for survival, and for the survival of the planet as a whole. Biologists accept the first part of this hypothesis without question, and the acceptance of the idea of food chains and similar forms of interdependence have been widely accepted by the scientific community for a long period. Lovelock takes this theory further in proposing that there is a natural intelligence behind this, which can be seen as the god/goddess concept of paganism and witchcraft.

Acceptance of this concept is one of the major ways in which the pagans' view of healing differs from that of the modern medical establishment. To the witch or pagan healer, there is no difference between healing the individual and the world we live in, because in effect it is the same principle.

This is echoed in Arthurian myth. As Arthur and the land of Logres waste away, he states: "I, and the land, are one." The offering of the Grail to Arthur to drink from heals both the land and Arthur. Percival cannot offer the Grail to Arthur until he has found it within himself. Percival's retrieval of the Grail on a personal level is the discovery within himself of his ability to heal, and an act of self-discovery and self-healing. This is an essential lesson for all healers. Surely the concept of *gaia* would not have been lost on the writers of this myth.

In modern society, somebody who is fit and healthy is more likely to be concerned and care for his or her environment than somebody who is ill. When we become ill, physically or mentally, we mentally withdraw from our surroundings and the people around us. We become egocentric, and concerned about ourselves before anything else. This is highly noticeable in our fast-moving, high-stress, ambition-motivated society. It is a natural defense mechanism, and in the right context allows others to recognize illness in a fellow human being. Unfortunately, in modern society, stress has become the norm and we have ceased to recognize it for what it is, with the result that people have forgotten how to heal each other and themselves.

It is important of course for the healer to recognize how illness is caused. For a long time modern medical science has ignored the spiritual aspect of disease and emphasized physical causes. Medicine has ignored the fact that we are holistic entities, and has consequently ignored seeing disease in the same fashion. Even the word "disease" has had its meaning changed, and it has come to mean, in common usage, an illness caused by a parasitic microbe rather than a dis-ease or imbalance of the body.

This emphasis on the physical has resulted in a booming pharmaceutical industry, with drugs being seen as the panacea for all ills, when in fact they treat the symptoms rather than the initial cause of the illness, and more often than not have unwanted side effects. For example, antibiotics are incredibly effective in destroying bacterial and viral infection, but they do not address the problem which allowed the infectious microbe to take hold. Apart from that, many antibiotics are becoming ineffective; their over use has resulted in the development of drug resistant super-bugs.

While modern medical science has concentrated on the physical body, the New Age movement has made a similar mistake by concentrating entirely on the spiritual. One reason for this polarization has been the New Age movement's theosophical basis. New Age philosophy has inadvertently held on to the concept of original sin, which sees physical matter, and therefore the human body, as spiritually corrupt. A good example of this is their view of the lower chakras, which are seen as the source of black magic by some New Age writers. Pagan healing practices ignore this polarized state, believing that true holistic healing can only occur with the balance of all elemental forces present, and therefore treat the physical and the spiritual equally. This has made pagan healers more likely to work in partnership with modern medical science rather than in opposition, seeing their healing practices as complementary rather than alternative.

Paganism recognizes the existence of this spiritual perspective to disease, and the belief that the body has a complex energy system governing it. This fits in with the pagan view of the elements, these being Earth, the physical body; Air, the mental functions; Water, the emotional realm; and Fire, the realm of energy. Up until the nineteenth century, the medical profession regularly referred to the presence of the elements within the human body by other terms;

the element Water was referred to as phlegm, and if there was fluid present in patients' lungs they were referred to as being "phlegmatic." The other three elements were called sanguine (Fire); choleric (Air); and melancholic (Earth). In traditional forms of paganism the combination of these four elements produces the quintessential element of spirit----the element of life itself.

Any imbalance of these elements, or "humors" as they became known, results in an imbalance in the other elements. For example, stress affects and imbalances the element of Water (the emotional realm). Its complementary element Air (the psychological processes), initially compensates for this, but if the stress continues it will also affect the physical body (the element of Earth), resulting in physical tiredness. This in turn leads to a drop in efficiency of the body's immune system, resulting in susceptibility to infection.

It is now widely recognized by physicians that stress can have this affect. Normally, if a patient's lifestyle is analyzed, a deep-rooted problem can be found in this area. In many cases, attitudes develop over a period of time, the commonest being the individual putting his or her physical or social needs above the spiritual. This imbalance in lifestyle is just as responsible for the illness as any physical cause. Hippocrates himself, the father of modern medicine, recognized how important lifestyle was in maintaining good health.

The Cabala of Health and Healing

(If you are not familiar with the Cabala skip this section and come back to it later after reading chapter 6.)

In terms of healing, the Cabalistic Tree of Life serves a useful function coordinating and clarifying the goals of the sufferer (see Fig. 3). For example, Kether, the Crown (pure being without form) can be identified with pure self and the idea of mental and physical well-being; Chokmah, the Supernal Father (raw directionless energy) may be perceived as the necessary action to begin the healing process.

Binah, the Supernal Mother who gives form to Chokmah's energy in the same way as the uterus contains the growing fetus, can be seen as the restraint patients must adhere to so that they can aid a recovery. The ideal state of health that a patient desires starts on the subconscious level, and manifests with the will and determination to attain that ideal: "I will become well and I will listen to

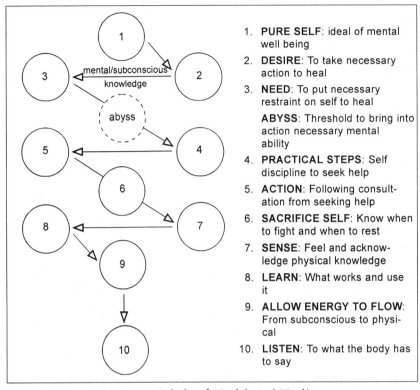

1. **PURE SELF**: ideal of mental well being
2. **DESIRE**: To take necessary action to heal
3. **NEED**: To put necessary restraint on self to heal
   ABYSS: Threshold to bring into action necessary mental ability
4. **PRACTICAL STEPS**: Self discipline to seek help
5. **ACTION**: Following consultation from seeking help
6. **SACRIFICE SELF**: Know when to fight and when to rest
7. **SENSE**: Feel and acknowledge physical knowledge
8. **LEARN**: What works and use it
9. **ALLOW ENERGY TO FLOW**: From subconscious to physical
10. **LISTEN**: To what the body has to say

Figure 3: Cabala of Health and Healing

myself and the advice I give myself. If that means restraining myself from overeating, eating and drinking the wrong things, etc., I will place that restraint upon myself and accustom my thinking to the aims I know that I can achieve." The Abyss is the threshold over which any negative desires must flow so that we can allow the mind to speak to the body.

Chesed is the sphere of organizing and administrating; in healing terms this applies to practical steps toward good health, such as seeing your doctor. Fear is the great killer, and the earlier treatment is obtained the greater the chances of full recovery. Geburah is about acting immediately and destroying the fear and panic which only decrease an individual's chances of recovery.

Tiphareth, the Tree's center of equilibrium, is the sphere of transformation between force and form. It is that part of a patient that tells him or her to sacrifice oneself to oneself, so that one can learn when to fight hard for recovery----and more importantly, when to rest. It is important that individuals do not martyr themselves by fighting when they require rest.

Netzach, the intuitive and emotional right-brain function, tells individuals to listen to the voice within telling them to feel their heart pumping and the blood flowing round their arteries and veins, to sense the extremes of their nerve endings. It also tells us to feel for the cause of our illness, the virus, cancer or broken bone that is present, and tells us to speak to our immune system and commence the healing process.

Hod, intellect, the left-brain function, governs the laws of learning. It reminds us that we need to learn about our bodies, our minds and our ailments. As healers we all need to read up on new developments, and when it comes to self-healing, we all need to find out what works for ourselves. A young Wiccan we knew and loved died because of her ignorance and sheer stupidity. She was a severe asthmatic, and disposed of her salbutamol and prednisolone inhalers in favor of a homeopathic treatment. On the occasion of her death, she was alone and desperately required the immediate effect of these drugs. She died from an asthma attack at the age of twenty-three.

Yesod, the astral and etheric sphere, transmits to Malkuth the emanations of the spheres above it. The unconscious mind speaks to us in our dreams, and answers to problems can often be found in these. Once when Janet had a fever, the affect of this sphere manifested itself. She had been running a high temperature for several nights, when she attempted to read the children's book *Tales of the River Bank*. That night several of the characters from this book appeared to her in a feverish dream. They climbed into her ears and proceeded to attack the virus she was suffering from. When she awoke the next morning the fever had gone and she felt wonderful.

Malkuth, the world of physical matter, is where the patient, after digesting the information from the other spheres, can proceed to the finer details. We should be aware of our relationship with the material world. The human body is a marvelous, finely tuned, piece of organic engineering. It becomes weaker with age, but with careful attention to its needs it will work for many healthy years. It is important to pay attention to diet and hygiene. If you can't cut it out, cut it down. Cigarettes, alcohol, fatty foods and lack of exercise all need to be addressed. Burning the candle at both ends does not allow the body to rest and recharge itself. If staying awake means popping a pill, then ask yourself, "Is this worth destroying myself for?" If the answer is a firm "No!" which it should be, then it is time to rethink your lifestyle.

The Cabala of health and healing is about wanting to be healthy, and the prime key to all of this system is the strength of self-worth; this is the single most important factor involved. If you do not value yourself, then no amount of magical exercises will make you well. That is why this system can be applied to the healing of self by using the following devotion:

Kether: "I will be a whole person."

Chokmah: "I desire to become stronger."

Binah: "I will reform my attitudes to myself."

Chesed: "I will step over my own Abyss and be firm."

Geburah: "I will put into action for myself the necessary steps to become a confident person."

Tiphareth showing us Kether: "I will throw away my crutches and have self-esteem so that I may keep my eyes on my goal."

Netzach: "I will love myself."

Hod: "I will teach myself knowledge."

Yesod: "All this is my divine right, and so I will allow my dreams to be fulfilled."

Malkuth: "All this makes me a person in my own right. I shall allow all of this into being, and like a great tree shall grow and flourish for all the years that my life span allows."

The Healing Process

The healing process is a variation of a system currently in use with the nursing profession. The widely adopted nursing process, developed by Nancy Roper in the 1970s, is a useful system for the healer because of its intrinsically logical approach to holistic philosophy. The healing process, which is divided into three sections, has been adapted for use by the practitioner using the healing methods described within this book. It is not essential to use it if the healing (of whatever sort) is only a one-time session, but we recommend it for a series of concurrent treatments.

Communication Skills

The development of good communication is essential if the

healing process is going to succeed. Transactional Analysis is the study of communication, and is used as a model by the medical and nursing professions. It is based on the precept that roles are taken by the participants during communication. In every day communication between adults, the communication is between equals, with both parties taking the role of adults (see Fig. 4).

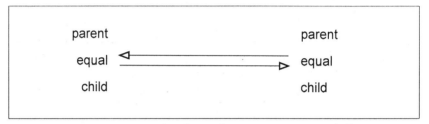

Figure 4: Example of Good Communication Skills

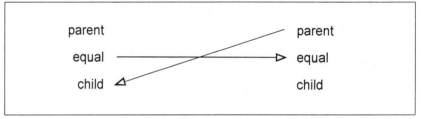

Figure 5: Example of Poor Communication Skills

As many doctors and nurses can contest, this relationship can change when adults become ill or require treatment. The patient may then take on the role of a child, seeing their healer as a parent. Successful communication will take place if the healer responds as parent, but individuals abdicating responsibility for their own health will not assist their recovery. Healers must avoid this situation from occurring, and this is best done by treating each client as an adult from the first moment. If the healer takes on the parent role, the client will adjust immediately into being the child (see Fig. 5).

A situation sometimes occurs where the healer takes on the parent role immediately, even though the client is expecting to be treated as an equal. This has no doubt been experienced by many readers who have been admitted to hospital and met a doctor or nurse "who knows best," a clear indication of the parent role. This results in the client adjusting to the child role, or the client feeling that the healer is being condescending and cannot be trusted.

Assessment

The first stage of assessment consists initially of the collection of information about the individual who requires healing. Healing is a holistic process, so as well as the more mundane information, such as name, date of birth and address, the healer should also include the client's social situation, including work or profession, and family details such as children or other dependents. Clients should be asked how they feel about their life to assess if they suffer from stress. Stress is one of the major causes of ill health in today's society.

Healers should also assess their clients' dietary habits, whether they eat regularly, whether they have a balanced diet, as well as their methods of relaxation, whether they take adequate exercise, and their smoking and drinking habits. They should also ask about past medical history, and obviously what problems they are suffering from at this moment in time. It is vital to find out if they have any allergies, particularly if you are intending to use essential oils or herbs. Many people can have serious adverse side effects to such treatments. All this information will give an overall picture of the lifestyle of the individual, which is essential in any form of holistic therapy.

It is best to collect this information in a relaxed atmosphere. Many important details are lost by members of the medical profession by a hurried approach in today's busy hospital environment. Take time to get to know your client, try to gather as much information in light conversation over a cup of tea or coffee. Exchange information about yourself with your client. This will help put him or her at ease, making it easier to get the information you need. Just as importantly, help to encourage trust prior to the healing session.

Remember that much of the information you receive will be of a personal and confidential nature. Be professional in your approach, in the same way a doctor or nurse is. On no account pressure your client into giving information (see Code of Ethics and Conduct for Healers, page 44). Lock your notes away from prying eyes when you have finished, and on no account divulge information about your client in idle tittle-tattle.

The last stage of assessment is to correlate all the information you have gathered and decide on what form the healing will take. For example, if an individual works long hours, has several young children that need care at the end of the work day, and is poorly paid, you can be sure the individual is suffering from stress, and this will be the root cause of many of the illnesses the individual could be suffering from. This indicates the need for a treatment which relaxes, and the treatment should be ongoing. In some such cases you may choose a therapy such as aromatherapy, using lavender or ylang-ylang essential oils.

This system of assessment can be applied to all the forms of healing mentioned in this book——it is just as valid for spellcraft as it is for aromatherapy.

Implementation

The next stage of the healing process is the application of the healing itself. We recommend that those who intend to follow the path of the healer should investigate and experiment with several forms until they find one that they have a natural aptitude for. Healing is an art, and it should be remembered that the application of any form of healing requires dedication, patience, knowledge and experience if a successful outcome is to be achieved.

Evaluation

This final stage is essential for discovering how successful the healing has been. Immediately after healing, any discernable effects——of a positive or negative nature——should be noted. The healer should of course confer with the client to see how he or she feels about the value of the session, and this should be the basis of any changes made to the next treatments. Any success in one area should be built upon. For example, if lavender is found to be more effective at relaxing the client than the existing ylang-ylang oil, you may want to replace it with this. And any part of the healing which has a negative effect should be discarded——such as an aromatherapy oil that causes a skin rash.

Many of the benefits of the healing session may not become apparent until a later date, and may be subtle and not noticed immediately by the individual who has been healed. Therefore, at the beginning of each visit, it is necessary to evaluate the individual and then adapt the healing appropriately. Even if no benefits are immediately noticeable, this does not mean the treatment is not having an affect. It may, for example, take several sessions of spiritual healing before aura damage is finally sealed.

Healers should not become discouraged at apparent continual failure with one client, but they should consider another form of healing—and if they are not adept at this other form they should consider referring the client to someone who is. This is covered in more depth in the following chapter on ethics, which is essential reading if you are going to use any form of healing and apply the healing process.

3

The Ethics of Healing

Why are ethics required in healing? Quite simply because those who heal soon realize that they can have a great deal of power over others if they so wish. This is well known to doctors, nurses, and others in health-care professions. Ethics in healing are by no means a modern invention. The ancient Greek Hippocratic oath is still accepted as a model by the modern medical profession, and it has remained a tradition for doctors to take the oath since the time of Hippocrates. The modern version reads as follows:

> I swear, by Apollo the physician, and Aesculapius, and health, and all-heal, and all the Gods and Goddesses, that according to my ability and judgment, I will keep this oath and this stipulation.

> To reckon him who taught me this Art equally dear to me as my parents, to share my substance with him, and relieve his necessities if required. To look upon his offspring in the same footing as my own brothers, and to teach them this Art if they shall wish to learn it, without fee or stipulation, and that by precept, lecture and every other mode of instruction, I will impart a knowledge of the Art to my own sons and those of my teachers and to disciples bound by stipulation and oath, according to the law of medicine.

> I will follow the system of regimen which according to my ability and judgment, I consider for the benefit of my patients, and abstain from whatever is deleterious and mischievous. I will give no deadly medicine to anyone if asked, nor suggest

any such counsel; in like manner I will not give a woman a pessary to produce abortion.

With purity and with holiness I will pass my life and practice my Art. I will not cut persons laboring under the stone, but will leave this to be done by practitioners of this work. Into whatever houses I enter, I will go into them for the benefit of the sick, and will abstain from every voluntary act of mischief and corruption; and further from the seduction of females or males, of freemen and slaves.

Whatever in connection with my professional practice, or not in connection with it, I see or hear, in the life of men which ought not to be spoken of abroad, I will not divulge, as reckoning that all such should be kept secret.

While I continue to keep this oath unviolated, may it be granted to me to enjoy life and the practice of the Art respected by men in all times. But should I trespass and violate this oath, may the reverse be my lot.

Of course the oath has been changed over time to suit the needs of the medical profession and changing cultural needs. The original version commenced "By the comforter in sickness, Apollo, and by Aesculapius, by Hygeia and Panacea." During the Middle Ages it was considered good Christian practice to remove the names of the gods; in this case Hygea and Panacea. It would have been impossible to remove Apollo, so it was inferred that he was an ancient physician like Aesculapius.

The statement "I will not give a pessary to produce abortion" existed in the original version; it was probably considered that it was a midwife's role, and not that of the physician. Paganism has never had a problem with abortion, and it was a well-known role of the village wisewoman to prescribe herbs for this purpose. It was the Romans who banned abortion in 211 A.D., a law carried forward from pagan Rome to modern Christian thinking. Most pagans are sensible enough to realize that abortion is neither a good, nor safe, form of birth control, but a last resort when the woman has no other choice. Most pagans feel that it is the woman's right to choose in this situation.

We have included this chapter on ethics because there is a tendency within certain New Age circles to assume that as long as healing is done with the best intentions, it will always be ethically correct to do it. This is far from the truth, as anyone involved in healing for any period of time will tell you, "The road to Hell is paved with good intentions." It would be better for the individual to avoid healing someone altogether, than to attempt healing without the required knowledge—"He who makes, can also break. He who heals can also curse!"

The practicing of the various branches of complementary medicine, from herbalism to aromatherapy, must always be thoroughly well-informed. Unfortunately, in many countries recognized qualifications for most of these healing methods do not yet exist or are in their infancy, so they can often be practiced without the patient having any way of checking whether the practitioner is truly an expert. This places great responsibility on would-be practitioners; they must conscientiously study the particular field in depth before making use of it. Mere enthusiastic dabbling can be dangerous and unethical.

It is also not enough just to learn a particular healing skill and then rest on your laurels. The art of healing is a dynamic process; it is in a continual state of development and change, as we ourselves evolve. This is part of natural law. Therefore ethics must include the importance of changing and adapting our healing practices, but we must not make the mistake that the modern medical profession made in the early days of its development: that of throwing a particular form of therapy out because it does not fit our own personal theories or world view.

Most modern healing professions are aware of this need to update their skills. In Britain, if nurses are not able to prove they have adequately updated their skills to the United Kingdom Central Council, they may lose their registration as nurses because they lack knowledge and are therefore placing their patients at risk. Those healers who use complementary therapies in a pagan environment must do the same or face the prospect of loosing their competency.

Every healing profession has a strong ethical code, which puts the patient's needs before anything else. The first ethic of healing for pagans must be the same as for any magical work: "An it harm none, do what thou wilt." In other words, don't do anything unless you are competent and confident enough to do it, and are sure it will have no harmful effect.

A good example of this is shown in *Egil's Saga*, an Icelandic manuscript written in the early Middle Ages. Egil, a rune master, is called to the bed of a sick girl. There he finds a rune stave (a form of spell) hidden under her bed. It had been carved by a boy with little experience in the runes, and it was obvious to Egil that the rune stave was making the girl's illness worse, so he immediately destroyed the charm: "A man should not carve runes unless he knows how to read; it befalls many a man who is led astray by a dark stave. I saw on the whalebone ten secret staves carved, that have given the slender girl her grinding pain so long."

Secondly, never perform any type of psychic healing without first taking precautions to protect yourself. You put your own health in danger if you try to heal someone when you are, or have recently been, ill or run down. It is just as unethical to put yourself in danger; you have a responsibility to maintain your own health.

Thirdly, never heal someone without his or her permission. This may seem a strange ethic at first, but by doing so you are denying the free will of that person. Also, you may not know the full case history. Every medical practitioner takes a full case history of a patient for diagnostic reasons. This includes a social history, which is vital for correct diagnosis. The psychic healer and the alternative therapist should do the same.

A good example of this happened to Gavin. He was asked to do specific healing work in Circle for a frail old lady who was becoming increasingly ill. Gavin asked about her social situation, only to find out that her husband (whom she had loved deeply) had recently died. The old lady was in fact pining for her husband and wished to join him; she did not actually want to be cured. To work to cure her would have been cruel; Gavin and his priestess therefore worked to free her of pain, rather than work to prolong her life. She passed away peacefully.

The moral is simple: there are times when it is ethically wrong to cure someone. It is important to realize that, psychically speaking, curing and healing are not necessarily the same thing. Curing may actually remove an ailment which is part of the healing process. A good example of this is giving patients a drug to reduce their temperature. In the past doctors would prescribe such drugs immediately. Now they are more careful, having realized that raised temperature is in many cases part of the healing process. Quite simply, curing is only about physically dealing with an ailment, while healing is about a holistic approach, taking into account the whole person's needs.

A great risk for the aspiring healer is to be seduced by the personal power that healing gives. This is something any nurse or doctor can attest to. They soon find some of their patients treat them as superhuman, ignoring their human fallibility; the public image of the nurse as the ministering angel is a good example. Aspiring healers soon begin to believe the image that has been laid upon them, and can make exaggerated claims about their abilities. They may also try to perform types of healing which are potentially dangerous, even though they are not competent to do so. This is probably the worst example of what can happen if the individual's ego takes control, but it is more likely that such people will begin to meddle in the lives of their patients. Those interested in healing need to examine their motives carefully and be honest with themselves.

There is a great deal of prestige attached to being a healer, and many junior doctors and nurses soon become aware of this during their training. They also become aware of how much power is attached to the white coat and the traditional nurse's uniform. This position of power gives healers the ability to control a person's life due to the amount of respect they are given in their society, and is particularly intoxicating if the individual is unaware and unable to control it. It is therefore unwise to come into healing purely for these two reasons, but unfortunately both in established medicine and in the forms of healing mentioned within this book, this sometimes happens. It can have disastrous results both for the healer and for the patient. The primary reason for coming into healing must be, and always remain, compassion for your fellow human beings.

One question on ethics which needs to be addressed is whether you should charge for healing. If healing is your whole profession, of course you have no choice; but if you earn your living in other ways, it becomes an ethical matter. During the writing of *The Pagan Path* we asked the pagan community whether they charged for healing, spellcraft and divination. More importantly we asked their opinions about it. Only 5 percent stated that they would charge for healing, but most who said they would not, stipulated that they would charge for time and expense. We have listed some of the replies below to give an indication of the way individual pagans feel about the matter and we hope that they will help readers develop their own views on what remains an emotive subject within the pagan community:

"It is my view that work such as these is not-for-profit, and should never be done as such. As far as I am concerned, the Craft is a gift in some ways, and the powers of the goddess and god should never be exploited for money. If someone asks me to give a tarot reading, or cast a healing spell for someone or something else that requires my knowledge, if I am prepared, I will gladly perform that task. It is the least I can do to help others."

Chris Strout, Wisconsin, USA

"Some people regard it as appalling to charge----fine if they already have an income. Besides, all these things are about an EX-CHANGE of energy. Not everyone can, for example, keep someone's garden in trim in exchange for healing, run errands for a tarot reading. The only exchange most of us have is our cash. This has become our substitute for energy exchange. It is of course up to the individual reader/healer to do what they feel is correct. It is not only their choice, but what is best for themselves and their 'client' at that particular time, for that particular situation and that particular 'client' that is important. There can be no hard, fast rule; every situation is different. If you always give for free there is always someone who will take advantage, only be interested in receiving and never giving. This has to be balanced."

Kate Westward, Birmingham, UK

"Charging for healing seems a bit dubious. Surely we're obliged to help the sick if we can. As a commercial venture, as with charging for spell work, surely it suggests that all considerations needed in such a situations, e.g. is another course of action more appropriate, may not be considered because of financial desires."

Paul Crawte, Hampshire, UK

"I do not charge for healing because I feel it is unnecessary. I do not disapprove of charging for these services. Money is merely a flexible way of accepting a payment. I believe that it is the person's motive that is important in this issue. Money itself is neutral, it is a person's attitude that counts."

Terry Johnson, Essex, UK

As pagans we must remember that in the past we did charge for healing work. This is how witch-craft came into being; it was just that, a craft like any other. In a village there would be a blacksmith, a carpenter, a butcher and of course, the village wisewoman or cunningman, the predecessors of the modern Craft. They would ply their trade by collecting herbs and producing various healing salves, potions and other concoctions. They would also counsel the heads of the village and the villagers themselves, on matters of importance. Like all other trades within that village they would be paid by goods and services and by barter.

But we certainly do not feel it is ethical to come into healing purely for financial gain. Our personal answer would be not to charge, but to ask for a donation to cover time and any expenses. We recommend that you do not ask for a fixed fee; to overcharge would of course invite the Threefold Law (that harmful occult work will bounce back threefold on the worker). Of course, not charging means that you get a nice tidy sum collecting in your karmic bank account for a rainy day!

Code of Ethics and Conduct for Healers

1. Healers must recognize that their primary obligation is toward those they are healing. At all times they must practice their skills to the best of their ability for the benefit of those they are treating. The comfort, welfare and safety of their client must take priority over any other consideration: "An it harm none, do what thou wilt."

2. Any knowledge gained by healers during treatment about the individual they are working for must be considered confidential. It must not be divulged to anyone without the consent of the client concerned.

3. At all times, be self-critical, and acknowledge any limitation of competence when appropriate to the needs of the individual who is being healed. Do not be afraid of saying, "I don't know," and referring the individual to a qualified medical practitioner or other healer.

4. The healer should work in cooperation with other health care professionals, including the client's doctor. In serious cases, they should not treat individuals without first referring them to their own doctor.

5. Take into account the customs, values, and spiritual beliefs of your client.

6. In healing practices such as herbalism, and other areas where there are potential dangers, the healer should seek professional training and recognition as soon as possible.

7. Healers should try to continue their own education and update their knowledge of their own field of interest and practice within healing, as well as other relevant areas, including conventional medicine, whenever possible. They must also seek to understand the workings of the human body on all levels, and have a basic understanding of anatomy and physiology before performing any form of healing.

8. They must not act in a way to bring Wicca (or whichever path they follow) or the wider pagan community into disrepute.

9. It is the responsibility of healers to look after their own health and well-being. They should do whatever is necessary to protect their own physical soundness when caring for those they heal. They should not attempt to heal an individual unless they are able to do so.

10. Always remember that you have the right to refuse healing if you feel uncomfortable with the situation, and you are obliged to do so if you feel ethically or morally compromised.

Healer's Self-Dedication Ritual

Introduction

We decided to write the following ritual for self-dedicants in the healing path because many people are diffident when it comes to writing their own rituals. Some of you may wish to embellish upon the following ritual, or to simplify it, or to change it completely; please do. Nothing should ever be static or dogmatic. Over the years, as we have been writing books, we too have changed, altered our opinions, and we have included among those changes some of the things we have written. Such is the nature of positive development.

Many of you may wish to fast for a period before this ritual. Certainly one should abstain from alcohol, tobacco and caffeine; and it is advisable to cleanse the body of its own toxins, to drink lots of fresh water, to eat green vegetables, to have a sauna if you can, and above all to be healthy in yourself before embarking on such a rite.

Role of the Healer

The role of the healer encompasses many elements, not the least of which is compassion. Many good healers become empathic with their clients, and although this is not necessarily a bad thing, it can be exhausting both mentally and physically for the practitioner concerned. For this reason, this dedication rite should educate the healer into closing down at the end of the day.

Never let the clients' suffering be an albatross around your neck; feel for them, but not through them. And if ill or emotionally fatigued yourself, do not work during your own recovery. A relaxing bath at the end of the day can work wonders, especially if you burn candles in the bathroom, listen to gentle music, and inhale the fragrance of musk, lavender or pine needle in an aromatherapy pot. While enjoying the soothing oils or salts of the bath, allow your etheric body to be cleansed of the toxins caused by the stress of the day.

Consider carefully before dedicating yourself as a healer. No oath should ever be taken lightly. Remember the healer is the servant of mankind. Egotism, self-glorification, and a hefty bank balance have no place in the healing arts. Spiritual healing is a god-given gift, and to misuse that gift mocks the face of the divine, no matter what you personally perceive your creator to be.

As Wiccans, we work ritual in a Magic Circle. Other pagans mark their sacred space in a variety of ways. For this rite we have used the Circle, a symbol of wholeness, and in the time-honored fashion quoted the symbolism of the four elements: Air to the east symbolizing intelligence, Fire to the south symbolizing drive and energy, Water to the west symbolizing emotion and compassion, and Earth to the north symbolizing steadfastness and practicality. This quartered Circle is suitable for practitioners from other paths and religions; for example, it is also the significance of the Celtic cross, a much-favored Christian symbol.

The Preparation

Thoroughly clear your intended working space, and place your altar in the center of it. Place two unlit candles, light blue in color, upon the left and right of the altar.

On the front of the altar place two blue glass bowls––the one on the left containing sea salt, the one on the right fresh spring water. Between these two keep a vial of olive oil. Place a bowl of healing herbs in the center of the altar, such as self-heal, wound wort, camomile, feverfew, sage––whatever plants appeal to your personal olfactory sense.

Behind the bowl, place the symbol of your deity. If you do not believe in a creator/creatrix, put a symbol that has meaning to you as a healing practitioner: a microscope, for example, or a stethoscope.

At each of the cardinal points, place a white candle, and in front of each candle the following symbols. To the east, an aromatherapy jar with lemon essential oil floating upon the water. To the south, a clinical thermometer or a bottle of liniment. To the west, a jug of water. And to the north, a pestle and mortar, preferably containing myrrh resin.

Beneath the altar, or on either side of it, place a chalice of wine or fruit juice, and a dish of sweet biscuits and honey.

On the floor in front of the altar, place a blue silk sash, the oath (preferably handwritten and decorated, if you are artistically inclined), and a kneeling pad.

For this ritual, we suggest that a new white robe (hand-sewn if possible) would be the best attire. All other clothing should be discarded. For those whose feet suffer without suitable attire, soft white shoes or slippers are permissible.

When your working space is ready and you feel comfortable with the results (add gentle music to the atmosphere if you so wish), it is time to proceed to the pre-ritual preparation. Remember this is a *self*-dedication; if you wish for companions to witness it, then keep your company small and intimate----family, close friends, those who are sympathetic to your wishes.

Relax in a bath of warm water and lemon oil (using only three drops of the oil, and not directly on skin which has been affected by the sun or exposed to ultraviolet light----and none at all for small children). Burn the candles, inhale the flavor of the oil, and prepare yourself mentally for the lifetime commitment ahead of you. If you have self-doubts, now is the time to consider them. Remember you are not infallible, and you will not be right all the time. Learn from mistakes, and always strive for your future development. You will face life with all its joys and woes. Even if you work as a spiritual healer from afar, you will still smell the odor of some cancers, diabetes, gangrene and so on; illness is often a very nauseating process. You will cope with death and the sorrow it brings, and with birth and its joys. You, the practitioner, are now living with the healing art, lock, stock and barrel.

The Ritual

After your bath, sit quietly with your companions if you have any, and explain to them what you are about to do. Go ahead of them into your sanctuary and light your candles——clockwise from the east, and then the altar candles. (Do not yet light the aromatherapy pot.) Start the soft music if you wish. Then invite your guests in, and ask them to sit quietly in the Circle, always moving clockwise, the way of the sun.

Opening your hand over the water, say:

O waters of life, cleanse me and bless me, so that my ideals may be pure.

Opening your hand over the salt, say:

O purifying salt, heal me that I may in turn heal others and administer to their needs.

Pour the salt into the water, and wetting your index finger in the saline solution, anoint your forehead say:

I ask for wisdom

Then your mouth:

That I may speak truth.

Your eyes:

For clarity of vision.

And the palm of each hand:

That my hands may work honestly with the healer's art.

Again with your index finger, anoint each point with the olive oil, saying:

O most holy of oils, healer of healers, bless me that I shall serve humanity to the best of my ability, never asking favor or reward for that which my spirit freely gives.

(If you are going to be a veterinarian, or if you are going to work with animals as well as humans, amend the words accordingly.)

Walking clockwise from the eastern candle, say:

As I walk this Circle of wholeness, and follow in the footsteps of Aesculapius, and of the great healers and teachers who have gone before me, I dedicate myself to the health and nourishment of this Earth on which I was born,

48

to the well-being of this world and all her creatures, to the study of her plant life so that I may benefit from the knowledge that it gives to me; to her creatures that they too may benefit from my endeavors; to her waters, that they may remain pure and refreshing for those who thirst; and to my fellow humans, that I may learn from each race and creed how better to understand the work of the healer. Let my healing extend to my beloved Earth, that I may be nurtured by her all the days of my life, so that my actions shall benefit her for generations as yet unborn.

At the eastern candle, light the aromatherapy pot and say:

By Air, may I acquire the knowledge to serve.

At the southern candle, lay your hand on the thermometer or liniment, and say:

By Fire, let me have the drive and energy to pursue my desires.

At the western candle, put your working hand in the water, and say:

By Water, give me love, compassion and understanding for those I heal.

At the northern candle, grind some of the myrrh in the mortar and say:

By Earth, teach me to be patient and steadfast in all I undertake to do.

Taking the blue silk scarf in both hands, repeat the oath. (The following is a form of the classical Hippocratic oath, amended to suit modern conditions. The "gods and goddesses" may be left out if they are not in accord with your personal philosophy.)

I swear by Aesculapius, and by all the gods and goddesses, that I shall teach this Art to those who wish to learn it, without fee or stipulation, according to the Law of Medicine. I will follow the system of regimen which according to my ability and judgment I consider for the benefit of my patients, and abstain from whatever is deleterious and mischievous. I will give no deadly medicine to anyone if asked, nor suggest any such counsel. With purity and with holiness I will pass my life and practice my Art. Into whatever house I may enter, I will go into it for the benefit of the sick, and will abstain from every voluntary act of mischief and corruption, and further from any seduction of females or males. Whatever in connection with my professional practice, or not in connection with it, I see or hear in the life of men or women which ought not to be spoken of abroad, I will not divulge, as reckoning that all such should be kept secret. While I continue to keep this oath unviolated, may it be granted to me to enjoy life and the practice of the Art respected by all mankind in all times. But should I trespass and violate this oath, may the reverse be my lot.

Then gird the sash round your waist, and bow to the altar. Go to each quarter in turn, and bow to it.

Now is the time for the first healing act. Take the wine or fruit juice and sip it, then pass it to each friend in turn, saying:

May you be strong and healthy, yet always thirst for knowledge.

Do the same with the biscuits, dipping each in the honey, and say:

May you never hunger, and may the sweetness of life be yours for ever.

Thank your companions for their support, and quietly extinguish the candles from the east to the north, but leave the altar candles to burn out completely.

Grounding

Now is the time to retire to the kitchen and have a good feast, flavored with laughter and conversation. After a serious ritual, grounding yourselves is necessary for your own health. An excellent way to achieve this result is a full stomach and lively talk.

4

The Physical Body

Many New Age books on healing ignore altogether the subjects of physiology and anatomy----the study of the physical body. This is a serious oversight on the part of their authors, and shows a lack of understanding of the holistic principles which govern our existence, on both the spiritual and the physical planes. To cover a subject as wide as this would be impossible in a book of this size, let alone one chapter. We have therefore tried to provide the reader with a brief sketch of the structure and workings of the human body in the hope that it will help them in their study of the healing arts.

For the purposes of this chapter, and to keep it in line with pagan philosophy, we have divided the body into six distinct systems relating to the chakras. There are seven major chakric centers (see chapter 6), including the Ajna, which governs the mind. (The Ajna is covered in chapter 5.) Modern Western dogma has always kept the mind separate from the body, and for the purposes of this chapter we have maintained this. However, the healer must always remember that the body and the mind are part of an integrated holistic system (see page 29) and it is not possible to study one without the other.

The physical body is of course governed by the element of Earth; the element of structure and stability. Hence, the human body is the vessel of the spirit on the physical plane, and to be more precise, the spirit can be said to reside within the nervous system (ancient European belief has always maintained that the spirit resides within the head). This is the manifestation of spirit within Earth.

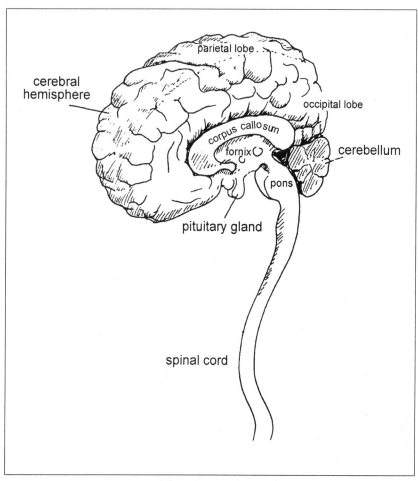

Figure 6: The Brain and Spinal Cord

Likewise Fire, Air, Water, and also Ether, manifest in a similar fashion. Hence a bodily system such as the genito-urinary system can be said to be governed by the element of Water in Earth. We have given the elemental correspondence, and the chakra center related to bodily functions where appropriate (also see chapter 6 regarding chakras).

The Nervous System (Spirit in Earth: The Crown Center)

The nervous system is divided into two parts by anatomists----

the central nervous system (the brain and the spinal cord) and the peripheral nervous system (the eyes, ears, nose, and the vast network of nerves which exist within the human body). We have decided to concentrate on the central nervous system, this being the more important area of study for the healer (see Fig. 6).

The brain's purpose is to act as a command and control center for the whole body, and as such it is responsible for coordinating and integrating all the bodily functions.

It has developed the ability to receive and respond to stimulus from outside, and within, the body by messages transmitted along the sensory nerves. It also has the ability to transmit messages to and from coordinating centers within the system; these are transmitted along the motor nerves and cause movement and action. Hence, the millions of nerves which reside within the human body are divided between sensory and motor functions.

The Brain

The brain, situated within the head, is protected and surrounded by the skull. It is the largest collection of nerves within the body; about 90 percent of all the nerves in the body are located within this one organ. The weight of the average brain is 47 ounces (approximately 1.3 kilograms), but weight or size appears to be no indication of intellectual ability. Its complexity is of more importance than its actual size.

It is surrounded, as is the spinal cord, by three membranes. The outer membrane being the dura mater, the inner being the pia mater, and sandwiched between the two, the arachnoid. The gaps between these membranes are surrounded by fluid which helps protect the brain from damage by acting as a shock absorber.

Forebrain: The forebrain is divided into two lobes; the left and right cerebral hemisphere, also known collectively as the cerebrum. The surface of the forebrain shows many folds and convolutions. This increases the amount of surface area, and the amount of gray matter present. The gray matter forms the outer layer of the cerebral cortex, and contains the cell bodies of the nerves arranged in a three-dimensional network. The gray color is caused by the pigmentation of these nerves.

The sensory and motor areas of the cerebrum are well charted, and we know that the central areas of the hemispheres are concerned with these. The rear, or occipital lobe, of the hemispheres is concerned with vision, hence a headache may occur at the rear of our head if we strain our eyes. The speech area only occurs on one side, the left hemisphere, and is positioned cranially. The front of the hemispheres is known to be concerned with conscious thought, but large areas of the cerebrum remain uncharted, and these areas are believed to be concerned with intelligence, memory, judgment, imagination, and creativity.

The left brain is primarily concerned with logical thinking and speech, and the right brain with instincts and intuition----the two halves complementing each other (see chapter 5).

Beneath the cerebral hemispheres lie the thalamus and the hypo-thalamus. The thalamus acts as a relay center for sensation, and therefore is responsible for giving us the warning we call pain. The hypothalamus contains the centers responsible for our automatic nerve functions----the autonomic nervous system. It controls our heart beat, blood pressure, body temperature and metabolism. The pituitary gland hangs beneath it, forming the link between the nervous system and the endocrine system.

Midbrain: The spinal cord starts to form at the midbrain which consists of white matter. This area of the brain links all the others, and is therefore responsible for acting as a center for all visual and auditory reflexes. It is connected by the cranial nerves to both the ears and the eyes, as well as all the other sensory organs.

Hindbrain: The hindbrain is beneath the midbrain and consists of three distinct areas: the pons, the medulla oblongata and the cere-bellum. The pons appears as a bulge beneath the midbrain and links all the other existing nerves, while the medulla oblongata is the dividing line between the brain and the spinal cord, and is where some of the nerves cross over. The result of this is that the right brain governs the left side of the body in motor functions and vice versa. These areas are also responsible for controlling the autonomic nervous system: functions which continue without the need for conscious thought such as breathing and heart rate.

The cerebellum is the largest and most noticeable part of the hindbrain. It is positioned at the rear and beneath the cerebrum, and consists of a hemisphere of nerves. Its main functions are concerned with maintaining balance by controlling muscle movements.

The Spinal Cord

The spinal cord runs from the base of the brain (medulla oblongata) down the back where it finishes just between the buttocks (the sacrum). It is on average about 17 inches (43 cms) in length. Like the brain, it is surrounded by the dura mater, arachnoid and the pia mater, which encase it within the vertebral column to form a tunnel. It is composed of both white and gray matter, but their position is reversed with the white matter being external.

The function of the spinal cord is to relay nerve impulses to and from the body and the brain. Major nerves branch off its length at regular intervals for this purpose, normally at each vertebra. These subdivide even further until every area of the body is covered; this is the peripheral nervous system.

Several control centers exist within the spinal cord, most of these being concerned with reflex actions——automatic responses to danger where action is immediately required (withdrawing a hand from a flame when it is being burned). It is believed that such response centers are located in the spinal cord so that reaction to such stimuli is quicker.

The Endocrine System

The endocrine system is comprised of ductless glands which release chemical messengers, or hormones, directly into the blood stream. Like the brain, the main function of the system is the control and coordination of various processes throughout the body. These processes include metabolism, growth, resistance to stress, and reproduction. Although each gland has specific functions, over-activity or under-activity tends to effect the whole system.

The endocrine system is an important area of study for anyone interested in spiritual healing because of the correlations between the positions of the glands and the chakras (see chapter 6). Apart from anything else, the endocrine system is a perfect example of a self-balancing holistic process.

The Pituitary Gland

Situated at the base of the brain, which it is connected to via the hypothalamus (see Midbrain), the pituitary gland is divided into two: the anterior and the posterior lobes.

The anterior lobe governs the functions which make the pituitary the master gland of the system. It regulates the activity of the other glands by monitoring the bloodstream for the amount of hormones present. It releases hormones which influence other glands to produce more or less hormones as they are needed. It also produces several hormones which act directly on body tissue to stimulate growth, and influence protein, fat and carbohydrate metabolism.

There are two main functions performed by the posterior lobe. The first is to produce hormones which act on the kidneys to reduce the output of urine when the body needs to conserve its fluid balance (anti-diuretic hormone). This also increases the blood pressure by constricting the blood vessels. The second function is to release a hormone (oxytocin) which contracts the uterus after childbirth, and commences lactation (milk production).

The Thyroid and Parathyroids

The thyroid consists of two joined lobes positioned on either side of the windpipe, or trachea. The four parathyroids are hidden beneath it, two on each side of the trachea. The main function of the thyroid is to produce thyroxin, the hormone which acts on cell tissue to hasten oxidation (the feeding of the cells with the nutrients they require) and to control energy metabolism (the storing or releasing of energy for the tissues as it is required). The thyroid therefore effects the growth and repair of all the body's tissues. Its secondary function is to secrete the hormone calcitonin. This is responsible for lowering high levels of calcium in the blood by preventing it from leaving the bones.

Like the thyroid, the parathyroids are also concerned with calcium metabolism. They regulate the amount of calcium taken from food and excreted, as well as retaining or releasing it via the kidneys. They regulate phosphates (also a constituent of bone) in a similar fashion.

The Thymus

The thymus gland is situated beneath the breast bone or sternum. In childhood it is relatively large because it plays the important role during growth of stimulating the tissue which produces white blood cells (lymphocytes). This assists in the formation of antibodies which help prevent infection from microorganisms in later, as well as in early, life. At puberty it reaches its maximum size, and decreases in size after this.

The Adrenal Glands

There are two adrenal glands, one positioned above each of the kidney's two lobes. The gland consists of the cortex and the medulla. Each of these structures produces specific hormones.

One of the hormones released from the cortex effects the retention and excretion of salts, such as sodium and potassium, through the kidneys. It also produces a hormone which helps the liver produce sugar from protein. Both of these hormones are referred to as cortico-steroids and have anti-inflammatory and antiallergic properties----hence their use medically in such conditions as asthma. The sex hormones androgen and estrogen are also known to be produced in the cortex.

The hormone produced in the medulla of the adrenal glands is probably one of the most well known. This is the fright-and-flight hormone, adrenaline. The medulla is under the direct control of the hypothalamus. During times of threat, excitement, or circumstances which demand extreme effort, adrenaline is released into the blood stream. It stimulates the heart and circulation by increasing the heart rate and increasing the volume of the blood vessels. It also re-routes blood supply to vital organs. This is done to increase the efficiency of the body to cope with the emergency.

The Islets of Langerhans (Pancreas)

The pancreas is situated within the abdomen, lying beneath the liver (see Gastrointestinal System). Within the pancreas are areas of tissue called the islets of langerhans. It is these which are responsible for producing two hormones: insulin, which promotes the absorption of glucose sugar into the tissues for fuel, and glucagon, which promotes the breakdown of sugars in the liver (glycogen) with the aid of the gluco-corticoids from the adrenal glands.

The Gonads

Gonads is the collective term for the sex organs of both genders. In the male, the specific endocrine glands within the gonads are the two testes, and in the females, the two ovaries.

In the male, the testes produce one hormone, testosterone. This is responsible for the development of the sexual organs during puberty. It also produces the secondary sexual characteristics, such as deepening of the voice, the development of facial hair, and the change in body shape.

Unlike the male glands, the female ovaries produce two hormones, estrogen and progesterone. As in the male, these help develop the gender's sexual organs during puberty, as well as producing the secondary characteristics----the developments of breasts, pubic and axillary hair, and the typical feminine proportions of the body. They also trigger the start of menstruation, the monthly cycle which results in the periodic shedding of the lining of the ovary.

Puberty, the development of physical, mental and emotional sexuality, normally commences between the ages of 12 and 14, and finishes by the age of 17. During this time, adolescents of both sexes develop their interest in each other and in sex.

The Respiratory System
(Ether in Earth: The Throat Center)

The principal purpose of the respiratory system is to take oxygen into the body, which is required for cell metabolism, and to dispose of carbon dioxide, which is a waste product of this process. This is done by breathing air into the lungs, where oxygen and carbon dioxide are exchanged across the lungs' internal surfaces (alveoli) into, or out of, the blood stream.

At rest, an adult normally breaths in about 16 times a minute, moving just below 1 pint (0.473 liters) of air in and out of the lungs with each breath. This increases with exertion, with the breathing rate increasing and the amount of air inhaled going up to 4.25 pints (2.011 liters), but the amount exhaled never goes above 1.75 pints (0.828 liters). These figures are referred to as the tidal volume of the lungs. A certain amount of air always remains in the lungs, this is referred to as the residual volume, and in an adult is normally between 1.75 and 2.25 pints (0.828 to 1.064 liters).

The Respiratory Tubes

The respiratory system starts with the nasal passages called the pharynx, moves down to the top of the throat or larynx, and then to the windpipe or trachea. It finishes in the lungs with the bronchi, which divide into the left and right sides of the lungs.

The pharynx is covered with soft tissue, and contains the cells

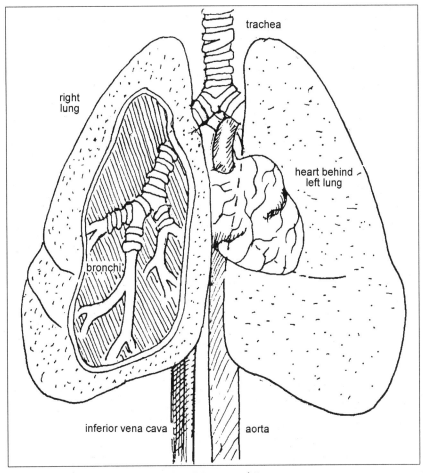

Figure 7: Heart and Lungs

which give us our sense of smell.

The larynx consists of cartilage (tough connective tissue) and is surrounded at the front by the thyroid gland. It contains the vocal cords, and because of this, it is sometimes referred to as the "voice box." In the male it becomes larger in size during puberty, and is sometimes referred to as the "Adam's apple," visible at the front of the neck.

The trachea is surrounded by tough cartilage rings which follow its whole length down into the lungs. On the inside, its surface is covered in hairs called cilia. These help to remove any dust and foreign particles which are inhaled. In smokers these are destroyed, hence the typical smoker's cough.

The bronchi start when the trachea enters the lungs and divides. It divides further into three more branches on the right side, and two on the left, consistent with the lobes of the lungs. They subdivide even further after this, with the cartilage rings gradually disappearing.

The Lungs

Comprised of two organs, the lungs are situated in the chest (or thorax) where they are surrounded and protected by the rib cage, the breast bone (or sternum) and the spine (or vertebral column) at the back. This protection is required because the lungs are composed of a soft tissue which is vulnerable to injury. The lungs are surrounded by the pleura, two tissues which hug the surface of the lungs and are filled with a thin film of fluid. The muscles within the rib cage help in the process of breathing by pulling the lungs open to receive air when breathing in (inspiration). When relaxed, they help breathing out (expiration) by pushing air out. Breathing is also aided by the diaphragm, a strong dome-shaped sheet of tissue which separates the thorax from the organs below it in the abdominal cavity.

The right lung consists of three lobes, while the left consists of two, hence the division of the bronchi. Within these lobes the bronchi divides into bronchioles, which end in alveoli. These are small, round sacks with a high surface area; it is within these that the exchange of gases takes place by diffusion, the movement of gas molecules from a high to a low density. The alveoli are surrounded by capillaries from the pulmonary veins and arteries for this purpose.

The pulmonary veins take oxygenated blood from the lungs to the heart for distribution to the tissues of the rest of the body, while the pulmonary arteries bring blood full of carbon dioxide to the alveoli for expiration.

The Cardio-Vascular System
(Air in Earth: The Heart Center)

The principle purpose of the cardio-vascular system is the transportation of needed nutrients, oxygen and hormones to the tissues. In astrological tradition, any form of transport is under the control of the planet Mercury, and henceforth of its governing element, Air.

All the body's tissues are bathed in fluid so that oxygen and food materials may be absorbed into them, and waste products such as carbon dioxide may be removed. The cardio-vascular system is the method of transportation for these materials.

The Heart

The heart is the pump for this system. It is positioned between the lungs, but slightly to the left. In size, it is slightly larger than a male fist. It consists of four chambers. The two top chambers receive blood and are known as the atrium, while the two lower chambers pump blood away from the heart and are known as the ventricles. Valves separate the atrium from the ventricles; there are also valves at the openings of the blood vessels going to and from the heart.

The pumping action of the heart is controlled by a complex system of nerves and an area of tissue within the heart known as the pacemaker. The action of the heart is involuntary, being under the control of the autonomic nervous system.

The Systemic Circulation

The heart is in fact two pumps. The left side of the heart receives oxygenated blood in the pulmonary veins from the lungs via the left atrium, and then pumps it around the body through the aorta via the left ventricle. The aorta is the largest blood vessel within the body, and descends from the heart until it branches into the left and right femoral arteries. It divides three times further before it reaches these vessels: firstly into the hepatic artery feeding the liver, secondly into the artery which feeds the gastrointestinal system (this is where nutrients are received), and thirdly into the renal arteries which feed the kidneys.

These arteries all divide and subdivide further into capillaries, which are smaller blood vessels the diameter of a blood cell, that feed the tissues with nutrients. From this point the system moves back toward the heart as veins ending in the second largest blood vessel, the inferior vena cava. The blood supply leaves the kidneys through the renal veins, and from the liver through the hepatic vein. The venous blood vessels from the gastrointestinal system go directly to the liver and merge with those of the hepatic vein.

The nutrient-depleted blood from these organs moves up the

inferior vena cava and into the heart via the right atrium.

The Pulmonary Circulation

From the systemic circulation, the depleted blood is pumped from the right ventricle, through the pulmonary artery, and into the lungs to be oxygenated. It then leaves the lungs in the pulmonary vein (see Lungs), bringing oxygenated blood to the left atrium.

Circulation to the Head and Upper Limbs

Arterial blood from the aorta feeds the head and upper limbs. Among the several subdivided arteries are two carotid arteries and two vertebral arteries. These feed a circle of blood vessels at the base of the cerebrum. Venous blood supply leaves the brain via the jugular veins, which join the superior vena cava before entering the right atrium.

The shoulder areas of the body are supplied with blood via the subclavian arteries which branch off the aorta. These divide further to supply the arms on both sides of the body via the axillary arteries. Venous blood supply returns to the heart from the arms via the axillary veins, which joins the subclavian veins, before draining into the superior vena cava.

Blood

Blood is the fluid which runs through the circulatory system and acts as the transport medium. It accounts for about 8 percent of body weight, and on average we have about a gallon (3.8 liters) of blood within our bodies. Visually, it is red in color, but contains both red and white blood cells, as well as salts, body nutrients, hormones, and waste materials.

Red blood cells carry oxygen. The red color is caused by the action of the oxygen on their main chemical constituent hemoglobin, which is rich in iron.

The purpose of the white blood cells is entirely different from the red. Their role is defense of the body from microorganisms. Because of this specialized role, there exist different types of white blood cells for different tasks.

There are four types of blood groups; A, B, AB and O. These blood groups were developed as a system to show the compatibility of blood for transfusions. Blood group O is a universal donor group, meaning that it can be given to anyone of any other blood group. AB is a universal recipient, meaning it can receive blood from any of the other groups. Groups A and B cannot be given to each other, but can give or receive appropriately to the other groups. Groups A and O are the commonest blood groups.

The Lymphatic System

Shadowing the main circulatory system is the lymphatic system. Clear tissue fluid passes through it (lymph), aided by muscle movement rather than the action of the heart. It is an important part of the body's defense system, providing antigens and white blood cells to destroy invading microorganisms.

The Gastrointestinal System
(Fire in Earth: The Solar Plexus Center)

The gastrointestinal system, also referred to as the alimentary canal, starts at the mouth and finishes at the anus (see Fig. 8). Its principle purpose is to deal with food and fluids, their preparation, digestion, absorption and finally the rejection of undigested matter. This system is concerned with providing energy for the body, and produces heat as a by-product. Not surprisingly it is attributed to the element of Fire.

The Mouth

The mouth contains the teeth, palate and tongue, as well as several salivary glands.

In a full-grown adult there should be 32 teeth, which are divided into groups which perform particular functions. At the front of the mouth, top and bottom, are the incisors for biting into food; and then moving back, the canines for tearing, and the premolars and molars for chewing. During our lives we have two sets of teeth. The first set appears after we are six months of age, and are often referred to as the milk teeth. These are replaced after the age of six years by the full 32 teeth of the adult; normally, these are fully in place by the age of 25 years.

The palate is situated in the roof of the mouth and consists of the hard palate at the front and the soft palate at the back of the mouth. The tongue is situated in the floor of the mouth; it is a muscular organ attached to the back of the mouth. The tongue

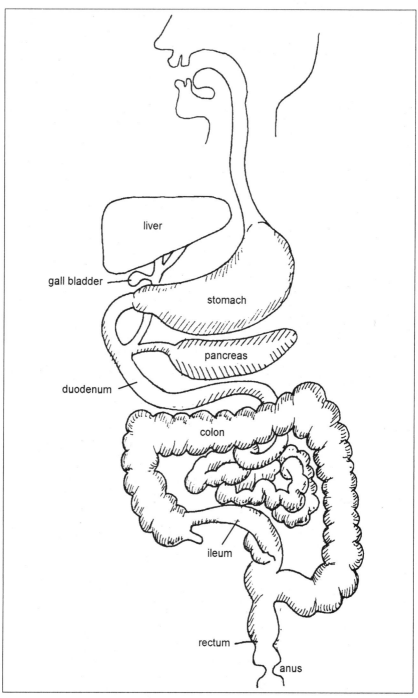

Figure 8: The Gastrointestinal System

pushes food against the hard palate to pulp it, after it has been shredded by the action of the teeth.

The three sets of salivary glands release saliva, which cleans, moistens, and starts the process of digestion within the oral cavity. The sets are composed of two glands each, positioned one on either side of the mouth. The sublingual glands are situated at the front, below the tongue; the submandibular glands are situated at the rear of the mouth, also below the tongue; and the parotid glands are situated in the roof of the mouth.

The action of all these organs produces a ball, or bolus, of food which is soft and easy to swallow. This is pushed to the back of the mouth, where the soft palate closes to prevent the food from entering the nasal cavity. It then enters the pharynx, where an involuntary action causes the bolus of food to be swallowed. During this action the entrance to the larynx is closed off, and breathing pauses.

The Esophagus, Stomach and Duodenum

The esophagus is a length of tubing which starts where the pharynx finishes at the entrance to the trachea, which it runs behind down the neck. It is about 10 inches (25 cms) in length, and travels down to join the stomach, which sits beneath the rib cage.

When food enters the esophagus from the pharynx, waves of contraction push the ball of food down to the stomach entrance.

The stomach itself is formed by a ballooning in the tubing of the upper alimentary canal to form a kidney-shaped structure. This organ is separated from the rest of the tract by two valves: the cardiac sphincter at the entrance, and the pyloric sphincter, where the digested food exits.

After food enters via the cardiac sphincter, it is churned up by the action of the stomach muscles (the same waves of contraction, known as peristalsis, which pushed the food down into the stomach). During this process mild hydrochloric acid, and several other enzymes, are released by areas within the stomach to break down the food into simpler molecules for absorption. This is the process we know as digestion, and it normally takes about three to five hours before the soup-like contents of the stomach exit through the pyloric sphincter and enter the duodenum.

The duodenum is the first length of the small intestine which leaves the stomach. It is about 10 inches (25 cms) in length and conveys the digested foodstuffs to the ileum, the length of the small intestine which absorbs nutrients. Before it reaches the ileum it passes the entrance to the pancreatic and bile ducts which lead to the pancreas, gall bladder and liver.

The Pancreas

The pancreas is a large gland which lies at the back of the abdomen. The pancreatic duct leaves it to meet with the bile duct, and then join with the duodenum.

Two secretions are released by the pancreas: one is hormonal (see Endocrine System) and the other is a digestive secretion. The secretions leave the pancreas and travel down the pancreatic duct. The secretion neutralizes the stomach acid which has entered the duodenum with the digested foodstuffs, and starts to digest the more complex molecules, such as proteins, which the stomach could not.

The Liver and Gall Bladder

The liver is the largest single organ within the body, and weighs about 3.25 pounds (1.5 kgs). It is triangular in shape and divided into two lobes. It sits beneath the diaphragm, with its entire upper surface in contact with it.

Many functions are associated with the liver—the two most important are the breakdown of toxins within the bloodstream, and the production of bile. This is a greenish-brown fluid which is used to break down fat, and gives excreta its distinct color and odor. Toxins can also be found within bile, which the liver removes from the bloodstream.

The gall bladder is a small pear-shaped sack, approximately two to three inches in length, which lies beneath the liver. The cystic duct leads from it to a junction with the bile duct. The liver produces 1 to 1.75 pints (0.47 to 0.83 liters) of bile a day, which is secreted continuously. The gall bladder stores much of this, and periodically releases it into the duodenum, via the cystic and bile ducts, to break down fat. The resultant solution of digested food from the stomach and the duodenum is referred to as chyme.

The Small Intestine

A long muscular tube over 20 feet (6.1 meters) in length, the small intestine is about 1 to 1.5 inches (2.5 to 4 cms) in diameter. It is surrounded by the large intestine in the central abdomen. The small intestine starts with the duodenum (as already mentioned) and then proceeds as the jejunum which starts after the bile duct, and then becomes the ileum. The jejunum and ileum continue the process of digestion and absorption. Their inner surfaces are coated with small finger-like projections called villi, which increase the surface area through which nutrients are absorbed.

The chyme passes into these areas of the small intestine by the action of peristalsis—waves of contraction which push it along. These movements further mix food with digestive juices released from the walls of the small intestine. Starch, and the remaining constituents of protein and sugars, are all broken down by the actions of these enzymes and absorbed, leaving fluid, waste products and indigestible matter (faeces) to enter the large intestine (colon) at the ileo-caecal valve.

The Large Intestine, Rectum and Anus

The large intestine, or colon, is much shorter than the small, being only 6 feet (1.8 meters) in length. It is much wider though, being 3 to 4 inches (7.5 to 10 cms) in diameter. It surrounds the small intestine to form a square in the abdominal cavity. The ileum merges into the colon at the caecum, an area close to where the appendix lies. The appendix is the remnants of an organ which was originally used for the digestion of vegetable matter. It is no longer of any use in humans.

The remnants of the chyme pass through the colon, where fluids and remaining salts are absorbed through villi into the colon wall. This helps to conserve fluid levels within the body and to dry out the faeces before excretion.

The rectum is the last length of the colon. It stores faeces before they are excreted through the anus: the canal which leads to the exterior of the body. The amount of faeces excreted in a day can vary according to diet, but is normally about 0.25 to 0.5 ounce (7 to 14 gms) a day.

The Genito-Urinary System
(Water in Earth: The Sacral Center)

The genito-urinary system is basically two systems: the reproductive system and the urinary system. They are generally grouped together by the medical profession.

The reproductive system consists of the testes and penis in the male, and the ovaries, uterus and vagina in the female.

The urinary system consists of the kidneys and bladder. These are identical in both sexes, except for the route of the urethra. Its elemental correspondences are self explanatory.

The Male Reproductive System

The main organ of reproduction in the male is the testes. These are two round organs about 0.75 inch (2 cm) in diameter. They occupy an external sack known as the scrotum, which is situated at the lowest part of the abdomen, between the upper thigh joints.

These produce two secretions; the hormone testosterone (see Endocrine System) and sperm, the carrier of the male genes in sexual reproduction. The production of sperm starts at puberty.

During sexual intercourse sperm passes from the testes into a length of tubing called the epididymis and then into the vas deferens duct. Here the seminal vesicle organ releases seminal fluid as a lubricant for the sperm. The prostate gland, positioned at the base of the bladder, then adds more fluid into the urethra to aid ejaculation. In a relaxed state the penis lies over the scrotum, being joined to the abdomen just above the scortum. During sexual arousal, the penis hardens and rises for penetration into the the female vagina.

The Female Reproductive System

The main female organs of reproduction are the ovaries, the female counterpart of the testes. Unlike the testes, these sit inside the abdomen. They produce two hormones (see Endocrine System) and every month release an egg containing the female genes. This egg is transferred to the uterus, via the fallopian tubes.

The uterus is the organ where the egg is fertilized by male sperm. The uterus is approximately 5 inches (13 cms) in length, but expands after conception (the fertilization of the egg) to accommodate the growing fetus during the nine months gestation period. At birth, the baby is expelled through the opening to the uterus, the cervix, and then passes through the muscular-walled vagina.

The Urinary System

The purpose of the urinary system is to expel the waste products of cell metabolism and excess fluid. It also excretes some toxic substances and maintains the balance of body salts (electrolytes).

The Kidneys and Ureters

We each have two of these connected on either side of the aorta and inferior vena cava (see Cardio-Vascular System), where they receive more blood than any other organ, with the exception of the heart. Each organ is just larger than a clenched fist and is positioned at the back of the abdominal cavity just below the rib cage. The left kidney is normally slightly higher than the right.

The kidney is a filtration unit, with its main unit being the nephron, a microscopic tube which selectively expels and re-absorbs the waste products of protein metabolism by the processes of osmosis and diffusion. During this process it also balances electrolytes and fluids in a similar fashion. Blood enters the kidney by the renal artery, which passes into the organ through the area known as the pelvis. This blood vessel subdivides to form renal arterioles and capillaries which encircle the nephrons to form a ball called the glomerulus. This area of the kidney is known as the medulla. If components of the blood are re-absorbed, they leave the medulla via the renal venuoles, passing into the renal vein and back into the general circulation.

Components of the blood which are expelled from the kidney enter the nephrons. They then pass down them into the calyx, an area where the stems of the nephrons join, and out into the ureter. The ureters are long tubes coming from each kidney which connect them to the bladder.

The Bladder and Urethra

The bladder is a large sack which acts as a reservoir. It is positioned at the base of the abdominal cavity, close to the sexual organs. When fully expanded with urine it can hold as much as 0.5 pint (140 ml). The ureters join it close to its base, feeding it with urine from the kidneys.

At its base, there is an opening for the excretion of urine. This is closed off by an internal sphincter, a circle of muscle which, when relaxed, opens and allows the urine to pass into the urethra.

The urethra conveys urine to the exterior of the body. It varies in length according to the sex of the individual. In males it is considerably longer due to the length of the penis and also has an extra set of sphinctal muscles guarding its passage located at the prostate.

The Musco-Skeletal System
(Earth in Earth: The Root Center)

The skeleton acts as a rigid frame for the body giving it shape and support. Most of its bones are hinged for the purposes of movement. The muscles, which are anchored to it, provide this movement. Because of this, it is also sometimes referred to as the locomotor system.

Bones are the individual units of the skeleton. They consist of calcium carbonate and calcium phosphate, which makes them hard and rigid. There are generally three classifications for bones: flat bone, such as the skull and the pelvic girdle which provide protection for delicate organs; long bones, such as the femur (thigh bone) and the humerus (upper arm bone), which act as levers for the muscles to aid movement; and short bones, such as the carpels (wrist bones) which help to confer strength. Internally, there are cavities in most of bones. These are filled with blood vessels, as well as marrow, a fleshy substance which is important in the production of red blood cells.

The Vertebral Column (Spine)

All the bones of the body are attached to the vertebral column or are attached to bones which are. There are 24 Vertebrae (of which there are three sorts), 5 fused sacral bones, and 4 fused coccyx bones within this structure. Through each of the vertebrae there is a hollow canal which encases and protects the spinal cord. Protrusions on the sides of the vertebrae act as anchoring points for muscles. The vertebrae are separated by discs of cartilage, known as the intervertebral discs, which allow movement between them.

The 7 vertebrae in the neck are known as the cervical vertebrae. These include the atlas and axis vertebra at the top, which support the skull and allow it to move horizontally and vertically. These are followed by the 12 thoracic vertebrae, which continue to protect the spinal cord, and act as anchoring points for the rib cage. After the thoracic vertebrae, come the five lumbar vertebrae. These are the largest of the vertebrae, and help to support the trunk of the body during movement.

The five fused sacral bones, along with the flat bones of the pelvic girdle, curve under to protect the organs of the lower abdominal cavity, as well as transmitting the body weight to the legs. The tail of the spinal cord finishes its journey down the column within them.

The four fused coccyx bones protrude below the sacrum. They actually serve no purpose, being the remnants of the mammalian tail within humans.

The Skull

The skull is a dome-like structure which sits above the first cervical vertebra. Its purpose is to protect the brain from damage, and to provide a protective structure for the eyes and ears, and the start of the upper alimentary tract (see Mouth). There is only one moving part within the skull, the lower jaw, which moves to aid mastication. Most of the skull consists of flat bones, which fuse together shortly after birth.

The Rib Cage and Sternum

The rib cage and sternum protect the lungs, heart and other organs within the thoracic cavity. There are 24 ribs: 12 emerging from each side of the vertebral column, curving round to form the rib cage and meet the sternum.

Like the ribs, the sternum is also a flat bone. It sits at the front of the rib cage protecting the heart and forming an anchoring point for the ribs. It starts at the base of the neck and finishes at the diaphragm or solar plexus.

The Arms

The arms are attached to the body at the upper back of the rib cage. Two flat bones, the scapula (shoulder blades), sit on either side where the thoracic vertebrae commence. These are also attached to the top of the sternum by two long bones, the clavicles, which form the shoulders. Each scapula has a cup-like structure on its outer edge so that the ball of the upper arm bone (the humerus) can attach.

The humerus ends at the elbow, where it divides into the two lower arm bones, the radius and ulna. These bones allow rotation of the arm at its lower length, and are approximately the same length as the humerus.

The radius and ulna divide into the carpels. There are eight of these forming the wrist. These divide further to form the metacarpals, the five lengths of the fingers which finish with the three phalanges.

The Pelvic Girdle

Protecting the genito-urinary system in the lower abdomen, the pelvic girdle also acts as an anchoring point for the thigh bones or femurs. Flat bones curve round from either side of the sacral bones joining at the base of the abdomen (the synthesis pubis). This forms a hollow opening through which the female organs of reproduction and the rectum can protrude.

Hollow cups are formed on each side of the pelvic girdle. These act as anchoring points for the ball-like structures at the top of the each femur.

The Legs

The legs start with the femurs, the long bones of the leg, and follow a similar pattern to the arms: dividing at the knee to form the fibula and tibia, and then dividing into the tarsal and metatarsals (the equivalent of the carpals and metacarpals). The only difference in this structure, apart from size and proportions, is that a small bony plate, known as the patella or knee-cap, protects the joint between the femur and the fibula and tibia.

The formation of the foot differs considerably from that of the hand. A bony protrusion, the calcaneum, sticks out to form the heel and to aid balance.

Further Study

As we said at the beginning of this chapter, this is only intended as a sketch of the human body; there is a great deal of fine detail missing. We recommend further reading on anatomy and physiology to anyone who is interested in doing any form of healing work, and suggest that they refer to the bibliography of this book for information.

5

The Mind: How It Works

Much can be learned from mythology about the nature of life (for more on this see chapter 8). This is certainly true when you explore ancient mythology for examples of psychology----this word itself being composed of the name of the ancient Greek goddess Psyche, which meant soul, and *logos*, which meant "word" or "science." The myth of Psyche first appeared in *Metamorphoses,* one of the many works of Apuleius, about the middle of the second century A.D. The myth no doubt preceded this work by many centuries, and as a Platonist, it is highly unlikely that Apuleius believed in the myth as a physical reality. Nevertheless, he used it to show how myth could be used to express the secrets of the soul, and of the mind.

Psyche was the loveliest of three beautiful princesses. In fact she was such a stunning beauty that she was hailed as the new Aphrodite, and the people came from far and wide to admire and worship her. All her sisters married, but Psyche was unable to find a husband, so stayed in her father's house alone.

Her father, the king, was saddened by her lack of suitors, and sought advice from the nearby oracle, which gave a worrying reply. He was told to dress the princess as though she was to be wed, and take her to the top of the mountainside and abandon her there. There, a hideous monster would come and take her away with him. The king and the queen were in despair, but knew they must obey the oracle or face the wrath of the gods.

It was Aphrodite who had spoken through the oracle. She was jealous of Psyche's beauty and the attention that was being paid to her. She had decided on a course of revenge, and commanded her son, Eros, to make Psyche fall in love with the ugliest and poorest of mortals imaginable. But Aphrodite's plan failed; when Eros saw Psyche, he fell in love with her himself, and planned to court her secretly. Instead of condemning her to the hideously ugly monster, Eros arranged for Zephyrus, the West Wind, to carry her off gently to a secret valley.

Exhausted by the journey, when she awoke she found herself lying on a flowery bank outside a palace of gold. Curious, she entered its open gates. She was welcomed by voices and, after bathing, was invited to sit and eat at a banquet table, while the voices entertained her with singing.

After the meal, the voices led her to a bedchamber where she settled down to sleep. It was then that she felt a presence beside her, whom she immediately assumed to be the husband the oracle had spoken of. He did not feel monstrous as she had been led to believe, even though she was unable to see him.

When she awoke at dawn, her husband had gone. During the day, invisible servants saw to her needs, and entertained her, until he returned after dark. This continued for several days, and Psyche was becoming used to his disappearance at dawn, and to the invisible servants waiting on her. She began to miss her family, especially the company of her sisters. She told her husband of her loneliness, and he warned her that to dwell on the past and the companionship of her sisters might well lead her into danger.

In the end, her husband gave in to her and commanded Zephyrus to bring her sisters to the palace. They were immediately struck with bitter jealousy over Psyche's good fortune, and Eros repeated his warning to his wife. She should not attempt to see him; she should be content with her happiness and not yield to curiosity. In this way her happiness would last, but if she did not pay heed she must expect disaster to befall her.

The sisters plagued Psyche with endless questions, and tried to fill her with fear over her husband. They said that he was a monstrous dragon, who was fattening her up as a meal. That she must do something immediately before it was too late. Psyche followed their advice. That night she hid a lamp and a knife within the room, to kill her husband, the dragon.

When she shone the lamp on her husband she was astonished by what she saw. Instead of a dragon, as she had been made to fear, she saw Eros, the beautiful adolescent son of Aphrodite, asleep with wings folded by his sides. She was so startled when she recognized him, that she tipped the lamp and a drop of hot oil fell on Eros's sleeping body. He awoke startled, and realizing that he had been betrayed, flew out of reach of Psyche's outstretched hands.

"Psyche, you wished to see me. You know who I am. Now I must leave you; you will never see me again."

Psyche collapsed with grief as her husband flew out of sight.

Realizing her own betrayal by her own sisters, she avenged herself on them by telling them that Eros was asking to see them. They threw themselves from the top of the mountainside, expecting to be carried off by Zephyrus, and fell to their deaths. Psyche, in desperation, traveled the world looking for Eros, but to no avail. No one was willing to help her, fearing the wrath of Aphrodite if they did.

Eventually Psyche had no choice but to surrender herself to the mercy of Aphrodite. Aphrodite first of all tortured her, and after becoming bored with this decided to set Psyche some tasks for her own amusement. One of these tasks was for Psyche to descend into the underworld to ask Persephone for a beauty ointment. Aphrodite forbade her to open the box, but Psyche's curiosity got the better of her, and she opened it. A vapor of sleep enveloped her, and she collapsed to the floor.

Meanwhile, Eros realized that he still loved Psyche, and had become desperate to retrieve his wife. He saw her sleeping from the vapor, woke her, and carried her to Olympus. He asked Zeus for protection for her, and asked his permission to marry her, which Zeus granted. Aphrodite and Psyche were reconciled, and Psyche had a child by Eros, who was called Voluptuousness.

There have been many attempts to interpret this myth, which is a more in-depth working of the old folk tale of Beauty and the Beast. It may have been Apuleius's way of describing the journey of the soul; the reflection of pure beauty chained to the earth by its baser aspects, such as curiosity. The soul cannot bear the sight of divine beauty, before it has been prepared and tested. It must be helped by the concept of love, which allows access to the world of ideas.

Other interpretations have included: that loving involves the necessity to make oneself vulnerable; that unity grows out of separation; and that the soul must make a journey into night, if it is to become unified with the darker half of its own personality. The number of potential interpretations continues with each individual who reads it, but maybe this is the whole point of this myth, because in the end the examination of our own minds will always be subjective, however hard we try to be objective.

The Theories of Carl Gustav Jung

Jung is one of the most popular psychologists among pagans and occultists. The reason for this becomes obvious when you study his work and his own life. A biography, *Lord Of The Underworld: Jung and the Twentieth Century* was written by Colin Wilson in 1984. This book outlines Jung's study of the occult and his personal experiences. There is little doubt that he was a gifted psychic, and he confounded his colleagues, including Sigmund Freud, with his predictions on many occasions.

By the time he became involved with Freud, he had already made a name for himself, having received an honorary degree for pioneering word-association tests. He first met Freud in 1907, but after working together for five years Jung broke away through disagreement. Jung published his first major work shortly afterwards, and continued to develop his theories.

The Unconscious Mind

Jung developed his concepts on the unconscious mind from his work with Freud, but elaborated considerably upon it. He divided the unconscious mind into two levels: the personal unconscious, which sits beneath the active conscious mind (see Fig. 9), and the collective unconscious, which sits below this. The true self bridges both the conscious mind and the personal unconscious, but is dominated most of the time by the persona and the underlying ego (see page 83). The personal unconscious bridges all the areas of the mind and, from Jung's viewpoint, was the most important area to work with.

The Personal Unconscious: Here, the unconscious mind holds feelings and emotions which have been repressed. It also holds on to the distant memories of past events of importance in our lives.

The Collective Unconscious: At this deeper level of mind the collective, inherited symbolism is housed. It is the place where dreams and visions arise. Freud had assumed it to be an area of darkness and impulse, but Jung developed the concept of it being a primordial structure, protecting the secrets of the mind which cannot be seen directly by the individual.

These secrets can only be grasped by the conscious mind in the form of archetypal symbols, metaphors for the instinctual base of the mind. Within the unconscious mind these archetypes are described as forming a crystalline structure, with multiple facets and axes. This results in the formation of conceptual polarities: mother/father, good/bad, light/dark and so on. Other axes are also forming, involving the same archetypes----for example: light mother/dark mother, the concepts of black Isis/white Isis in Egyptian mythology, and Kali/Laxmi in modern Hindu symbolism.

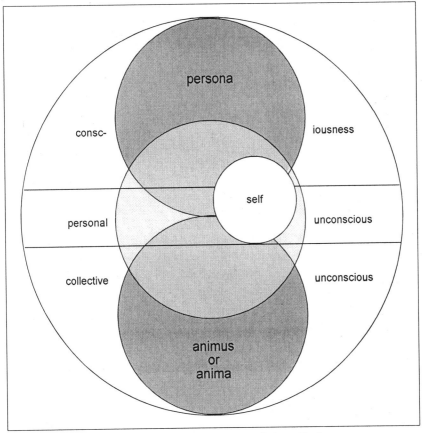

Figure 9: Jung's structure of the Mind

As pagans we are all familiar with these concepts put forward by Jung. The archetypal concept of "mother" can be seen as a point on a crystal with axes converging on it, and this applies to all of the other major archetypes. This structuring collects the memories and experiences of the individual, polarizing them in the process and integrating them into its structure. The result is that unconsciously we apply archetypal concepts to our everyday lives.

The conscious and unconscious aspects of our selves are also divided among the four functions. In modern Western society, thinking remains in the consciousness, while feeling, being its polar opposite, is relegated to the unconscious realm. Sensation and intuition are found on the edges of the boundary between the conscious and the unconscious.

The Four Functions

All of Jung's work is dominated by the idea of the unity and the wholeness of the psyche, symbolized by the circle. He divided this circle into four functions----thinking, feeling, sensation and intuition----which he defined as the four major forms of psychic activity (see Fig. 10). These functions work independently. When looking at an image such as a painting, we may therefore think about it: "Is this a true depiction?" We may feel for the picture, either accepting or rejecting, liking or disliking, the content of the image, for no conscious reason. We may examine it from the aspect of sensation, for example by touching the painting to feel where the brush strokes have deposited the paint and then making a judgment from this. Or we may examine the deeper meaning of the painted image on an intuitive level.

Jung paired these functions into those that involve judgment----thinking and feeling----and those that involve perceptive processes----sensation and intuition. He concluded that the constituents of these pairs are opposite poles, and only one can function at any one time. Hence, we cannot think and feel at the same time about the same thing, but we may alternate these functions. Jung also concluded that individuals have a preferred function with at least one auxiliary: the empiricist would mostly think about sensation, the theorist would think about his intuitions, the aesthete would feel about his intuitions, and the sensualist would feel about his sensations.

Jung considered that our Western culture overemphasized the thinking function; Western society had gained the whole world but

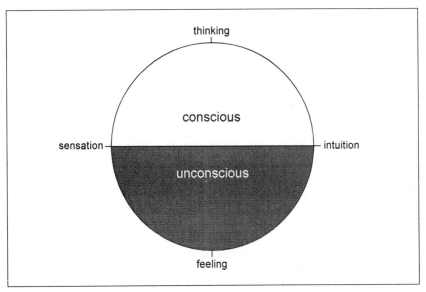

Figure 10: Jung's Four Functions

lost its soul. This was fine for the younger generation, but he felt that the object of age was the rounding off of the psyche to precipitate the achievement of insight, wholeness and advanced spirituality. This was the path of the functions, from thinking to intuition, from intuition to sensing, from sensing to feeling---a journey to the depths of the unconscious mind.

Introversion and Extroversion

Apart from being divided into the four functions, Jung also put forward the idea that the psyche is polarized between being introvert or extrovert. The extrovert has a positive relationship with the physical world, is generally more outgoing, while the introvert tends to have a positive relationship with the internal world, making him or her appear withdrawn and meditative.

This results in the four functions being influenced, making them either extroverted or introverted in their attitude. The unconscious mind compensates for the conscious mind; hence an individual who appears quiet and introverted, may be unconsciously loud and sensationalist internally, and vice versa. This may come out into the consciousness in times of stress.

Combined with the four functions of thinking, feeling, sensation and intuition, Jung defines eight distinct personality types based around introversion and extroversion:

1. **Extroverted Thinking Type**: Persons of this type are ruled by their need to be objective in their understanding of the world around them. They are typically scientists, who devote their lives to learning as much as possible about natural phenomena, natural laws, and theoretical formulations. They tend to repress the feeling side of their natures, appearing to others cold and impersonal. In extreme cases the feelings are forced to find another route to manifest themselves within the personality. This may make them autocratic, bigoted and vain. A good example would be Dr. Jekyll and Mr. Hyde: the mad scientist who periodically turns into a psychopathic monster.

2. **Introverted Thinking Type**: This personality is inward-seeking, exemplified by the philosopher. It seeks to understand the reality of its own being, and in extreme cases the exploration can bear little resemblance to reality. Many schizophrenics are the extremes of this type for this reason. Like the extrovert types, they try to protect themselves from their own feelings, and therefore share many of the same personality traits as those types. They may appear to be emotionless and distant because they do not seem to welcome or value the interaction of others in their thoughts. They do not feel the need to be accepted by others, or to have their ideas accepted for that matter. They are therefore inclined to be stubborn, standoffish, arrogant and inconsiderate.

3. **Extroverted Feeling Type**: One of the most noticeable traits of this type is mood swings. This type's feelings change as frequently as the situations they find themselves in. Even a slight change in environment can cause a change. They can be emotional, ostentatious, and moody. They form strong attachments to people, but these are normally transitory; love can turn to hate very easily with them. Regardless of these swings in mood, their feelings are fairly conventional. When this type's thinking function is over-repressed, their thought processes become noticeably primitive and undeveloped.

4. **Introverted Feeling Type**: Unlike the extroverted feeling type, they tend to hide their feelings from the world. They tend to be quiet and inaccessible, and may also appear to have a feeling of depression around them. Interestingly, they may also appear to

80

have a feeling of inner harmony and self-sufficiency about them. This can result in them having a mysterious and charismatic quality; a quote often said about them is: "Still waters run deep." They have incredibly deep and intense emotions which can often erupt, much to the surprise of those who know them.

5. **Extroverted Sensation Type**: Realistic, practical, and hard-headed are the traits of this type. They delight in collecting facts about the external world, but may not be all that concerned about what these facts actually mean. They accept everything around them at face value, without any thought. Their feelings can be shallow as they are attracted to thrill-seeking and physical pleasure through sensation. In its extreme they can become crude sensualists, living purely for these experiences. This can make them susceptible to addictions and compulsive behavior.

6. **Introverted Sensation Type**: The archetype which best defines this kind of personality is that of the hermit from the tarot; they separate themselves from the world, immersing themselves in their own psychic sensations. They consider the world to be dull and uninteresting compared with their own inner sensations. They have difficulty expressing themselves, except through art, although this may be devoid of any deeper meaning. To the outsider, this type can appear calm and self-controlled, although uninteresting as they are deficient in both thought and feeling.

7. **Extroverted Intuitive Type**: They are flighty and unstable. They leap from situation to situation looking for new possibilities within the external world. They start their new intuitions with strong enthusiasm; they make excellent promoters of new causes and enterprises, but they never seem to complete what they are doing, having moved on to their next project. This is because of their deficiency in the thinking function, which results in their inability to pursue their intuitions for too long without getting bored. They tend to fritter their lives away on a succession of these intuitions, and find it hard to hold down steady employment. They tend to treat friendships in the same way, becoming easily bored after a period of time. As a result they are prone unwittingly to hurt those they love.

8. **Introverted Intuitive Type**: These are the artists, dreamers, prophets, visionaries and cranks. They are a mystery to their

friends, and normally consider themselves to be misunderstood geniuses. They can be poor at communication, due to being out of touch with external reality or its conventions; Vincent Van Gogh is a good example of such a personality type. They are isolated in a world of primordial images which they do not understand. Like the extroverted intuitive type, they jump from intuition to intuition, never developing any of them to their full potential. Since they are unable to sustain an interest for too long they cannot make as much a contribution to the under-standing of the psychic processes as do the introverted thinkers. They tend to leave their work for others to build upon.

Ego, Id, Persona, and Shadow

Jung's concept of the ego was adopted directly from Freud. Freud believed the human personality consisted of two compo-nents, the ego and the id. These terms are Latin and mean, respec-tively, "I" and "it." In everyday life we normally refer to ourselves in the context of the semiconscious ego, hence we refer to ourselves as "I."

If we become controlled by our instinctual impulses----hunger, thirst, sexual and aggressive instincts----we fall under the control of our id. When this happens we may very likely refer to these forces as "it."

In a normally adjusted individual the function of the ego is to serve, and to a certain degree control, the instinctual id. Hence we are prevented from taking off all our clothes in a public place in hot weather by our ego, which fears ridicule. This is a good example of the ego controlling mechanism that develops with age; in a child the ego has not yet developed, so a youngster may very likely strip without fear. An example of the serving function arises in hunger: the id only knows the hunger and the demand to be satisfied, but the ego knows how to open the can of food!

When the ego finds itself trying to cope with over demand from the id, which is only interested in satisfying itself, the ego defense mechanism copes by using several strategies. It may push the un-wanted impulses, thoughts, and ideas into the unconscious. This is called repression. It is also responsible for projecting these impulses and ideas onto others, so sometimes what we most hate in others is what we are trying to repress within ourselves. It may also displace the unwanted impulse, such as when a person takes out their anger on someone who is not connected with the cause of the anger.

We may try to intellectualize and rationalize these impulses, developing elaborate excuses for our behavior. Other ways of coping with the demands of the id. are as follows: to regress to a childlike state where the ego is less demanding; to deny consciously the cause of an impulse, whether it be fact, feeling or memory; and to sublimate the channeling of unacceptable impulses into acceptable everyday behavior. Many sports perform this function by channeling unwanted aggression. While the ego remains partly conscious, these methods of ego defense always remain unconscious.

Jung differed from Freud, believing that we develop a persona at the outer edge of our functioning egos. This is a mask, and a compromise between what the ego aspires to be, and the limitations and social functions imposed upon it. If there is no compromise between the ego's aspirations and the social limitations, then the persona becomes a rigid stereotyped mask. In a balanced state it is supple and pliable, being able to adjust to life's everyday situations.

The shadow is the antithesis of the persona. Just as the persona lies in front of the ego, the shadow hides behind it. It is the part of the ego which has been rejected, its unacceptable face. This concept has appeared in mythology and literature for centuries. In Norse mythology, Odin's shadow is Loki; in Egyptian, Osiris's shadow is Set. Biblically, Satan can be seen as God's shadow, and in modern writing, the concept is typified by the characters of Dr. Jekyll and Mr. Hyde.

Because of the ego's rejection, the shadow is often found portrayed as evil in nature, as can be seen from the examples given previously. This is an oversimplification; when the ego sublimates some of its aspects, it sometimes throws the baby out with the bath water, so to speak. For example, if aggressive aspects are sublimated, individuals may also lose their ability to be assertive and make decisions. Sometimes exploration of our shadows (an essential aspect of many forms of occultism) can restore these lost aspects and complete the wholeness of the individual's psyche.

Anima, Animus and Libido

The anima is the buried feminine element in a man, and the animus the buried male element in a woman. Both are often found, like the shadow, in art, literature and mythology. In Welsh mythology, the Arwen is the female soul-spirit of the poet and artist, and in Irish, the Leannán Sidhe fulfills the same function. Arthurian Nimue is the anima representation of this within Merlin. Many male pagans relate to the goddess principle via their anima, as do female pagans to the god principle via their animus. Mary Shelley, when she wrote *Frankenstein*, not only portrayed her shadow (the monster), but also her animus, Professor Frankenstein himself.

When we first fall in love, or have crushes on the opposite sex, we tend to fall for this soul image, unconscious of the fact that we are falling in love with ourselves. The result, if we remain unaware of what is really happening, can be disastrous, as with Lancelot and Guinevere within medieval Arthurian mythology. (The original Guinevere was a very different woman, but that is another matter.) If recognized and harnessed, the soul-spirit can act as an inspiration and a guide.

An example of this can be found in the Welsh bardic tradition where the anima is referred to as "the Arwen": the female spirit of inspiration which eventually comes to claim the bard's soul while he is still young. Perhaps within this myth there is a veiled warn-ing----that the exploration of the anima can go too far, eventually destroying important parts of the individual's persona. A similar concept appears in Norse myth, with the Valkyries coming to claim the souls of the warriors, and within the Celtic myth of the Morri-gan, the crow goddess who claims Cuchulain. Even the myths revolving around various pagan deities show the importance that the anima/animus concept has played in the formation of the hu-man psyche.

Jung proposed that all aspects of our psyche are driven by our individual life-force, which he referred to as the libido. In its higher form he suggested that it energized our will, and affected our per-formance mentally. In its lower form it is responsible for energizing our attitudes, interests, and our hidden potentials. The libido swings like a pendulum between the higher and the lower forms. Jung called this action the principle of emantridomia, and believed that the action of the ego could make one of the forms dominant in our own psyche, but it was still governed by this pendulum effect. Eventually the pendulum swings to the other side, so we experience polarities of tension and relaxation, evaluation and decision, and the like, within our lives, causing a dynamic balance.

The Development of Personality

Jung believed that the development of personality was inherent within all of us from the moment we are born; that we start life in a state of undifferentiated wholeness. The eventual goal of this development is to differentiate fully all the aspects of the psyche—such as the persona, ego, id, shadow—while maintaining the balance between them and unifying the personality (Jung called this process individuation). He believed that very few people reached this unity (he considers Buddha such an individual).

In the process of individuation, not only do the structures of the personality become more differentiated during one's life, but the structures themselves also become more differentiated internally. Each system becomes more complex, allowing it to express itself in more ways—the undeveloped ego, for example, has a few simple ways of being conscious, but as it develops these increase. Eventually this process enables the ego to make fine perceptual discriminations among ideas and the meaning of objective phenomena. This process affects the persona, shadow, anima/animus, and the personal unconscious in the same way.

In the collective unconscious this ability to express in more subtle and intricate ways can be seen in the way that archetypes important to the personality develop. In childhood we are satisfied with simple nursery rhymes and games, but as the process of individuation develops we strive for more complex archetypal forms within religion, art, literature and society.

Although individuation does not require external stimulation to come into existence (it is part of our genetic makeup), it does require stimulation in the form of healthy experiences and education to prevent its growth from being stunted. Normally there is little problem for most of the aspects of the psyche. However, the shadow is generally repressed within modern society: children are punished and taught to suppress their animal instincts. These return to the unconscious sphere of the personality. However, the goal of education is to bring all of the personality's aspects into the conscious, including the shadow.

In later life the undifferentiated shadow manifests these repressed feelings in crude and inadequate ways; Jung points out that modern society's preoccupation with developing more savage forms of warfare are a result of this repression. Only by becoming conscious can a system of the personality (such as the shadow) individuate successfully. Psychotherapy, the healing of the mind, is primarily a process of individuation.

Individuation is the first step in the process toward integrating all the systems of the personality. The second step is called transcendence. Jung states that the aim of the transcendent function is "the realization, in all of its aspects, of the personality originally hidden away in the embryonic germplasm; the production and unfolding of the original potential wholeness."

Individuation and the integration of all the systems of the personality are co-existing processes, this unification is brought about by the transcendent function; the realization of selfhood. A good example of transcendence at work is the integration of the anima with the masculine nature of the male persona. As both the persona and the anima are permitted to individuate by being expressed in conscious acts, they are also integrating with each other. A man who has integrated his anima is one whose behavior is not solely either masculine or feminine but a synthesis of both. Instead of opposition or separation, there is a harmonious blend. Like individuation, Jung believed that this selfhood brought about by the transcendent function was rarely achieved.

Several factors can hinder the development of a completely individuated and integrated personality. Jung believed that it was possible that genetic factors could influence personality development; a person being predisposed toward a strong or weak anima/animus, or extroverted rather than introverted, or a thinking rather than a feeling type. Jung felt that this heredity could be overcome, believing that the greatest influence was the environment that the young personality developed in.

Every psychologist accepts that the influence of the parents on an individual's development is one of the greatest factors. Jung takes this belief a step further. In Jungian psychology there is the belief that the child has no separate identity during the early years; that the psyche of a child is a reflection of its parents. Psychological disturbance within the parents is therefore reflected by the child. In one case, Jung even describes a child's dreams being identical to those of his disturbed parents; the child mirrored his father's Psyche.

When children go to school, they begin to develop their own identities; the process of individuation begins to take place. As long as a child is not over protected, does not have decisions made for him or her, and is not prevented from having a wide range of experiences, this process will develop unhampered. If either or both of the parents do try to force aspects of their own personalities onto the child----their introversion----the child will develop imbalances in his or her own personality. Jung believed that schoolteachers were surrogate parents in the educational field, and could have a similar effect on children.

6

The Psychic and Spiritual Body

The Aura

The aura is the visual expression of several levels that surround the physical human body (see Fig. 11). These seven (or eight if we include the etheric) levels of the human entity are divided into two groups, generally called the individuality and the personality. The individuality (upper spiritual, lower spiritual, and upper mental) is the immortal part, the spiritual aura which survives from incarnation to incarnation. The personality (lower mental, upper astral, lower astral, etheric, and physical body) is the transient part, the mental/emotional aura and the etheric body. It is built up during a single incarnation and discarded when it ends.

These various levels also act as a psychic shield, an interface, and a form of communication with other organisms. They can indicate the emotional and mental state of individuals, as well as the state of spiritual development. Every living organism has an aura, and with practice it is quite possible to see it.

The easiest aura to see is that of a tree at dawn or twilight. It normally manifests as a misty gray field around the topmost branches. In humans, the aura is generated by the action of the chakra centers spinning. The result is that three distinct auras exist, layered like the skin of an onion (see Fig. 12). Some advanced psychics are able to see all the eight levels within these auras, but generally most are only able to see the following three main auras.

The Etheric Aura/Body

The gray misty area closest to the body is generally referred to as the etheric body, which normally extends about one to three

---

Seventh Plane UPPER SPIRITUAL

Pure or Abstract Spirit. The Divine Spark. Substance and energy directed from the Great Unmanifest. Astrological symbol: the Sun

---

Sixth Plane LOWER SPIRITUAL

Concrete Spirit. Tendency for one of the Seven Rays to predominate and set keynote. Astrological symbol: Jupiter

---

Fifth Plane UPPER MENTAL

Abstract Mind. Qualities differentiated into types. Astrological symbol: Mercury

---

Fourth Plane LOWER MENTAL

Concrete Mind. Definiteness, form, memory. Astrological symbol: Saturn

---

Third Plane UPPER ASTRAL

Abstract Emotions. Attraction, desire for union. Astrological symbol: Venus

---

Second Plane LOWER ASTRAL

Instincts and Passions. Desire to attract or possess. Astrological symbol: Mars

---

ETHERIC

The tenuous energy-web of near-matter which links the physical with the subtler planes and maintains it in being. Astrological symbol:the Moon

---

First Plane PHYSICAL

Dense matter, the material body. Astrological symbol: the Earth

---

Figure 11: The Component Levels of a Human Being

inches over the body. The term "ether" refers to a state between energy and matter. Gifted psychics often describe the etheric body as being composed of energy lines forming a sparkling translucent web along which sparks of bluish white light move. This gives a pulsating effect. It is generated by the first four chakra centers, these being related to the elements of Earth, Air, Fire and Water.

The action of these four centers in conjunction with the fifth, the etheric chakra, results in the formation of this part of the aura. The etheric body vibrates at the same frequency as spirit, and acts as a vehicle for it. It therefore helps to shape and anchor the physical body, which is why it hugs the surface of the body so closely. For this reason it is sometimes referred to as the etheric double. Its main purpose is to feed the body with life force or prana, as it is called in the Vedic scripts.

The Mental/Emotional Aura

Second is the mental/emotional aura. It is generated by the sixth chakra, the brow center or third eye. It is made up of even finer energy than the etheric body, and unlike that body it is normally ovoid in shape. How far it projects depends on the immediate mental and emotional state of the individual; in someone who enters a room full of strangers, the aura will withdraw closer to the body. When that person feels more comfortable with the people around, it will begin to return to its normal size.

In an extrovert person it can project out as far as several feet, but in an introvert, it may always remain close to the body, almost withdrawing into the etheric body. A trained psychic sees this part of the aura as made up of a variety of colors. These, like the size of the aura, indicate the mental, emotional and occasionally the physical state of its owner.

Sometimes thought forms can be seen within this body. These manifest as blobs of varying brightness, color and form. The clearer and more well-defined the idea, the clearer and more well-formed is the thought form associated with it. The color of the form represents an emotion attached to it----such as red for anger. These thought forms are in a continual state of flux. Those we focus on regularly remain static within the aura, becoming important forces or convictions within our lives, and thus transfer themselves to the spiritual body.

The Spiritual Aura

The last, and the least easy for even a sensitive to see, is the spiritual body. This connects with the last of the chakras, the crown.

In a spiritually developed person it can extend from the body for some distance; it is said that the spiritual body of the Buddha Gautama, in his last incarnation, could be seen for six miles. This part of the aura exists on the astral plane, and is the individual's connection with the world of spirit.

It is in this, combined with the mental/emotional body, that the individual's consciousness moves during astral travel in the higher planes, but during out-of-body experiences on the physical, material plane, it is only the mental/emotional section of the aura which detaches from the physical body. This happens involuntarily sometimes during sleep, giving what is often referred to as lucid dreaming.

Because of the etheric body's responsibility for continuing the life functions, it remains attached to the body until the moment of death. Like the mental/emotional body there are colors present, but these indicate the character and personality of the individual rather than just his or her present emotions. After physical death the consciousness leaves the physical body and withdraws into the astral.

The Chakra System

The inclusion of the Hindu/Buddhist chakra system into Western occult thinking occurred at the end of the nineteenth century, and was almost certainly introduced into European thinking by Madame Blatavsky and the Theosophy movement. In Indian philosophical thought, the understanding of chakras in their present forms has existed since at least the seventh century, the time of the first transcription of the Vedas. An early form of the system probably existed well before this date, and there is some circumstantial evidence that a proto-chakra system was known throughout the earlier migratory Indo-European culture. This would have brought this bodily energy system into pre-Christian Germanic, Celtic and Greek mystical thought.

The significance of the caduceus, used in Greek healing practices, bears a striking resemblance to the chakra system, the serpents

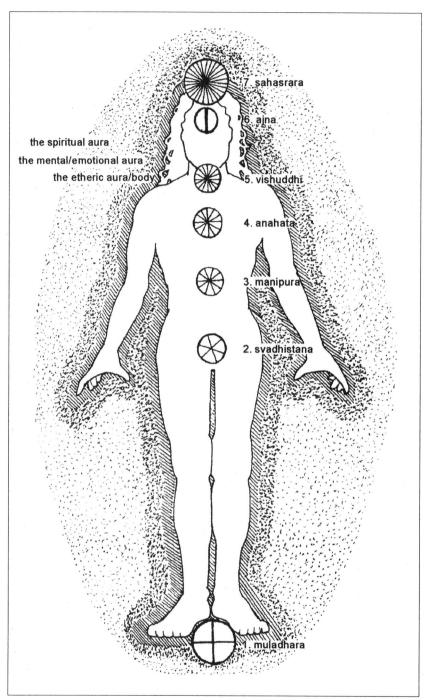

Figure 12: The Body's Energy System

representing the path of Kundalini and where this crosses the centers. This was cited as evidence by the Theosophy movement, and notes on this relationship were first published in C. W. Leadbeaters *The Chakras----A Monograph* as early as 1927.

Within Western occultism there has always been a belief that it is dangerous to mix magical systems----that Western philosophical thinking does not always readily combine with Eastern. Regardless of whether you believe that the evidence for the existence of a Western system of energy points to Indo-European origin, after working as a healer it soon becomes apparent that the chakra system, and the energies it represents, is as real as the physical organs of the body.

Chakra (or chakram as it was earlier known by the Theosophists) is Sanskrit for "wheel" and is used to signify the idea of a turning center of energy within the body. To the gifted psychic, chakras manifest as revolving discs of light emerging from the body, sometimes described as funnel-shaped when viewed side on. These centers are normally arranged within the human body in a vertical fashion.

It is important for anyone studying them to realize that there is more than one descriptive system; this will help to prevent confusion during study and further research on the subject. Different systems quote different numbers of centers, as well as positions and functions. These range from seven major chakras (see Fig. 12) to ten, exclusive of the 21 minor chakras. The commonest system in use is the seven major centers and we feel this system is the most beneficial for would-be healers until they sufficiently understand the nature of the energy they will be working with.

The chakras act as connection and transferal points for the energy of the body. They also vitalize each auric body, thus affecting the physical body likewise. As we explained in chapter 2, the physical body consists of all four elements, and four of the chakras are responsible for movement of that elemental energy between the etheric, mental and astral bodies of man.

Just as the elements exist in the physical body, so they also simultaneously exist in these other three bodies. Hence the first four lower chakras are dedicated to these elements. The next three upper chakras are for the purpose of generating these auric bodies. The result of this is a complex interwoven system of energy, which is sometimes seen by the clairvoyant as a web of colored energy enmeshing spinning colored vortices.

Rather than energy actually spinning out from each chakra center as at first suggested, the force actually pours into each center and is then pushed out by the spinning motion at right angles to itself (see Fig. 13). This action is like the effect of a bar magnet that is pushed into the field of an induction coil, resulting in an electrical current which flows around the coil at right angles to the direction of the magnet. One effect of this action is to cause the formation of petals, an effect caused by the primal energy present which is described as undulating as it passes through the chakra. The number of petals within each center increases as you move up from the root center.

In most individuals the chakras remain in a closed, dormant state, and each center is only opened when its action is required in everyday life. Normally, only five centers are open at any one time. They enlarge as spiritual development increases. When all the centers are opened simultaneously, in perfect balance, and have reached their full development, each center spins in the opposite direction to its two adjacent chakras, similar to a series of cogs.

This action is responsible for moving two flows of energy----one positive, one negative, up and down the whole system from the root chakra to the crown----when the centers are consciously opened in various spiritual exercises such as Yoga. This is the mystical Kundalini, the serpent fire, which the Eastern yogis attempt (though only with full understanding and control) to raise through the other chakras to bring about psychic enlightenment. If aroused early in the unprepared, the Kundalini is potentially highly dangerous. We recommend those interested in these practices find a competent instructor.

One interesting aspect of the system is its relationship with the physical body's endocrine system (see chapter 4). This would seem to suggest that chakric meditation acts as a color-coded trigger system for controlling these glands. There is certainly a correlation between each chakra and its corresponding endocrine gland. For example, the Manipura or sacral chakra which is governed by the element of Fire. This center is responsible for governing the body's vital energy. It can be no coincidence that it is positioned over the adrenal glands, which are responsible for stimulating energy for the body's fright-and-flight reflex.

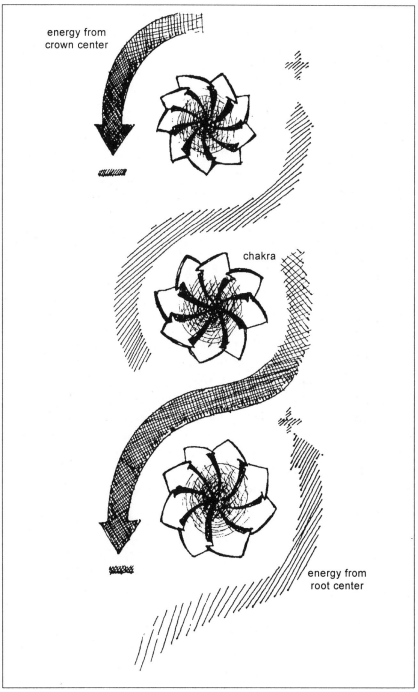

Figure 13: Energy Flow around the Chakras

The Seven Major Centers

1. **The Muladhara**: Located at the base of the spine, this center is commonly referred to as the root chakra. It is the seat of the mystical Kundalini, which is sometimes referred to as a goddess. There are differing views on its actual position. If the body is in the lotus position, it is certainly at the base of the spine (the fourth sacral bone), but there is one view that, when standing, the normal position of this center is at the base of the feet. This would make sense as it is the center which links us with the earth. As such, it is responsible for picking up energies within the earth, and therefore allows dowsers to detect the item they are searching for.

   The root chakra is normally seen as a rosy red when at rest and fiery orange-red when active. It is divided into four segments or petals due to the effect of the energies present. Being the center related to the element of Earth, it is responsible for the disposal of unwanted, impure energies which may pollute the three levels of the aura and the other centers. Within the physical body it governs the spinal column and the urinary system, including the kidneys. This chakra is also associated with physical sensation----feeling physical pain or pleasure.

2. **The Svadhistana**: This is the sacral center, and is positioned in the genital area. Early Western practitioners of Laya Yoga avoided this center altogether, replacing it with the splenic center, which was described as being several inches off center and to the left of the other centers.

   The reason for the avoidance of the original sacral center and its replacement with what was regarded as a minor center was the Theosophist's worry that concentration on this center would result in the awakening of sexual feelings. Such an act was considered inherently black in nature, as much of the Theosophist literature of the period testifies.

   It appears as orange in color and relates to the element of Water. It is traditionally divided into six petals. It has obvious associations with sexual love, controlling energy to the reproductive organs. Psychologically it is associated with the emotions. It is actively involved in all forms of intimacy and interpersonal feelings and strongly affects the sense of emotional well-being. It has obvious connections with the endocrine glands situated in the gonads.

3. **The Manipura**: There is often confusion over the color of this center, which is placed in the solar plexus. Early literature states that it is a blend of several shades of green and red, and also divided into ten petals, but modern writers tend to portray it as yellow, as do many psychics and healers. We tend to agree with the latter, as this makes more sense logically.

Because of its association with Fire, it is seen to be responsible for expansion and self-preservation. For this reason it is sometimes referred to as the survival center. Physically it is related to the nervous system and the adrenal glands (although some relate these endocrine glands to the first center). The lower gastrointestinal tract, including the stomach, liver, and gall bladder, is also governed by this center, probably because it is the system responsible for producing the body's energy.

4. **The Anahata**: This center relates to the heart, which in Western culture has been traditionally associated with love and the emotions. This chakra is related to the emotions and is said to be responsible, on the etheric level, for the individual sympathizing with others and allowing people to become instinctively aware of their joys and sorrows.

Because of its relationship with compassion, it is important for those involved in the healing arts to study this process in depth. This center is also responsible for metabolizing the energy of love that we receive from others.

This chakra is the first center to deal with the concept of self, which separates it from the other lower chakras. For this reason some have placed this center with the higher chakras regardless of its elemental nature.

On the physical plane it governs the heart and the associated vagus nerve and circulatory system. This center is also positioned in the same area as the thymus gland, connecting its actions to the immune system of the body. It is related to the element of Air, and modern healers tend to see it as green or turquoise in color. Early Theosophical works list it as a golden color and divide it into twelve petals.

5. **The Vishuddhi**: The first of the upper centers is positioned at the throat. As it relates to the concept of ether, it is the center responsible for generating and connecting us with our etheric aura. It is positioned over the larynx and has obvious associa-

tions with communication and speech—the power of the word, listening to others and taking responsibility for what we say.

Physically, it is related to the respiratory system, the upper alimentary canal and the vocal apparatus. The throat center also affects metabolism due to its relationship with the thyroid and parathyroid glands. All traditions agree on its blue color. It is divided into sixteen petals.

6. **The Ajna:** This is the mystical third eye positioned on the brow. It rules the mind, and is responsible for generating the mental body. It is well-known for being the center that controls clairvoyance and psychic experience. For this it is referred to by some as "the doorway to eternity."

Within the physical body it affects the lower brain, ears, eyes and nervous system. It is positioned perfectly over the pituitary and hypothalamus glands, the control system for the whole endocrine system. Again, there is no dispute among traditions about this center's color which is violet or indigo. The number of segments of this center suddenly leap to ninety-six petals.

7. **The Sahasrara:** The final center is known as the crown chakra because of its position at the top of the head. It is the ultimate link with the person's astral body, and is where the soul enters the body. It is therefore governed by Spirit.

Its color is said to vary depending on the individual's spiritual development. It is generally visualized as white which is made up of all the colors of the spectrum. In a spiritually developed person it becomes quite large, and when fully open covers the whole head, producing the classical halo effect. This effect is also due to the amount of petals present in its form, which is a staggering nine hundred and seventy two.

In oriental pictures and statues it is often shown quite prominently, as it is in early Christian iconography. This is considered to be the highest chakra connecting the individual to ultimate Kether (which means crown) in Cabalistic terms, or god and goddess in general pagan terminology. In the physical body it controls the higher functions of the brain.

Variations of the Major Chakras

As we have previously mentioned, some systems refer to more than seven centers. Spiritualists tend to work with an eighth center for which they have no name. It is located 18 to 24 inches above the crown chakra. This puts it outside of the physical body, but within the aura. It is said to act as an intersection between the body's aura and the soul's energy, and as such can be considered to be nothing more than an extension of the crown center.

The ten-center system is a recent development based on the principle that the original seven-center system is now outdated. It adds a further three centers----one just above the root center and positioned on the feet, which is responsible for movement and balance; one at the base of the spine, similar to the old Theosophy system; and finally, one positioned just below the brow center, with the function of power and activity.

The root chakra in this system is relegated to the role of nurturing, with its functions being taken over by the new base center. Protagonists of this system point to the fact that the old system has Chaldaean/Hebrew origins, which only took into account seven planets (Mercury, Venus, Mars, Jupiter, Saturn, the Sun and the Moon). They claim that this system was incomplete due to the exclusion of the three other planets (Uranus, Neptune, and Pluto) which were not discovered until much later. This argument is of course based on the theory that the Vedic chakra system was based on the planets, when in fact planetary correspondences have only been placed on the centers in recent times.

The Minor Chakras

There are 21 minor centers, but they can not be considered to be chakras in the true sense of the word. They differ considerably in the way they are formed compared with the seven major centers, being produced by the effect of over a dozen energy strands crossing within the etheric body. They are only about three inches in diameter and stand out from the body by about one inch.

They start at the feet with one on each sole, one behind each knee, two pelvic centers positioned on either side of the genitalia, a center over the spleen, plus one nearby, one over the liver, one connected to the stomach, one near the thymus gland, and one near the solar plexus. There are also centers related to each of the eyes and ears, and one on the palm of each hand.

Six of the minor centers are of particular relevance to the healer, these being the spleen, liver, two pelvic, and two hand centers.

The spleen center is said to absorb energy from the sun and feed it into the aura. This has the effect of balancing the nervous system and giving added vigor. It interacts with the solar plexus center, assisting in its functions.

The liver center is positioned at the bottom of the rib cage on the right. This is not even considered to be a minor chakra by some, but it is important for the healer to consider it during healing because it can store violent emotions. This has the effect of upsetting body chemistry, which it is responsible for on a physical level.

The two pelvic centers help to transfer energy from the sacral center to the root chakra. Their health therefore affects both of these centers. They are positioned just below and to either side of the sacral center.

The centers in the palm of each hand are important for a different reason. They act as tools for healers, allowing, with practice, the transfer of energy outside of their own aura.

The Sephiroth and the Chakras

The Cabala was adopted by the Western Mystery Tradition during the sixteenth century. It was originally a collection of works known as the Zohar, which emerged from Spain during this period. Since then it has continued to develop, producing the system that emerged with the Order of the Golden Dawn in the late nineteenth century. It is still in common use among those practicing ritual magic and among the wider pagan community, particularly within Wicca.

What the Cabala is best known for is the Sephiroth: the components of the Tree of Life, which is the graphic description of its philosophy (see Fig. 14). As it requires an entire book in its own right to explain this philosophy, we only offer a brief outline and explanation of how the Sephiroth relates to the body and to the mind. Of particular importance to the healer is the Cabala's relationship to the chakras which fit, with some acceptable adjustment, onto its spheres or Sephiroth.

The Tree of Life consists of ten Sephiroth arranged on three pillars. On the center pillar are four spheres. Starting from the bottom these are Malkuth, which is Hebraic for kingdom. This sphere is labeled number ten and represents the external world, and more importantly to us, the physical body. On a psychological level

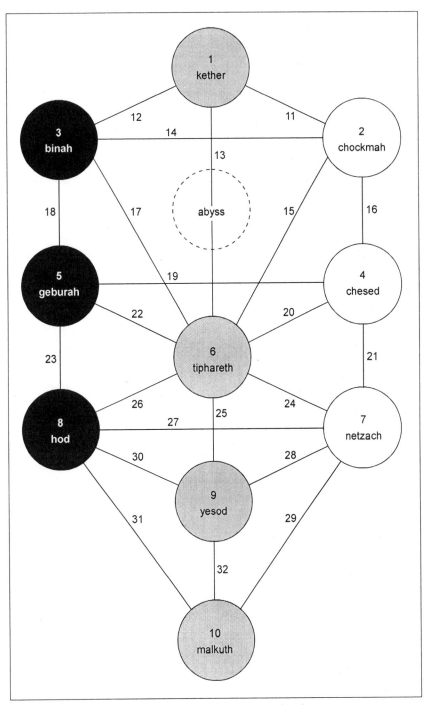

Figure 14: Cabalistic Tree of Life

it represents sensation and bodily awareness. The Muladhara or root chakra is placed here, and not surprisingly, the planet attributed to it is Earth.

The next Sephira up on the center pillar is Yesod or foundation. This sphere is labeled nine and represents sexual energy; hence it is considered a repository for repressed feelings. More importantly it governs instincts and the autonomic nervous system, which link it psychologically to the unconscious mind. It is associated with the Moon and the element of Water, and it performs the same function as the Svadhistana or sacral chakra. It also represents the etheric body which exists behind the outer reality of the physical body or Malkuth.

We now move to the two Sephira which are placed above Yesod on the left and right pillars. Together they perform the balancing function of the Manipura or solar plexus center. The sphere on the left is known as Hod, splendor, and is numbered eight. It represents the intellect and is assigned the planet Mercury. The Sephira on the right, Netzach, victory, numbered seven, represents feelings and intuition. Quite naturally, it is represented astrologically by Mercury's counterpart Venus. These two spheres are responsible for the balancing of the left and right sides of the brain, which is essential if the solar plexus center is to be fully opened.

The four spheres we have mentioned so far come together to form the personality: the "I am." This is represented by the next sphere on the tree, Tiphareth, beauty, which is positioned above Yesod on the middle pillar. Just as it is the center of the Sephiroth, it represents the center of the self, the real self or as some express it "the real me." It is the sixth Sephira and governed by the Sun.

As with Yesod, we move up to the two Sephiroth above Tiphareth on the left and right pillars. On the left is Geburah, strength, and on the right is Chesed, mercy. They are numbered five and four and attributed the planets Mars and Jupiter respectively. They represent the principles of will power and organizational ability, and when combined with Tiphareth they form the Anahata or heart chakra, which can only be opened when the two are in balance. These three spheres in harmony represent the superconscious and soul. Geburah and Chesed come below a boundary which is traditionally known as the Abyss; this divides the individual from the next spheres above which represent universal spirit. A similar boundary exists passing through Tiphareth. This is known

#	Pathway	Body System or Part	Tarot Card	Astrological or Elemental Association
11	joins 1-2	Respiratory System	The Fool	Air
12	joins 1-3	Nervous System	The Magician	Mercury
13	joins 1-6	Lymphatic System	The High Priestess	Moon
14	joins 2-3	Reproductive System	The Empress	Venus
15	joins 2-6	Head and Face	The Emperor	Aries
16	joins 2-4	Shoulder and Arms	The Hierophant	Taurus
17	joins 3-6	Lungs	The Lovers	Gemini
18	joins 3-5	Stomach	The Chariot	Cancer
19	joins 4-5	Heart	Strength	Leo
20	joins 4-6	Back	The Hermit	Virgo
21	joins 4-7	Digestive System	Wheel of Fortune	Jupiter
22	joins 5-6	Liver	Justice	Libra
23	joins 5-8	Organs of Nutrition	The Hanged Man	Water
24	joins 6-7	Intestines	Death	Scorpio
25	joins 6-9	Hips and Thighs	Temperance	Sagittarius
26	joins 6-8	Reproductive System	The Devil	Capricorn
27	joins 7-8	Muscular System	The Tower	Mars
28	joins 7-9	Urinary System	The Star	Aquarius
29	joins 7-10	Legs and Feet	The Moon	Pisces
30	joins 8-9	Cardio-vascular System	The Sun	Sun
31	joins 8-10	Brain, Arteries and Veins	Judgment	Fire/Spirit
32	joins 9-10	Skeleton	The World	Saturn/Earth

Figure 15: Table of Cabalistic Correspondences

as the Veil of Paroketh and divides the soul from the "I" of the personality.

The bridge between the individual and the universal spirit is the Sephira which has no number, Daath. It is assigned to the throat chakra or Vishuddhi. It is the final crossing point across The Abyss to the trinity of spheres known as the Supernal Triangle.

The first of these spheres is Binah, understanding, positioned on the left hand pillar. It is also sometimes known as the supernal mother; its number is three and corresponds planetarily to Saturn. It represents the goddess principle of universal love and awareness. It is balanced with the masculine principle on the right-hand pillar by Chokmah, wisdom. This is referred to as the supernal father, and provides Binah with raw directionless energy to shape. It is the second Sephira and astrologically is assigned to Neptune. These two spheres when balanced form the brow chakra or Ajna. They give purpose and awareness.

The final and third Sephira in the Supernal Triangle is Kether: crown. The association with the crown chakra or Sahasrara is obvious. It represents pure being without form. For this reason it is labelled as the first sphere.

Apart from the ten Sephira or spheres, there are the paths which connect the spheres. There are 22 of these in all, and they are generally represented by the major arcana of the tarot, as well as a combination of the signs of the zodiac and the elements. More importantly, each path also represents a system or part of the human body. This gives a useful correspondence table for those using Cabalistic practice for healing (see Fig. 15).

Astrology and the Human Body

Physicians first started to relate the effects of the stars and planets on the human body during the fifteenth century. The Renaissance boosted the popularity of astrology; the stars were seen to have an influence on all areas of human life, and it was inevitable that this would include illness and health.

The first accepted theory was developed by Marsilio Ficino (1433-1499), who published the first zodiacal and planetary correspondence tables of the human body in his work *Liber de Vita*.

Paracelsus (often referred to as the first modern scientist) developed the microcosmic-macrocosmic approach to astrology. He saw the stars affecting man internally as well as externally. He used astrology to analyze and prescribe medicines. He did this by comparing the area affected by the illnesses' zodiacal and planetary attributions with that of the available medicines. It was through this

Sign	Ruling Planet	Traditional Associated Body Part	Traditional Associated Body System
Aries	Mars	Head	Nervous System
Taurus	Venus	Neck, Throat	Alimentary Canal
Gemini	Mercury	Hands, Arms, Lungs	Respiratory System
Cancer	Moon	Breast, Stomach	Upper Gastrointestinal Tract
Leo	Sun	Heart, Spine, Lower Arm	Cardio-vascular System
Virgo	Mercury	Abdomen, Hands, Intestines	Lower Gastrointestinal Tract
Libra	Venus	Lower Back, Kidneys	Renal and Urinary Systems
Scorpio	Mars	Pelvis, Sex Organs	Reproductive System
Sagittarius	Jupiter	Hips, Thighs, Liver	Hepatic, Digestive System (Gall Bladder)
Capricorn	Saturn	Knees, Bones	Musco-skeletal System
Aquarius	Saturn	Shin, Ankles	None
Pisces	Jupiter	Feet	Lymphatics

Figure 16: Astrological Correspondences

process that mercury was first prescribed as an effective cure, the reasoning behind the initial prescription being that a Mercurial substance would negate the effects of the heavier influences of Saturn and Mars.

Up until the eighteenth century, astrology was still being used by physicians to decide on treatments, and the prescription of herbs by astrology continued until much later.

We recommend anyone intending to use herbs for healing to avoid the astrological approach. It is now a very much dated and potentially dangerous system. We have listed the traditional astrological correspondences (see Fig. 16 and Fig. 17) and recommend that these only be used for magical purposes such as spells or talismans.

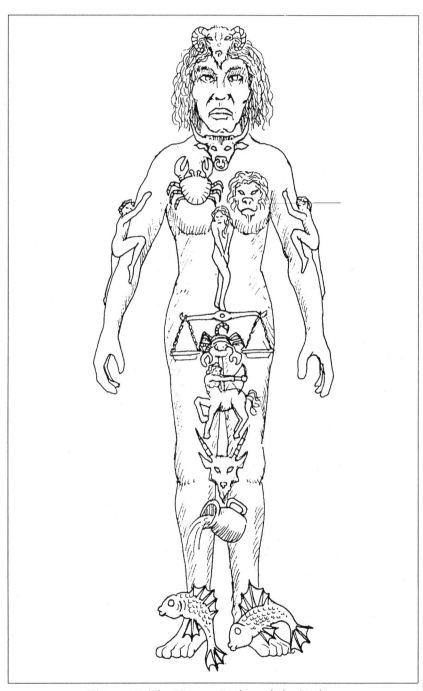

Figure 17: The Human Body and the Zodiac
(based on a seventeenth century German woodcut)

7

Healing Sanctuaries

Sacred space is an essential requirement for working magic, as well as for any other form of psychic or spiritual healing. Within witchcraft and ritual magic this space has always been the Magic Circle----a portable temple which could be set up anywhere with a minimum of ritual equipment. This is still the practice of these traditions today, with the living room of a suburban house quickly becoming a temple when required.

Within paganism, generally, this use of temporary places of worship was not always so. Before the coming of Christianity, and the persecution of pagans, temples would have been permanent structures taking the form of stone buildings, as well as Druidic groves. Such structures were not only common in ancient Greece and the Roman Empire, but also within the rest of Europe. A good example of such a structure is at Yeavering in Northumberland, England. This is the site of one of the last Anglo-Saxon temples which was destroyed by Christians around 632 A.D.

The destruction of such sites, and the persecution of pagans, forced ritual practices to be hidden. This resulted in what we now call "witchcraft," a form of hidden pagan practice with the need for temporary ritual space to avoid detection. Of course since the repeal of the Witchcraft Act in England in 1951, and the use of the First Amendment by pagans in the United States, permanent temples are beginning to reappear.

Casting the Circle

The first act performed during magic by witches and ritual magicians is casting the Circle. Within witchcraft its original purpose was to preserve and contain the power; in other words to consecrate an area so that it remained sacred and maintained the level of energy raised. With the fusion of ritual magic practices into witchcraft, the Circle also becomes a form of psychic protection to prevent unwanted influences invading the sacred area.

The Circle sets the practice of ritual aside from the mundane world, in the same way that a Church does in Christian services. This helps the magic work by allowing the practitioner to concentrate on the job at hand without the distractions of the outside world.

Both witches and ritual magicians may use elaborate and decorative ritual equipment for casting a Circle, but it is not essential. Good practitioners of magic require nothing but the knowledge of what they are doing and somewhere to do it.

We have given an example of Circle casting below, and have catered it for the solitary practitioner. We have used the Greek deity Aesculapius (see page 124) for an understanding of the symbolism used as an example of a healing deity, but healers can use any deity they relate to (see page 126).

Within many pagan traditions, weapons were banned from healing sanctuaries; we have maintained this ban in the ritual below, with the traditional witch's athame (ritual knife) and ritual sword being omitted for this reason. We have also replaced the pentacle with a bowl of earth, as this is more representative of the physical realm.

Preparation

The area to be used is cleared of everyday items, and a small table, or a similar item of furniture, is placed in the center for use as an altar. (If the magical working is going to require space, the altar may be set up in the northern quarter.) The altar is covered with a cloth, which can be of plain or ornate design. Arranged on the altar are the following:

• A bowl of earth in the center (representing the element of Earth).

• A candle behind this (representing the element of Fire).

- A pair of altar candles.
- A wand entwined with thread.
- A chalice of red wine (representing the element of Water).
- A small bowl of water.
- A small bowl of salt.
- A knife for any cutting.
- An incense burner or joss-stick holder.
- A dish of cakes or biscuits.
- An empty bowl (for libations).

A figurine to represent the healing deity should also be placed on the altar. These are now widely available from occult and New Age shops. Some initiative and imagination can also be used: for example, a stick entwined with thread can represent the snake-entwined wand of the healing deity Aesculapius (see Fig. 1).

A candle should be placed at each quarter: east, south, west and north. These can be colored appropriately according to the element they represent. (The elemental placings are east, Air; south, Fire; west, Water; and north, Earth). Matches or a lighter should also be available to light these, the altar candles, and the incense.

The easiest form of incense to use comes in the form of joss sticks, and many healing incenses are readily available pre-made from occult and New Age shops. Those who are more adventurous and experienced may wish to make their own incenses.

Music is also helpful to set the mood. Again, there are plenty of New Age music tapes available for this purpose (Gavin regularly uses one called *Chakra Dance,* which he finds useful when working with chakra centers).

The Ritual

The healer priest or priestess kneels in front of the altar, and clears his or her thoughts and meditates. The altar candles have been lit, as has the incense.

The healer places the wand into the bowl of water and says:

> Water is life. I consecrate and purify this water; may it aid me in this rite of healing, and may it be blessed in the names of Apollo and Aesculapius, and of Hygeia and Panacea.

109

The wand is then placed into the bowl of salt:

> Salt is life. I consecrate and purify this salt; may it aid me in this rite of healing, and may it be blessed in the names of Apollo and Aesculapius, and of Hygeia and Panacea.

The healer then pours some of the consecrated salt into the bowl of water.

He or she then casts the Circle, starting and finishing in the east. Proceeding clockwise, the Circle is drawn with the wand. While this is done, the healer imagines the working area being enclosed in a blue sphere (the Circle being where the sphere is cut by the ground). The healer invokes as the Circle is drawn:

> O Circle of power, I consecrate thee as a place of purity and healing; a meeting place of love and truth; a shield against all that would harm and weaken us; a boundary between the world of men and the realms of the gods; a rampart of protection that shall contain the healing power used within it. Wherefore do I bless thee and consecrate thee, in the names of Apollo and Aesculapius, of Hygeia and Panacea, and of all the gods and goddesses.

The healer lays down the wand, and picks up the bowl of consecrated salt and water. Moving clockwise, the bowl is carried around the Circle, and its contents are sprinkled on the perimeter. When the healer reaches the altar, the bowl is replaced and the process is repeated with the incense burner, and then finally with one of the altar candles.

The healer then picks up the wand in his or her right hand, and holds it forward, and faces the east:

> O Guardians of the East, Lords of Air. I do summon you to aid me in this rite of healing; protect this Circle, and give me the knowledge to heal. Air is breath.

The healer then bows, and brings the tip of the wand to the heart. After a pause of three breaths, he or she then lights the candle and moves to the south, presents the wand again:

> O Guardians of the South, Lords of Fire. I do summon you to aid me in this rite of healing; protect this Circle, and give me the motivation to heal. Fire is energy.

Bowing the head, the tip of the wand is brought to the solar plexus, for the same pause of three breaths. The healer then lights the candle and moves to the west, and presents the wand again:

> O Guardians of the West, Lords of Water. I do summon you to aid me in this rite of healing; protect this Circle, and give me the compassion to heal. Water is blood.

The tip of the wand is this time brought to the genitalia, with the same pause of three breaths, and the candle is lit. The healer then moves to the north and presents the wand:

> O Guardians of the North, Lords of Earth. I do summon you to aid me in this rite of healing; protect this Circle, and give me the stability to heal. Earth is body.

The tip of the wand is this time pointed downwards toward the feet for a pause of three breaths, and the final candle is lit.

The healer then faces the altar, and with the wand still in the right hand, raises both arms in invocation:

> Aesculapius son of Coronis; born in death, and saved from the flames by Apollo.
> He who was taught the art of medicine by Chiron the centaur.
> He who raised the dead with Athena's blood.
> He who incurred the wrath of Hades, and was killed by Zeus's thunderbolt.
> I invoke thee to this temple of healing. Aid me, thy priest (priestess) of the art, in my work.

The arms are lowered and the tip of the wand is first placed on the throat, and the healer says:

> By the words of Chiron.

The tip of the wand is then placed on the forehead (third eye):

> By the knowledge of Aesculapius.

The tip of the wand is placed at the top of the brow:

> By the inspiration and wisdom of Apollo.

The Circle is now prepared for the healing work to take place.

Consecration of Wine and Cakes

Taking place after the work has been completed, the consecration of wine and cakes is a time to relax. It is also worth noting that eating helps to close the chakric centers down. In Wiccan practice

111

both a priest and a priestess are required to consecrate the wine, but a single person performing this blessing can be just as effective.

The healer holds the chalice of wine in front of the altar with both hands and says:

> Water is life; water is blood. From the chalice of life we are born. May this wine be consecrated, by Apollo and Aesculapius, by Hygeia and Panacea.

A small amount of wine is poured into the libation bowl, and the healer then sips from the chalice. The chalice is then placed on the altar, and the plate of cakes or biscuits is picked up in both hands:

> Earth is life; earth is body. From the earth we are made, to the earth we return. I bless these cakes, by Apollo and Aesculapius, by Hygeia and Panacea.

One of the cakes or biscuits is placed in the libation bowl. The healer can then relax and partake of the wine and cakes at will.

The Closing Ritual

A closing is performed after every ritual to banish any energy that remains, and to ground the healer.

The healer faces the east, places the tip of the wand to the heart, and says:

> O Guardians of the East, Lords of Air. I thank you for attending this rite of healing. Go if you must, stay if you will. So mote it be!

The wand is then presented to the quarter, the healer bows and pauses for three breaths. He or she then extinguishes the candle and faces the south. With the tip of the wand on the solar plexus, he or she says:

> O Guardians of the South, Lords of Fire. I thank you for attending this rite of healing. Go if you must, stay if you will. So mote it be!

The same gesture is made with the wand, pausing for three breaths, and the candle is extinguished. The healer then turns to face the west. The tip of the wand is placed over the area of the genitals:

> O Guardians of the West, Lords of Water. I thank you for attending this rite of healing. Go if you must, stay if you

will. So mote it be!

The same actions are repeated as with the other quarters. The healer then turns to the north, and has the tip of the wand pointed at the feet:

O Guardians of the North, Lords of Earth. I thank you for attending this rite of healing. Go if you must, stay if you will. So mote it be!

The actions are repeated, and the healer then stands, arms raised, in the center of the Circle:

This Circle of healing is closed. I thank Apollo and Aesculapius, Hygeia and Panacea for their presence here. Merry meet, merry part and merry meet again. So mote it be!

The rite is then over.

Healing Temples

The first recorded existence of permanent healing temples comes from Egypt. At first healing practices took place in all temples dedicated to Isis, but later as specific healing deities developed, with their own priesthoods, so did the practice of having specific healing temples and sanctuaries. Many of these temples had an oracular function as soothsaying and prophecy had long been associated with healing. This model soon spread throughout the near east, but particularly to Greece, where the records of the temples dedicated to Aesculapius are quite detailed.

It is said that the first temple to Aesculapius was built by his grandson, Alexana, who erected it to his memory at Titania in Sicily. The most celebrated temple, though, was at Epidaurus, in Peloponnesus. It is from here that the cult of Aesculapius, and the building of his temples, spread throughout the known world.

Epidaurus was said to have been his birthplace, and was therefore regarded as particularly holy; only initiated priests of his cult were allowed access to this sanctuary without prior purification. It was a well-known site of pilgrimage, with a continual stream of sick visiting the site to regain their lost health and receive enlightening dreams (Aesculapius was often referred to as the dream-sender). The temple was situated near the sea, but was surrounded by sacred groves and pleasure gardens on all sides. Situated within these gardens was accommodation for the sick, and a marble bath for purification prior to entering the temple.

In the forecourts of the temple were tablets inscribed with records of diseases and their proven remedies. Other records were engraved in writing or in hieroglyphic paintings on the pillars and walls of the temple. These were left by those who were cured within the temple, as votive offerings.

The temple had several rooms. The antechamber held statues of the gods and goddesses of good fortune, dreams and sleep. Aesculapius himself was said only to be present within the central room of the temple. Within this room sat Trasimenides' statue of Aesculapius. It was made from ivory and gold. One hand of the statue held the staff, while the other lay upon the head of a serpent (the serpent was thought to bring oracular vision). A dog stood next to him. Only on rare occasions was anyone other than a priest admitted into this chamber to view the statue.

All of the temples dedicated to Aesculapius were laid out in a similar manner. Some had gymnasia, others had healing springs, but all were surrounded by a sacred grove and had the facilities for bathing and purification.

Practices within these temples were all similar, and the preparation of the patient for healing was of particular importance. These practices all seemed to follow the same pattern:

1. Any sick person wishing to enter the temple had to agree to the rules laid down by the priesthood. Those that would not conform with these laws were duly banished from the temple grounds. These rules included a period of fasting, normally about 24 hours, and abstinence from wine, so that the ether of the soul may not be defiled.

2. The priesthood led their patients through the anteroom showing them the paintings and tablets left as offerings by the healed. They extolled the virtues of their methods, and of their deity.

3. Prayers, sacred songs, and poetry, were recited. The priest read or sang these, and the sick were expected to repeat them aloud. They were often accompanied by musical instruments. Young boys were also employed within these temples, and at a later date they were often ordained into the priesthood.

4. Sacrifices, libations and offerings were made. These were of various kinds.

5. Bathing was essential before any form of healing was attempted, and before any divination. The drinking of water was also required from the springs within the grounds of the temple.

6. Baths were often accompanied by massage and body manipulation. Oils and salves, made from essential oils and other ingredients, were often used. Those who performed this task were chosen and trained especially for it. This took place both before and after entering the interior of the temple.

7. Patients were fumigated with incense before entering to see the oracle. They were, reportedly, "touched, stroked, and rubbed with the hands" a second time.

8. After all these preparations the person was considered fit to receive *incubatio*, the prophetic sleep of dreams. The patient was reclined on a sheepskin, or on a magnificent bed which was often kept in temples for this purpose. All lights were extinguished so that a solemn silence and sacred darkness might aid the visions of the dreamer.

9. When the patient awoke, the priest would interpret the dream and prescribe any further treatment.

10. After successful treatment, the patient would leave a votive offering describing the success of the cure given to him or her.

Setting Up a Temple

There are several advantages to having a permanent healing temple, particularly if you regularly do healing work. Temples generate a healing energy of their own, unlike temporary Circles. This is mainly due to the constant presence of the deity or deities invoked within its confines, which produces an incredibly relaxed and healing atmosphere, beneficial to both the healer and the client. Casting a circle every time you wish to do healing work is a time-consuming and overt affair. Clients who are not occultists or pagans are likely to feel much more relaxed if they are not subjected to a ritual that they do not necessarily understand.

The first requirement for setting up a permanent temple is a room large enough for the type of healing you wish to perform. When deciding on the room you are going to use, you must take into account two things. First, you must ensure that there is enough space for the type of healing work you wish to perform. Massage and aromatherapy work will require a space large enough for the patient to lie down, as will some types of chakra work. Second, ensure that the room will only be used for the purposes of ritual and healing work. The area will be consecrated space separate from the mundane world. To use it for any other purpose would be desecration. If you do not have the space within the spare room you wish to use, or if you find yourself needing it for some other purpose, you will have to rely on setting up temporary temples for healing work in the Wiccan fashion (see Casting the Circle earlier in this chapter).

Healing temples are traditionally dedicated to particular deities. So deciding to set up a temple means that you must have already decided on which healing god or goddess you best relate to (see chapter 8). Study their myths carefully and read as much as you can about their worship. Finding such information may not always be easy; their is plenty of information about healing deities in the classical world (Greece, Rome and Egypt) but very little about those in Northern Europe.

In the information you have gathered about your deity there will be important clues on how your temple should be set up; for example, in a temple to Aesculapius, a private corner should be set aside for the statue or likeness of the deity away from all eyes except your own.

A statue or likeness of your deity is essential. There are many statues of various deities now available, so it is worth searching through the catalogues of various occult and New Age stores to see what is available. You may of course dedicate an easily available statue to your deity (we have a marble garden ornament of a Greek nymph covered in amber as a representation of Freya). If you are an artist you may wish to create your own likeness of the deity; this is an invocation to that god or goddess in its own right, being a form of sympathetic magic (see chapter 9) which can be very powerful.

Items associated with the deity should also be present. In the case of Aesculapius there should be a wand serving as a caduceus, a statue of a dog and one of a snake. Again, you can improvise; the important thing is that they act as a focus for you when you are healing. So get to know the symbolism of your god or goddess.

The ritual for dedicating your temple initially takes the same form as Casting the Circle (see above). You may wish to change the words of the ritual to suit the dedication of the temple by substituting "I do summon you to consecrate and protect this temple" for "I do summon you to aid me in this rite of healing; protect this Circle," when you call the elemental guardians. You may also wish to anoint the walls of the temple with consecrated water and with wax from the candle facing that wall. These actions help to strengthen the consecration of that temple. When you have finished you do not close the Circle and banish the elemental guardians as you do with normal Circle casting; this is only done when you close down the temple permanently.

The next act, after consecrating the room as a temple, should be to affirm your dedication to your deity within it. This may take the form of a revised self-dedication (see page 45). Meditation and contemplation on your deity should take place regularly within the temple, at least every other day for the first month and then weekly after this. Regular libations should be left on the altar after these meditations. These actions strengthen the link between the temple, the deity and yourself. After awhile you will find that you enter a meditative or healing frame of mind the moment you pass the threshold of the temple.

You must always remember that the temple is sacred space. As such, it should be the cleanest room in the house, with fresh flowers placed on the altar and kept in a neat and decorative condition. Remember that it is a reflection of your spirituality, and a home for your deity.

All temples have rules, and yours should be no exception. Again, look at the myths and customs of your deity for guidance, but we recommend the following rules, as they are applicable to all sanctuaries. These rules can be applied to all areas of sacred space, including healing wells and springs.

1. Footwear should be removed before entering the temple, as you are stepping on sacred ground. It should be fine to enter with everyday clothes as long as they are not excessively dirty—such as builders' overalls covered in dust.

2. Washing should also be considered compulsory before entering the temple; face and hands should be sufficient.

3. All entering the temple should be purified by being dowsed with incense from the burner.

4. No smoking or drinking (except ritually) within the temple.

5. No swearing or profanity within the temple.

6. Those receiving healing within the temple should leave some sort of offering in the libation bowl before leaving. This can be anything from crystals to money. (It is important to remember that this is not payment; this money should be used for the temple's upkeep, such as for candles or altar flowers.)

Healing Wells and Springs

Consecrating water sources as sites of healing and fertility is an inherently pagan practice. The early Northern European cultures saw them as entrances to the underworld. In the Norse cosmology many of the nine worlds that surround Yggdrassil, the World Tree, are interlinked by wells. The three Norns or Wyrd Sisters sit at the Well of Urd weaving man's destiny, and Odin himself, hanging above the well, snatches the runes. In *The Great Mother: An Analysis of An Archetype*, Erich Neumann makes the following observation:

> To the realm of the earth-mother belongs not only the pond and lake but also the spring. While in the well the elementary character of the feminine is still evident----it is no accident that in fairy tales a well is often the gate to the underworld and specifically the domain of the earth-mother----in the spring the rising, erupting motif of "being born" and of creative movement is more strongly accented than that of being contained.

After reading this passage, it is worthy to note that many deities associated with wells and springs are associated with all these qualities. A good example is the Celtic Bríd (see chapter 8).

Well worship, which was widespread within early Celtic culture, has remained surprisingly intact due mainly to its absorption into mainstream Catholicism. Such wells have become linked with saints, the commonest being Saint Bridget who of course is the Christianization of the goddess Bríd. Wells dedicated to this saint are most common in Ireland, which is hardly surprising; there are over 60 wells in one county alone.

Not far from where we live in County Meath there is a site with three healing wells dedicated to Saint Kieran. Each well has a particular healing quality; one cures warts, one cures foot ailments, and the final one is for general ailments. They are still regularly visited by the local people. At Lammas (August 1), known in Ireland as Lughnasadh, it was traditional for the local horse breeders to bring their horses down to be blessed. The god Lugh was the deity of horsemanship, hence the date of these blessings. Myth has it that the monk Kieran on visiting these wells was approached by a stag, a boar, and a salmon whose head appeared from one of the wells. He was told by these animals, each in turn, that he should build a monastery on this land as it was holy. It is our belief that Saint Kieran is a Christianization of Lugh.

There are many such wells in Ireland, all open to the public who leave offerings indicative of their ailments. We have seen everything from prayer cards for help from a particular saint to a condom left as a plea to prevent pregnancy (see page 147, chapter 9, Libations). It is also common practice to decorate the surrounding trees with colored ribbons as an acknowledgment of the cure received there. At many wells one particular tree seems to be associated with this practice, and seems to have been grown next to the well for this purpose. In Ireland these trees are often blackthorn, the traditional Irish fairy tree.

The leaving of such offerings, and the decoration of a tree, is also common among the wells which remain in England. It is obvious that this practice has relevance to the Indo-European concept of the tree being the *axis mundi* of the world. Again, the Norse cosmology is a good example, combining both the tree and the well. Erich Neumann explains this link:

> As fruit-bearing tree of life it is female: it bears, transforms, nourishes... but in addition the tree trunk is a container, "in" which dwells its spirit, as the soul dwells in the body... But the tree is also the earth phallus, the male principle jutting out of the earth...

It is therefore very likely that the tree at the well served two purposes. Primarily it was planted to act as a guardian to the entrance of the underworld, but it also reflected the nature of the universe as a symbol of the cosmos, and represented the male aspect to the well's obvious female connotations.

Because of the continued practices surrounding these wells in Ireland, excavation by archeologists has been rare due to the belief that this would constitute desecration of a holy site. In England and Wales, though, much archeological work has been carried out, and the items found at the bottom of many wells have revealed that the practice of throwing offerings into the well itself was once common.

One well in Wiltshire was found to contain pottery, bones, coins and decorated pebbles. Another well at Hadrian's Wall was found to contain over 14,000 coins, pottery, glass and bronze figures. A bronze tablet close to the well shows that the Romano-Celtic goddess Coventina was obviously the deity associated with the well.

In England, many wells and springs that still have customs associated with them are often referred to as "plague wells." This goes back to the time of the Black Death when many wells were associated with healing, due to the fact that the water remained uncontaminated by the plague.

Worship, in the form of well-dressing, has continued in Derbyshire and Staffordshire. The dressing is done with flowers and greenery, which are fashioned into illustration of Christian themes. Most of the people practicing these rites are unaware of the pagan overtones attached to them, and believe that such practices only date back as far as the seventeenth century.

Psychic occurrences around wells and springs are common, not only healing, but also manifestations of entities. Lourdes, in France, is a good example of both, where there was a vision of the Virgin Mary in the nineteenth century and several miraculous cures. Such manifestations of white ladies are common around healing wells and springs. Of course, being venerated by Catholics means that any manifestation of such a figure is always interpreted as being the Virgin Mary.

In non-Catholic areas many wells are said to be haunted by white ladies. There is little doubt that what is manifesting is the image of the deity that was once worshipped there, because the area has become so psychically charged. In his book *Ghosts And The Divining Rod*, Tom Lethbridge suggests that such ghosts are caused by the fact that we imprint our imagination in the static charge of an area. He believes that this is more possible around water, and of course wells, because they have a high static charge.

In 1993 we received a booklet and some correspondence from Brian Slade, an archeologist who was working on excavating a well on the Isle of Sheppey. The archeological site was at Minster Abbey, a Saxon church built between 640 and 670 A.D. He had made several recent finds including a statue of a triple-headed goddess. He had already contacted Marija Gimbutas who had confirmed that it was obviously of pagan origin.

He had made the obvious conclusion that it was either representative of Coventina or possibly of Brigantia (the Romano-Celtic equivalent of the Irish Bríd). We wrote back to him to confirm his conclusions, and entered into several dialogues with him on the subject. He also wrote to tell us that he believed that it had cured his wife of infertility problems: exactly nine months after he touched the statue, his wife gave birth to their first child. Previously she had suffered four miscarriages. There was widespread newspaper coverage of the miracle, and Brian remains convinced, as do we, that it was the work of the deity of that well.

Dedication of a Spring or Well to Bríd

Of course, dedicating a spring or well first requires you to find one to consecrate. If you live in the countryside this may not be a problem, although there may be no privacy if it is regularly used by others. If in town, you may need to use your ingenuity. Our old friend Susa Morgan Black has solved the problem in several rather unique ways:

> I create mini-wells for ceremonies from a stone mortar that I surround with rocks and stones. This can be placed outdoors, or even in the living room during the winter! Outside for a more permanent well, I have a wooden wine half-barrel for my water magic. It is waterproof, picturesque and works!... Even man-made garden fountains can be used magically. A witch's cauldron can also substitute ritually for a healing well.

One problem this does solve is the problem of water purity. Unfortunately, the use of modern fertilizers has resulted in many wells being unsafe to drink from. Anyone planning to do healing magic at well or spring sites should take the purity of the water into account.

Once you have created a well or found a water source which is usable, if there isn't a tree overlooking it, plant one! Then create a ritual asking the tree spirit (dryad) to protect the well.

Stones, usually ovate in shape and about four to six inches in length, are often located at, or near, the sites of holy wells or springs in Ireland. Although the exact use of these ritual stones is now something we can merely speculate on, glimpses of their original use can be seen in many cultures around the globe. Prayer stones, as they are often called in Ireland, seem to fulfill a similar use to the

Catholic rosary or Greek worry-beads. Pilgrims to holy wells would roll them lovingly in their hands while praying to the saint whose shrine they were visiting.

When dedicating your holy well, spring, garden or indoor water shrine to Bríd, it is wise to consider ancient traditions. As Bríd is a triple goddess, it would be fitting to use three such stones to support an offering bowl for your shrine. The bowl should be filled with pebbles or minerals that you yourself have collected. If others wish to leave an offering to the deity, encourage them to leave a stone of their own in the bowl and take one that feels good to their touch in exchange.

If you are dedicating an established well or spring, remember that there may be other pilgrims of different religions who also use the shrine; be tactful in your approach to your rite. Bríd is more content with tracksuits, trainers and purity of intention, than robes, bells and upset to the other worshippers. If your shrine is on your own land, then go ahead, be elaborate and as colorful as you wish.

If the shrine is a public one, then merely place your three stones as near to the well as possible so that they form a natural triangle, and restrict your offering stones to beach pebbles, that way there will be a degree of protection from greedy fingers!

February 1 is Bríd's holy festival, and therefore the most suitable date to dedicate a holy well to her. Bríd is the goddess of healing, inspiration and craftsmanship, as well as the protectress of childbirth.

The Ritual

As near as possible to sunrise, carry your three stones, and your pebbles, to the well, and place them to the east of the water. Kneeling before the well, clear away any debris that may have fallen into the water and say:

> Holy Bríd, bright threefold lady, as I clean this well I ask for myself to be cleansed that I may be a pure vessel to heal those who have need of thee.

Anoint each of your chakra points (see chapter 6) with water from the well. Pick up your first and largest stone and walk clockwise around the well saying:

> Great Bríd, mistress of healing, I dedicate this pure water to your honor so that all those who would seek health, and

hope, might gain their desires through your gentle touch.

Place your first stone in its permanent position. Taking the second largest stone, repeat the process, this time saying:

Mighty Queen, divine inspirer, fill me with your knowledge. By gazing deep into your watery depths may I become filled with the inspiration required to make me a fitting vessel for your work.

Kneel before the well and spend a few moments in contemplation of its depths. Place the second stone in position. Take up the final stone, and walk for the final time around the well and say:

Lady of the artisans and craftsmen, I ask for your blessing upon my endeavors. Let this healing well bring color and joy to weary hearts, sweet smells and peace of mind to saddened souls, hope and renewed vigor to enfeebled bodies. Inspire me to plant strong herbs for healing, and colorful flowers for your delight, here, in your honor.

Place your final stone in its resting place (the stones should form a triangle). Now take the pebbles and rinse them in the well water. Visualize each one as a molecule of Bríd's healing power. Place the pebbles in the center of the triangle of stones.

Return to the well, bow three times and say:

Spirit of this well, I ask you in Bríd's name to watch and guard this water for our lady. For this service I thank you.

If there is a tree nearby, decorate it with rags and ribbon every time you perform healing at the well, and thank the guardian for its protection. Now thank Bríd for her aid. Do this in whatever way your heart tells you to, for her inspiration has now begun!

8

Gods, Goddesses and Myths

As we have shown earlier, healing in ancient pagan tradition was considered to be an integral aspect of the priesthood of certain deities. Such priesthoods developed, not surprisingly, because healing was considered to be divine in nature. Personification developed quickly in most cultures, first as healing spirits and eventually as gods and goddesses.

In many cases, such as Aesculapius, the deities derived from real people who developed healing into a fine art, bringing important benefits to the society they lived in. They were therefore deified in recognition of their achievement. This is a common practice within paganism, and was adopted by early Christianity in the form of the canonization of saints.

Most of the myths associated with these deities were allegories, or symbolic stories, which developed to make important points about morality, society, and life in general. The myths surrounding Aesculapius are a good example of this. Aesculapius becomes such an accomplished healer, thanks to Athena's gift of Medusa's blood, that he is soon able to bring the dead back to life. Hades is furious because his abode becomes empty. He complains to Zeus, who kills Aesculapius with a thunderbolt. There is the obvious association of the goddess giving life and the god being responsible for death. But what else does it mean? Quite simply, that it is the healer's responsibility to heal the sick, but not to bring the dead back to life or to attempt to prevent the inevitability of death. It also gives a warning to the healer; if you interfere with the divine scheme of the universe, expect divine retribution!

Myths surrounding the gods and goddesses of healing are full of such allegories, and the student of the healing path should try to understand their meanings. They are rich in important information that healers will find useful as they progress along their chosen path.

"Numinous archetypes" was Jung's term for powerful concepts symbolized in various aspects, which pagans tend to personify as gods and goddesses (the Horned God representing nature or Hestia representing hearth and home) and Christians as saints (Saint Francis expressing love and care for animals or Saint Barbara caring for gunners, miners and those in danger of sudden death). Though few Christians would admit it, a pagan invoking Hermes and a Christian appealing to Saint Christopher, both for safety on a journey, are doing exactly the same thing—attuning themselves to the appropriate numinous archetype.

But what are deities on a spiritual and psychic level? In their symbolic cultural forms, they are a tuning signal for the ultimate. Over a period of time their worship, and the associated reverence shown to them, has resulted in them developing into super thought forms on the highest levels of the collective unconscious and superconscious of humankind (see chapter 5). Unlike other thought forms that have developed, we have given them the ability to act independently of ourselves due to their divine nature.

But all the same they are still, in their visual and symbolic forms, only clothing for the ultimate divinity, which is undefinable and unimaginable in our present state of evolution. We symbolize them in human form because we are human ourselves. As somebody said: "If I were a horse, my god would have four legs."

Not surprisingly, the ancient healing deities of our pagan forefathers have remained in our consciousness, while other deities have been replaced by the monotheistic religions. Aesculapius has continued to be invoked since his deification, and there are hardly any members of the medical profession within the world who have not performed his invocation in the form of the Hippocratic oath (see chapter 3). His symbol can be seen on the sides of ambulances, on nurses' qualification badges and on hospital documents. All of these reinforce the super thought form of Aesculapius. This has resulted in him being one of the most effective deities to invoke for healing.

There are of course other deities who are just as effective for the same reasons. In many Roman Catholic countries, the symbolism of Isis and her healing functions were absorbed into the Virgin Mary (see page 132). Many deities which have not been invoked or worshipped for centuries are awaiting reawakening for healing purposes.

When pagans decide to follow the healing path, they are choosing to continue the tradition of the healer priests and priestesses. It is necessary for a priest or priestess to choose a deity as a guide on this path. We say "choose" with reservations, as in many cases it is a two-way process, with the deity having just as much say in the matter. Many who find themselves on the healing path (or indeed on other paths) realize that they have no choice about who their deity is going to be, feeling that the god or goddess concerned has chosen them!

Such a revelation can be due to a series of incidents which have led them to the path of healing and their deity simultaneously. This can take the form of omens or symbolic psychic messages which have occurred around them for a period of time. Many find that there is a cultural connection related to their racial heritage, while others just click with a deity when they first read about it. There are no hard and fast rules on the adoption or recognition of a deity, but in all cases the deity should be one that the healer can have a one-on-one relationship with.

The development of a personal relationship with that deity, and the ability to act as its advocate, is what sets aside a priest or priestess from other members of society. To develop this relationship takes time and dedication on the part of healer priests and priestesses. The first stage is regular worship or communion with the god or goddess in question.

Initially, a shrine should be set up to the deity, then the deity should be invoked, and regular libations should be performed (see page 147, chapter 9). This strengthens the deity within the healer's own psyche. It should be followed by regular meditations, where the healer visualizes that he or she is in the deity's presence. As time progresses, this can develop into the healer taking instruction from the deity during these meditative sessions, and into the ability to invoke the deity's assistance during healing. This ability is essential during spiritual healing (see chapter 10).

The Healing Deities

AH UINCIR DZ'ACAB (Mayan): Healing god/goddess who takes on the same sex as the patient. Patron of herbalists.

ARVAGASTIAE, THE (Nordic): Saxon goddesses of healing.

ASCLEPIAS (Greek/Roman): God of healing and medicine (known to the Romans as Aesculapius). He was introduced to Rome in 293 B.C. as a god controlling plagues. He was the son of Apollo and the human Coronis. While Coronis was pregnant with him she was unfaithful with the mortal Ischys, the son of Elatus. Apollo was told of her infidelity by a raven (who as a result of his indiscretion was turned from white to the now familiar black). In his anger, Apollo killed Coronis, but as her body was placed on the funeral pyre, he snatched Asclepias from her womb.

He handed the child to the centaur Chiron for his education, and Chiron taught him the arts of healing. He became a skilled physician, even bringing the dead to life, for which purpose Athena had given him Medusa's blood (from her right side, which could revive the dead, while that from her left was poisonous). Hades complained that this was leaving the underworld under-populated, so Zeus killed Asclepias with a thunderbolt. In due time he became a god. He was father of Hygeia, goddess of health, and of two sons, Podaleirios and Machaon, who also became physicians. His sanctuaries were places both of worship and of medical treatment.

His symbol was the snake entwined around the knotted staff, handed to him by Apollo. There is some confusion over his symbol; some feel it is actually the caduceus: a staff entwined by two serpents and winged. The caduceus has traditionally been associated with Hermes. One reason for the confusion may be that both gods are sons of Apollo; it is very likely that Asclepias took over the healing functions of the older god. It is also very likely that he was a real person who was a healer priest of Apollo who advanced the medical knowledge of the ancient Greeks at a time when a specific healing deity was needed.

ASOKOTTAMASRI (Buddhist and Tibetan, Lamaist): God of medicine. He is portrayed with stretched earlobes and is red.

AUŠAUTAS (Lithuanian): God of health. He is of Balto-Prussian origin.

BAST (Egyptian): Cat goddess who protected humans against contagious diseases. Her city was Bubastis in the Delta, founded as early as the second dynasty, ca. 3,200 B.C.. When Bubastis was the capital in the twenty-second dynasty, ca. 950 B.C., she became a national deity, surviving as such until ca. 400 A.D. Originally lion headed, she represented the beneficent power of the sun, in contrast to Sekhmet who personified its destructive power. Cats were domesticated very early by the Egyptians, being valued as snake destroyers (the Delta in particular was infested with snakes). They became much loved, and sacred, often being carefully mummified at death. Bubastis had a huge cat cemetery. (One Roman visitor to Bubastis who unwisely killed a cat was lynched by the horrified citizens.) One tradition says that Bast accompanied the sun god Ra's Boat of a Million Years on its daily journey through the sky, and at night fought Ra's enemy, the serpent Apep. She was said to be Ra's daughter (or sister) and wife, bearing him the lion-headed god, Maahes. A kindly goddess of joy, music and dancing, her rituals included light-hearted barge processions and orgiastic ceremonies. Like Sekhmet (with whom she sometimes overlaps) she became the wife of Ptah of Memphis, their son Nefertum completed the Memphis Triad. She is portrayed as a cat-headed woman, carrying a sistrum and basket, or as a whole cat. Often, in either form, there are kittens at her feet. Her city of Bubastis is mentioned as Pi-Beseth in Ezekiel xxx:17.

BEBHIONN, BE BIND (Irish and Manx): She is said to have originally been an otherworld healing and pleasure goddess. A large and beautiful dweller of the Isle of Women off the Irish west coast, she travels surrounded by birds. One legend says she came to live with the king of the Isle of Man, but that he was brutal and she left him; he pursued her and killed her.

BHAISAJYAGURU (Buddhist and Tibetan, Lamaist): One of several healing gods; his name means "Supreme Physician." He is portrayed with stretched earlobes and small curls on his forehead, with fruit and sometimes a bowl. His color is blue or gold.

BRÍD (Irish Celtic): In Ireland this healing goddess has migrated smoothly from paganism to Christianity, with all her characteristics and legends unimpaired. In Gaelic, she is Bríd (pronounced "Breed"), while the sixth-century Christian saint is known in English as Bridget. Frazer, in *The Golden Bough*, puts it bluntly: "It is obvious that Saint Bride, or Bridget, is an old heathen goddess of fertility, disguised in a threadbare Christian cloak."

In pagan times, Bríd was the goddess of healing, craftsmanship and inspiration. Her healing function was particularly invoked at her sacred wells; there are probably as many wells of Bridget in

Ireland as there are wells of Patrick (which he commandeered from the god Lugh). She is still appealed to for healing at these wells; at any one of them, you will find many offerings, often bits of clothing appropriate to the part of the body where healing is needed. No one would dream of tidying these up.

(Many hawthorn trees have similar bits of clothing tied to their branches. Lone hawthorns are regarded as inviolate----you will often see one left growing in the middle of an efficiently plowed field; but particular ones, often in hedgerows, have a long tradition of healing.)

Called "the Poetess," she was the daughter of the Dagda, the Good God of the Tuatha Dé Danann, last occupiers of Ireland before the Gaels in the mythological cycle, and generally regarded as the aristocracy of the fairy folk. She was married for dynastic reason to Bres of the Fomors, to whom she bore a son Ruadan. But peace between the Tuatha and the Fomors did not last, and Ruadan was killed in the second battle of Mag Tuireadh (Moytura); Bríd's lament for him was the first time crying and shrieking were heard in Ireland.

Saint Bridget took over the legends, aspects, and holy places of the goddess Bríd in their entirety, even taking her pagan Triple Goddess aspect, as popular tradition says that Saint Bridget was in fact three holy sisters of the same name.

Her Festival, *Lá Fhéile Bríd* (the Festival of Bridget, pronounced "Law Elluh Breed"), on February 2 is regarded as the first day of spring.

The popular Saint Bridget's Crosses vary widely in materials and design from area to area; most frequently they are made of straw or rushes, and may be diamond, swastika, three armed, wheel or many other shapes. It is the custom to make new ones at Lá Fhéile Bríd and to hang them in the home and outbuildings for Bríd's protection during the coming year. One form of Saint Bridget's Cross is the logo of Radio Telefís Éireann, the Irish television and radio network (see Fig. 18). On the Isle of Man, the day is *Laa'l Breeshy,* and in northern England, Wives' Feast Day. In all those places, it is marked by transparently pagan folk rituals.

Bríd has appeared in neighboring countries----in Gaul as Brigindo, in other parts of the continent as Brigan and Brig, and in north Britain as Brigantia, which was the name of an ancient kingdom there; and in the Hebrides, also as the goddess of childbirth.

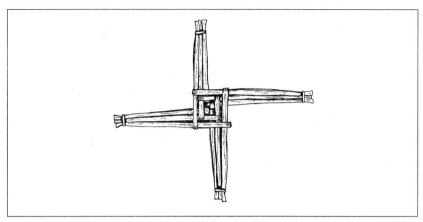

Figure 18: Bríd's Cross

DIANCECHT (Irish): Father of Medicine. His son Miach was also a physician. Miach and his sister Airmid made King Nuad's silver hand, for which Diancecht killed Miach; healing grasses grew on his grave.

EIR/FREYA (Nordic): Eir, goddess of healing, although called a handmaiden of Freya, is more accurately an aspect of her ("handmaiden" in Norse/Germanic culture is often a metaphor for "aspect"). She was probably invoked as Freya, and shared the same symbolism. She sat on the hill Lyfjaberg ("Healing Mountain") granting health to any woman who could climb up to her. This was a common practice of Vala', soothsayers and priestesses of Freya, during this period of history.

Freya was a fertility goddess, and probably the most revered of the Nordic goddesses. Daughter of Niord and Skadi, and sister of Frey. ("Frey" and "Freya" simply mean "Lord" and "Lady," as with the leaders of many cultures' pantheons.) She was originally of the Vanir (the original agricultural inhabitants of the area), in whose legends she and Frey were the children of Niord and his sister. The Aesir (warrior invaders who finally merged with the Vanir) welcomed her and Frey and Niord and accepted them; but they rejected incest, so Skadi became Niord's wife in their mythology and his sister disappeared.

Freya was the wife of Odin, or in some stories of Od, who is sometimes equated with Odin. She overlaps with Frigg; Frigg and Freya seem to have originally been the same goddess, or perhaps a

Vanir Triple Goddess with Skadi, then to have developed as two, finally tending to merge again. Frigg is given to introversion, Freya to extroversion. Both are named as the wife of Odin.

Freya owned a falcon-plumed robe in which she flew through the air, including to the underworld, to gain information in her role as a seeress. She was the mother of Baldur. She protected marriages and made them fruitful, but was not herself faithful to Odin. She was a goddess of sexual pleasure, and was said to have slept with all of the Aesir and with her brother Frey, as well as with giants and mortal men; her priests were regarded as her consorts. She is particularly called upon by women today who wish to regain the strength which Christian patriarchy has so long denied them. Medieval songs dedicated to her, called *mansongr*, or in German *Minnegesang*, were suppressed by the Christians, but later troubadours and minstrels revived the tradition, dedicating their songs to the Virgin Mary.

She is said to have been a mistress of magic and witchcraft, as well as a war goddess. As commander of the Valkyries (originally her priestesses), she often fought alongside Odin; she claimed half of the dead slain in every battle for her hall, Folkvangr (Field of Folk), Odin taking the other half. She also received the souls of unmarried women. She loved ornaments and jewelry such as her famous Necklace of the Brislings. She rode in a chariot drawn by two cats, and also on a boar called Hildisvini ("Battle-Swine") whose golden bristles showed him the way in the dark. She may have been a priestess of a hawk-totem clan. Animals sacred to her as Freya included the sow, the cat, the falcon, the swallow and the cuckoo, and as Frigg included the ram, the heron and the spider.

Although a goddess of Earth, she also had a watery side, and a dwelling in Fensalir ("Ocean Halls"). Her many titles included Heidh ("Witch"), Horn ("Flax"), Gefn ("Giver"), and Syr ("Sow"). Her symbols were the spindle and the distaff; she was mistress of the crafts of the home. She was associated with the zodiacal sign Leo and Friday was named after her. English place names recalling her include Freefolk, Hampshire (in the *Domesday Book* Frigefolk, "Frigg's People"), Froyle and Frobury, Hampshire (both Old English Freohyll, "Freya's Hill"), Fryup, Yorkshire ("the hop or marshy enclosure of Freya"), and Fridaythorpe, Yorkshire. She has two festivals: the first Monday after January 6 (Saxon Plow Monday) and November 21.

ISIS (Egyptian): Isis was unquestionably the most widely worshipped goddess of pre-Christian times; her worship lasted for at least 3,500 years, and before Christianity suppressed her, it extended from Nubia in Africa to Yorkshire in England, and from the Middle East to the Atlantic. Among her many aspects, she was regarded as an expert in medical science, taking pleasure in healing humans, and was the inventor of many healing drugs. She gave healing dreams, especially to those who spent a night in one of her many temples—— this was the practice of incubation followed by Egyptians of every class, and later in her overseas temples even by Roman Emperors. Egyptian medicine (including its priestly psychotherapy) was rightly famous throughout the ancient world, and Isis was its queen.

After her suppression, much of her symbology was transferred to the Virgin Mary. Even some statues of Isis cradling the infant Horus were adopted by Christian churches, particularly in the South of France, as representing Mary and the infant Jesus. Among grass-roots Catholics today, Mary is appealed to for healing more naturally than the austere male god.

The mythology of Isis is voluminous. She was the daughter of the sky goddess Nut by her brother the Earth god Geb. With her in the womb of Nut were Osiris, Horus the Elder, Set and Nephthys. Isis and Osiris fell in love and mated in Nut's womb, as did Nephthys and Set. Osiris and Isis ruled Egypt, and taught its people the basics of civilization. But Set (who symbolized the arid desert) was jealous of his brother, and in the twenty-eighth year of his reign succeeded in killing him, nailing his body in a coffin and throwing it into the Nile. His treachery alienated his wife Nephthys, who left him and thereafter was loyal to her sister Isis. The desolate Isis finally traced the coffin to Byblos in Phoenicia, where the currents had taken it. A tamarisk tree had grown around it, and King Malacander built the tree into his palace. Isis, incognito at first, became nurse to the son of Malacander and his queen, Astarte. When she revealed herself, Malacander gave her a ship to take the coffin back to Egypt.

She hid in the Delta marshes near Buto, to conceal from Set that she had magically conceived a child by her dead husband. Set found Osiris's body nevertheless, and tore it into fourteen parts which he scattered about the kingdom. Isis patiently searched for them, and as she found each one she held a funeral and set up a stele, hoping that Set would think all the parts had been buried in separate places.

The only part she failed to find was the phallus, which Set had thrown into the Nile and had been eaten by a crab. But Isis fashioned another. Osiris, now immortal, became King of Amenti (the West), the realm of the dead, and in due course Isis gave birth to Horus the Younger. These three became the Holy Family of Egypt, even overshadowing such important triads as Amun-Ra, Mut and Khonsu of Thebes.

Osiris was essentially a dying and resurrecting vegetation god. He was thus also a symbol of rebirth; the dead were identified with him, as a guarantee of immortality. In the funerary rites, the deceased, whether a man or woman, was referred to as "the Osiris Nebseni, victorious." The living Pharaoh was identified with Horus, the dead Pharaoh with Osiris; and the living Pharaoh was often depicted as being suckled by Isis, and therefore her son, because suckling was a ritual act of legal adoption in Egypt.

Isis, in addition to her role in the annual fertility myth, came to symbolize the ideal of a loyal and loving wife and mother. For the worshipper, her magical power was something which could be appealed to directly. She was the compassionate, motherly goddess who understood suffering from her own experience, and who could be asked to bend the rules in her supplicant's favor when a problem seemed humanly insoluble——a characteristic later (like so many other Isian attributes) taken over by the Virgin Mary. Yet bending the rules does not quite express it. Egyptians felt that her magic was in accord with deeper laws beyond their immediate understanding. This was reflected in the fact that Isis's magical collaborator, time and again, was Thoth, god of wisdom——whose wife, significantly, was Ma'at, goddess of the natural order of things and the inescapable laws of the cosmos.

The spread——one might almost call it an explosion——of Isis-worship outside Egypt was really set alight by Alexander the Great's conquest of Egypt in 332 B.C.. The Ptolemies, who ruled Egypt from then until Cleopatra, had great respect for Egyptian tradition, and strove to abide by it as Pharaohs; but they were also tidy-minded Greeks by descent, so they naturally tried to equate the Egyptian deities with those of their ancestry.

Ptolemy I, "the Great," appointed two distinguished priests, the Egyptian Manetho and the Athenian Timotheus, to advise him on the subject. They intelligently navigated the paradoxes to produce an Alexandrian pantheon acceptable to both Egyptian and Greek thinking. Isis, Horus, Anubis and some others presented few problems----but Osiris, a god of the dead and of fertility, having at the same time solar attributes----did not export easily. So they virtually invented a new god, Sarapis, an extension of the Apis Bull. Sarapis, absorbing Osiris yet equatable with Zeus and Poseidon, became Isis's consort in the international pantheon.

Losing nothing at home, she became increasingly cosmopolitan. Sarapis and Horus traveled with her, but Sarapis remained her Prince Consort rather than a King in his own right. The astonishing spread of Isis worship----to places as far apart as the Black Sea, Morocco, the Rhineland and York, and into emperors' palaces, private homes, and market places----would take pages just to summarize. The most comprehensive book on the subject is R. E. Witt's *Isis in the Graeco-Roman World* (see bibliography).

One attribute which hardly concerned the Egyptian Isis, or any other Egyptian deity, was a connection with the sea. But under the Ptolemies, the Western Mediterranean virtually became an Egyptian lake, with Alexandria becoming a major port of international shipping. So the cosmopolitan Isis soon added to her titles, Isis Pelagia, Star of the Sea, patroness of ships (many of which were named after her) and of sailors. She had become Isis Myrionymos of the Countless Names----a title still used by Greek Orthodox Christians for the Virgin Mary.

It was only one of the Isian features which Mary was given because of the Church's urgent need to fill the vacuum created by the banishment of Isis. The story in Revelation xii of Michael's battle with the dragon Satan, in defense of the "woman clothed with the sun, and with the moon under her feet, and upon her head a crown of twelve stars" who was "travailing in birth" is the source of much Marian symbology, and yet it follows the story of Isis, Set, and the birth of Horus so exactly, stage by stage, that the writer must have had it in mind. The Madonna and Child statues directly echoed those of Isis and the infant Horus, and some of them were actually Isis statues repainted. Mary, like Isis, was Star of the Sea, the Power that Heals the World, She who Initiates, Throne of the King, Mistress of the World, the Heifer who has brought forth the spotless Calf, and so on. And most significantly of all, Theotokos, Mother of God.

Isis's Festivals were January 9, February 5, March 5 and 10, May 14, June 24, July 3 and 19, August 12 and 27, October 28 to

November 3, November 13 and 14, and December 22. Her days were Wednesday and Friday. She was honored on the first and fourth days of the waxing moon.

IXCUINA (Aztec): Beautiful goddess of healing, fertility, love, sexuality, divination, magic and the Earth—also of dirt and its purification. Also known as Tlazolteol ("Eater of Filth"), Teteoinian ("Mother of God"), and Toci ("Our Grandmother"). She is identifiable with the mother goddess Tonantzin and is mother of the maize god Cinteotl.

IXLILTON (Aztec): God of health and medicine, known as "Little Black Face." His priests were physicians or shamans, and specialized in the healing of children.

KAMRUSEPAS (Hindu): Goddess of healing and magic.

KEDESH (Syrian): Goddess of life and health who was also worshipped in Egypt. Depicted as standing naked on a walking lion, with a mirror and lotus blossoms in her left hand and two serpents in her right. She overlaps with Hathor and Ashtart.

KHORS (Slavonic): A health and hunting god, portrayed as a stallion.

KINICH-AHAU (Mayan): God of medicine and sun god. He is lord of the face of the sun. His wife was Ixalvoh, goddess of weaving.

KWAN-YIN (Chinese): Goddess of healing and fecundity, she who bears the cries of the world. Of Buddhist origin, she sacrificed her Buddhahood for the sake of suffering humanity. Also known as Sung-tzu Niang-Niang, the Lady who Brings Children. Her image is in most Chinese homes, sitting on a lotus flower with a child in her arms, or sometimes on a lion. She is also described as a magician, a teacher of magic, an oracular goddess, and sometimes as a prostitute. In rural China, a man normally approaches her through a woman intermediary. If none is available, he approaches her himself, but apologizes for the omission.

LADY OF GOOD SIGHT (Chinese): Goddess who protects children from eye maladies.

LIBAN (Irish): Goddess of healing and pleasure. With Fand, she appeared to Cuchulainn in a dream, in which they beat him with horsewhips—but only to teach him a lesson which ended in happiness.

LIETUTIS (Lithuanian): A rain god whose water had healing properties. His rain was collected in boulders with chiseled impressions, in which offerings of money were left, and the boulders were strewn with flowers. The boulder was known as *lietus akmuo*, "the boulder of rain." His name may be the origin of the country's name, *Lietuva*.

MALLANA DEVA (husband) and **MALLANA DEVI** (wife) (Hindu, Kelihar, Muhl): Represented by a pair of dolmens at each of 15 villages. The shepherds offer wooden figures to them to avert death from sick people.

MANASA (Hindu, mainly Bengal): Invoked against snake bites. Her legends imply strong feminine counterattacks against male chauvinism.

MENES (Lithuanian and Latvian): Moon god prayed to for health and beauty. He is the husband of the dawn goddess Saule, but fickle, as he disappears for a few days each month to pursue others. Portrayed as a handsome man with a cape of stars, he drives a chariot drawn by gray horses.

NINKARRAK (Chaldaean): Goddess of healing and the alleviation of misfortune.

O-KUNI-NUSHI (Japanese): God of medicine and Earth god. He is the son of the sea and fertility god Susanowo. His sister and wife was Suseri-Hime. When his jealous brothers killed him, the seed goddess Kami-Musumi brought him back to life. He became ruler of Izumo.

ORUNMILLA (African, Nigeria, Yoruba): A god of healers and diviners. One of the original gods of the Yoruba pantheon, he accompanied the sky god Obatala on his first descent to the swamps of Earth. He travels around as the counselor of the destiny god Olodumare, to plead with him for the alleviation of human suffering. He was present when Olodumare fixed the destiny of every man, woman and child on Earth, so he knows our history before it happens. He has his shrine in almost every Yoruba household.

OSANOBUA (African, Nigeria, Benin, Edo): God of health, happiness, prosperity and long life.

OSUN (African, Nigeria, Benin, Edo): God of herbalists who collect leaves and roots from the forest both for healing and for divining and spell working.

PINGA (Eskimo, Caribou): A goddess who supervises the health and the souls of the living. She watches over hunting and game animals, especially the caribou. She is the one on high, balancing the sea goddess Sedna, and the one below, guardian of the dead. In very recent tradition, Pinga has come to be regarded as male.

ROHINE (Hindu): A cow goddess invoked to cure jaundice. She is variously associated with the constellations Scorpio and Hyades, and with the stars Antares and Aldebaran.

SALUS (Roman) and her equivalent **HYGEIA** (Greek): Goddess of health and welfare.

SASURATUM, THE (Phoenician, Canaanite): Seven midwife goddesses.

SETIK (West Slavonic, Bohemian): A domestic spirit who protects flocks from disease, and brings good harvests and money. He resembles a small boy with claws, and lives in the sheep shed, in the flour or the peas, or on a wild pear, while in winter he sits in the oven. The Styrian Slovenians believed he was a good spirit about the size of a thumb, who haunted places where salt was kept, or lived among the young cattle in their shed. A little of everything that was boiled or roasted was put aside for him, otherwise he might put the oven fire out, crack the pans, or cause the cows to give blood instead of milk.

SUITENGU (Japanese): A child god, protector and comforter of sick children, and a very popular protector of sailors.

SUL, SULLA (Gaelic *suil,* "eye"): British sun and wisdom goddess, and goddess of hot springs. Bladud, son of King Rud Hidibras, built a shrine for her near Badon on a spot where he had cured himself of a skin disease by rolling in the mud. This shrine became *Aquae Sulis* ("Waters of Sul"), the modern Bath. A perpetual fire was burned there in her honor. She was known to the Romans as Sul Minerva and she may have some connections with Silbury Hill, the Scilly Isles (Sylinancia), and Mousehole ("Place of Sul," pronounced *MAOW-z'l*) in Cornwall. Sally Lunn cakes recall the wheaten cakes offered at her altar. Her festivals are on February 2 and December 22.

SUNG-TZU NIANG-NIANG (Chinese): Goddess of healing and fecundity. She is depicted as draped in a large white veil, seated on a lotus with a child in her arms and corresponds to Kwan-Yin.

SURYA (Hindu): Sun god. Hymns or prayers are made to him for healing sickness, or by women wanting to have a son. In early Vedic times, he was one of the three chief gods, ruling the central sphere, that of the physical sun as the celestial form of fire, Agni, the source of life. In post-Vedic times, this role was taken over by Vishnu; but appeals to Surya continue to be widespread. Small images of him can be seen in other deities' temples. He has two wives, Sanjna and Suvarna; Sanjna left him for awhile because she could not control his brightness. He agreed to give up one-eighth of this brightness if she would return to him, which she did.

SVARTALVAR (Nordic): Mound-elves, to whom blessings are made for healing and a good harvest.

TLITCAPLITANA (Native American, Bella Coola tribe): Healing goddess, who descends from the sky to cure the sick. Sometimes her power is too great for the patient, who dies through her contact, but never through her ill will. She is ugly, with a snout and ropelike breasts, but her singing is beautiful.

YAKUSHI NYORAI (Japanese Buddhist): Divine healer who stops epidemics. Portrayed as a Buddha holding a flask of medicine, and often flanked by the Sun and the Moon, he was very popular from the eighth century onwards.

9

Healing With Magic

Using magic and ritual for the purpose of healing was one of the earliest religious practices of mankind. Modern adherents of paganism, Wicca, and ritual magic still use it for this purpose today. Not surprisingly, it is not regarded as coming under the category of complementary medicine, mainly because it is regarded as superstition and hocus pocus by the medical profession. Even those of the profession that accept that magic sometimes succeeds, dismiss its success as being due to the placebo effect, or that the illness was psychosomatic: "it was all in the mind!"

Most practitioners of magic would of course not argue with this statement, knowing that what affects the mind affects the body; but they would of course point out that this works in reverse---what affects the body also affects the mind! In theory this applies to the spirit as well so, in practice, working on the spirit can affect a cure in both the mental and the physical realm. This is the application of holistic principles in magical healing.

From a Jungian psychologist's viewpoint, magic works in the collective unconscious (see chapter 5) by the manipulation of symbolism within the group mind. Occult philosophy believes that there are seven levels of reality, and that magic works through interaction between these levels by this same process of symbolic manipulation. Individuals or groups who do any form of magical healing are therefore ritually manipulating this symbolism. This magic causes a change in the structure of the collective unconscious, and therefore affects the individual they wish to heal. Logically, it seems most likely that the first effect would be on that individual mentally, followed by the physical effect. Working magic, therefore, is a way of triggering an individual's own healing processes.

Occult philosophy names the different levels of reality as the spiritual, mental, astral, etheric, and physical levels, with some of these being subdivided. They are relevant, of course, both to the cosmos as a whole and to ourselves as individual human beings. One quote is used often by occultists to sum this up: "As above; So below." These levels are in fact reflected in the aura (see Fig. 11).

As the astral level is of particular importance in spell working, the above definition should be amplified a little. The division into upper and lower astral is something of an over-simplification; experience shows that the astral plane is a continuous spectrum. At its upper end, its images and thought forms are near-mental, but belong on the astral because they are infused with emotion. At its lower end, it is sometimes called the astral counterpart of physical manifestation in that each physical entity or object is closely associated with an astral image of itself; obviously it is the astral counterpart of a given object or person that magic seeks to influence through imagination (an astral function), concentration (mental), and willpower (something of both) as its direct path to influencing the physical.

Precise visualization of intent, concentration, and willpower are all essential if magic is to'work. Concentration is an ability built up by practice. Willpower includes confidence——and that demands an understanding of how magic works and the knowledge that it does work. Any form of magic will fail if the practitioners do not actually believe in what they are doing, or have no confidence in their own abilities.

The important thing to remember about the seven levels is that they speak and understand different languages. The mental level uses words and logical processes. The astral and the physical levels both work in the language of unconscious; the astral levels in symbols and images, the physical levels in sensations. Successful magical work therefore involves effective communication between them all.

In chapter 7, Healing Sanctuaries, we talked about creating sacred space and gave an example of Casting the Circle. In any form of magic this is vitally important in order to maintain a raised level of energy and to protect the area from psychic intrusion during magical working.

Spells and Charms

In *The Witches' Way* we defined "spell" as: "a ritual for raising psychic power and directing it to a specific and practical purpose." More precisely, it has come to mean a form of verbal magic sometimes involving hand gestures or a dramatic act of some description, such as knotting a cord. Charm (from the Roman goddess Carmina) basically signifies the use of a piece of prose or verse as a spell.

The use of charms is well recorded in classical literature, and we know from archeological finds that they were used for healing in Ancient Egypt. Malevolent charms were banned by Rome's earliest known code of law, the Twelve Tablets of the midfifth century B.C.

There is little doubt that charms and spells remained popular with the common people well past the Christianization of European culture, and many took on Christian overtones as well as pagan (see page 18, The Nine Herbs Charm). Many of these charms included a herbal cure, which was a typical feature of Anglo-Saxon charms pre-dating the tenth century. The following provide examples of typical charms and spells.

Against a Wen

This Anglo-Saxon charm can still be used today for the removal of a growth.

Wen, wen, little wen,
Here thou shalt not build, nor have any abode,
But thou shalt fare North to the hill hard by,
Where thou hast a brother in misery.
He shall lay a leaf at thy head.
Under wolf's paws, under eagle's wing,
Under eagle's claw, ever mayst thou fade.
Shrivel as coal on the hearth,
Shrink as dung on a wall,
Waste away as water in a pail.
Become as little as a linseed grain,
And much less also than a hand-worm's hipbone,
And also become so little that thou become naught.

From the British Museum; Manuscript MS Royal 4A.

There are no recorded rituals with this, but the words do give some indication of what was probably used, such as a leaf and an eagle's claw.

Egyptian Udjat (Eye of Horus) Charm for Good Health

Take a triangular piece of paper and draw the Eye of Horus upon it, while saying the following incantation:

The god Thoth has given us the Udjat.
I am healthy and it is healthy.
I am free from imperfection,
And it is free from imperfection.

Incantation taken from Egyptian Book of the Dead.

Keep the piece of paper in your wallet or purse.

Against a Headache

The following is a Chaldean spell to cure a headache (we originally published this in *Spells And How They Work*). Unlike the previously mentioned spells it does not use any form of incantation and relies purely on ritual actions:

A band of cords, with a knot on the right, is arranged flat and regularly with a woman's diadem on the left. Divide it twice into seven smaller bands. Wind it around the head of the sick one. Wind it around the seat of life. Seat him on his bed. And anoint him with charmed water.

We have quoted this spell—which we do not recommend—to prove a point. The tying of a band around the head is more likely to cause a headache than cure it! Spells work better if you create them yourself, using a little common sense, rather than taking them out of ancient dusty grimoires.

The best spells we have ever seen have come out of a person's mouth on the spur of the moment. To use an old quote—necessity is the mother of invention!

Sympathetic Magic

In sympathetic magic the practitioner creates an astral double and thereby influences the physical realm. The most well-known form of this is the use of a doll or wax image, known more commonly among witches as a poppet or fith-fath (see Fig. 19). Unfortunately, these have had rather bad press due to the influence of horror films and the like.

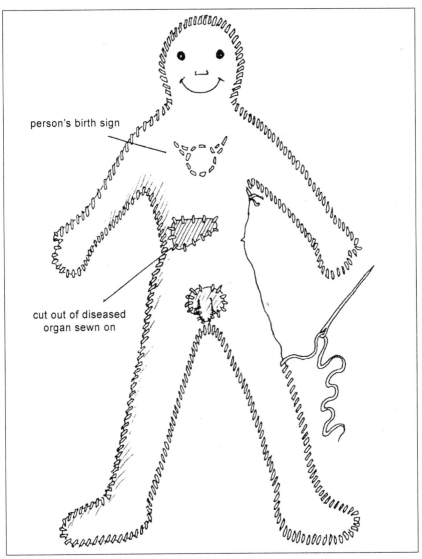

person's birth sign

cut out of diseased
organ sewn on

Figure 19: Example of Poppet Used for Healing

The original use of the poppet was for healing, for which it is highly effective. In many ways it accommodates what spiritual healers call "distance healing"----the sending of healing energy when the individual is not able to be present. Witches use poppets because they act as a focus for the healing rather than just throwing energy blindly. They also allow specific healing to be carried out on the area of the body that requires it.

143

Nowadays poppets are normally made out of cloth and stuffed with cotton wool or similar material. It may also be stuffed with herbs which are appropriate astrologically. In healing, these herbs are generally related to Venus such as rose, alder and sandalwood, to name but a few. Poppets are normally cut out in the shape of a person, and given features such as a mouth, eyes, nose and sexual genitalia. The act of making the poppet this way, rather than just using a cardboard cutout, is more creative and therefore endows the image with more magical power. Part of this process can also be to decorate a person's poppet with the astrological symbols related to the person and with something to represent the area of illness. For example, a cutout drawing of the liver may be pinned onto the poppet if the person has liver disease.

The first act of any ritual involving a poppet (after Casting the Circle of course) is to consecrate and name the poppet as the sick person. This creates the astral double and links it with the sick individual. One other act often used is the process of breathing life into it. This consists of breathing down a straw into the mouth of the image to endow it with life energy or prana (see page 90).

After the poppet has been charged magically, the healing magic is performed on it. This can take several forms, including spiritual healing, where the poppet is used as a surrogate for the sick person (see chapter 10). It may be useful to mark the chakra points on the poppet.

More commonly, the infirmity is magically banished from the poppet, and therefore from the sick person. The following outlines such a ritual.

Poppet Healing Ritual

The altar is set up as in chapter 7, Healing Sanctuaries. Included on the altar are a small bowl of anointing oil (jasmine is a particularly suitable oil to use, being governed both by Mercury, which will help form the connection between the sick person and the poppet, and by Venus, which is the planet of love and healing), a length of green thread or cotton (enough to bind the poppet three times and be tied) and a straw. The previously prepared poppet is also placed on the altar.

After Casting the Circle, and a brief period of meditation, the healer places his or her fingers into the bowl of consecrated salt and water, sprinkles the poppet with it, and says:

144

Water is life. I consecrate thee with water and salt, and name thee (name of ill person). As blood flows through his/her body, so it flows through yours.

The healer then dips fingers into the wine, sprinkles the poppet with it, and says:

Spirit brings life. I consecrate thee with wine, and name thee (name of ill person). As he/she lives, so does this image.

The healer then picks up the straw, places one end on the mouth of the poppet, and then breathes down the straw, visualizing light entering the poppet. When satisfied that there is enough life energy in the poppet, the healer replaces the straw and says:

Breath is life. I consecrate thee (name of ill person) with my life force. As I breath, so does this image.

The healer then repeats the process with the anointing oil, as with the water and wine, and says:

I consecrate thee with oil. The link is made. This poppet is thyself in every way; what ails thee, ails this image.

The image is then picked up in both hands and waved over the incense. The healer then says:

I banish from you the (name of the illness) in the element of Air. May this smoke purify you, and may you breathe freely and your life force flow.

The image is then waved over the candle flame:

I banish from you the (name of the illness) in the element of Fire. May this flame burn the illness from you, and may it energize your body.

The image is then placed onto the bowl of earth:

I banish from you the (name of the illness) in the element of Earth. May your infirmity be banished to the ground, and may your body replenish itself.

The healer then picks up the green cotton and binds it around the poppet while saying:

I bind good health into thee. May you be blessed three times with love, wealth and health. So mote it be.

145

The cotton is then tied off.

There is a good magical reason for repeating the naming of the poppet, and of the illness, three times. Most occultist believe the first time you name something it penetrates into the conscious, the next time into the subconscious (Jung's personal unconscious), and finally the third time into the unconscious and, of course, the astral realm.

We feel it is always good practice after such a ritual to offer the poppet to the person who the ritual was performed for (it has a good psychological effect on them). If you do keep it, put it away safely until the person is well and then reverse the consecration of the poppet (but make sure you do not reverse the banishing of the illness or the healing!).

Dough-Baby Healing Ritual

One of our coven developed the dough-baby healing ritual when a friend's newly born baby failed to thrive; she was born premature and was not gaining weight as the doctors had hoped.

The magic used for this baby was not only a good example of sympathetic magic, but also of kitchen witchcraft—traditionally using what would have been available to any country wise-woman within her kitchen. The intention of the ritual as presented here is to increase body weight, health and well-being in someone who is ill; however, the ritual can be adapted for a number of healing purposes.

All that is required is flour, water and yeast—and the knowledge of how to bake bread (there are plenty of good recipes available). These ingredients should be mixed and prepared as a dough, although you may wish to include some herbs associated with healing and the astrological correspondences of the recipient of this magic. The unbaked dough should then be formed into the shape of a person, and consecrated in a similar fashion to the poppet.

Once consecrated and named as that person the dough figure should be placed in the oven. The following spell should be recited:

In warmth and friendly darkness,
Dough gently rises on,
Growing now in strength,
So you too may grow strong.
So placed within the oven,
To turn from white to gold,

Now shall you gain in health,
A wonder to behold.
Take, eat the bread of life,
Proved and baked and true,
Ingest the spell we weave,
And make it part of you.

As this dough rises, may the health of (name of person) rise too. As this dough grows, may the well-being of (name of person) grow too.

A small piece of the bread should be left as an offering outside to the gods and goddesses. The rest of the bread should be given to the ill person to eat, to ingest the power of the spell. In the case of a baby, the bread should be eaten by the mother, so that it passes into her milk.

Libations and Offerings

The use of libations and offerings can be considered to be more of a religious than a magical practice, although it is unlikely that our ancestors would have distinguished between the two. The use of libations, offerings to gods for favors, can be found around the world. They are still an important part of Shintoism in Japan, as well as within India's Hindu culture.

Libations are probably one of the earliest forms of ritual practices used by mankind. It is logical to surmise that early Stone Age man, having developed the belief in some form of divine intelligence at work, would have asked for its help by offerings of gifts in return. Although mankind has developed both in intelligence and in his technological skill, it is interesting to note that the practice of leaving offerings has differed very little in 5,000 years. The Greeks and Egyptians both used libations. This differed slightly from the usual leaving of offerings in that wine was poured onto the shrine as a plea for divine intervention, and there are some good archeological examples of altars with channels carved into them for the wine to flow down. This practice spread to Rome in the early period of the empire.

In Europe, libations were adopted into the Christian faith from the rituals performed at temples within Rome. Testifying to this are some of the many archeological finds of small carved hands, feet and other body parts made from ivory. These were left at the temples by the sick and ill as a plea to the gods and goddesses to cure the appropriate ailment. In Roman Catholic Ireland this practice continues to this day at many of the wells and shrines which can be found in the Irish countryside. These are normally dedicated to saints who are obvious Christianizations of pagan deities. We have seen an assortment of offerings left at such sites, which have included everything from church-endorsed prayer cards (which are common in Roman Catholic countries) through to pairs of glasses as a plea for better eyesight, insulin syringes, and a salbutamol inhaler for asthma all as pleas for a cure.

Even during the Reformation and the rise of Protestantism it was impossible to completely wipe out this form of worship from the cultural memory. Go into any church at Harvest Festival and the evidence is there to be seen, with fruit and vegetables, and the odd can of baked beans, being left as offerings for an even better harvest next year.

After the Reformation, the Protestant Church attempted to outlaw these practices by claiming that they were deals made with the Devil. This was a claim continually levied against witches during the years of persecution. It probably comes from the pagan practice of making pacts with deities: "If you heal me, I'll build you a new shrine (but only if you heal me!)." Many of the temples built in Rome were built as a response to a fulfilled libation. Sometimes the deities were even threatened that if they did not respond favorably they would be denied worship; this seems to have been a common practice among the Norse and the Celts. Some of it even seeped into Christianity, with an example of such a threat existing in the Roman Catholic Prayer Book.

So why has this form of ritual practice survived for so long? The reason is of course a very pagan one----Darwinian natural selection----it survived because it works. Unlike other forms of magic, it relies on the intercession of the divine wearing one of its many masks----the deity being called upon within the ritual. It therefore requires belief in that deity, which is why priesthoods and the development of temples as institutions were an important part of religious growth.

As gods and goddesses can be seen to be thought forms supercharged by both mankind and the divine (see chapter 8), the development of priesthoods resulted in more power being accumulated by the gods and goddesses and therefore more ability to intercede on behalf of their worshippers. The Christian church is therefore responsible for the miracles that its god creates because it gives him the power to do it. This is the real meaning behind the Wiccan practice of Drawing Down the Moon, where the high priest and the coven give their power to the goddess.

Magically, using libations and offerings is one of the most ethically safe practices. Again, this is because it relies on the intercession of a deity. This means that the petitioners will receive what they need, not necessarily what was ask for. This is always true in the cases where a healing deity has been invoked, but may not always be true when it comes to other deities (they can be fallible).

Making pacts with deities is also a legitimate form, but is probably best left to a priest or priestess of that deity, because they understand the nature of their god or goddess more fully. It is important to remember that a pact is a binding agreement, so you must fulfill your end of the bargain or face the karmic consequences. We recommend avoiding the threatening of deities. Although there is historical precedence for it, it should be avoided as a disrespectful, and therefore unsafe, practice.

Because of the devotional nature of libations and offerings, they are best suited to permanent temples and shrines which are dedicated to the deity concerned. The rituals can be performed in temporary circles but it is necessary to invoke the goddess or god in a similar fashion to the Wiccan Drawing Down the Moon or Sun (more on these rituals can be found in our books *Eight Sabbats for Witches* and *The Witches' Way*).

We have listed two libation and offering rituals below as examples.

Libation to Aesculapius

The temple or Circle should be set up and prepared as described in chapter 7, Sanctuaries. It should be noted that it was traditional for Aesculapius only to be approached by members of his priesthood, never by members of the public. This is obviously adaptable nowadays, but nevertheless should be taken into account.

The priest or priestess stands before the altar, arms raised, and says:

Hail to thee, Aesculapius, son of Apollo, student of Chiron, slain by Hades. As priest (priestess) of your art, I call

149

upon your powers of healing; upon the powers of your daughters Panacea and Hygela; upon the powers of your father, Apollo. Bring the power of healing to (name of ill person) and banish his/her infirmity, the disease of (name of illness). As your priest (priestess), I leave this offering to you as a mark of my devotion and respect.

The red wine from the chalice is then poured into the libation bowl on the altar.

Offering to Bríd

Devotions to Bríd are best suited at an outside location, such as a consecrated well or spring. An example of a well or spring being prepared can be found in chapter 7. Offerings can be performed in a temporary Circle, but they need to be rich in related symbolism (see page 128). Unlike Aesculapius, Bríd can be approached by anyone, so it is not necessary to be a priest or priestess dedicated to her.

A piece of clothing from the part of the body which is ill is required, as is fruit and straw made in the form of a Saint Bridget's or Bríd's cross (see Fig. 18).

The following is said:

Hail to thee Bríd, Mother of the Gael; thou who art three sisters of the same name. I call upon you, bringer of craftsmanship, bringer of inspiration, bringer of healing, to heal (name of person), from his/her infirmity (name of illness). From his/her body comes this clothing, which shows you this sickness; I leave it for you to see.

The piece of clothing is held up, and then tied to the tree next to the well (in a temporary Circle this is done later).

O Bríd, Mother of the Gael, I leave you these offerings. This fruit from the field, and this cross of light. I thank you for your power of helping.

10

Spiritual Healing

Spiritual healing was revived as one of the healing arts by the Spiritualist and Theosophy movements during the nineteenth century. Its practice was well known by the priests and priestesses of various pagan traditions before the coming of Christianity.

It is often referred to as "faith healing" by the general public. A term adopted from the tabloid press, who have confused it with the "laying on of hands" performed by some evangelical sects of Christianity. This term is also often used to indicate that the results of this form of healing are caused by what doctors refer to as the placebo effect—the curing of a psychosomatic illness by deception. To call spiritual healing "faith healing" is a misnomer, as it relies on the body's energy system, the aura and the chakras, rather than on blind faith or deception.

Even though belief or faith is not essential for participants undergoing spiritual healing, it is an advantage if they are open-minded. Closed-minded individuals are likely to affect their auras and chakras, making them unresponsive to treatment.

It is essential that healers understand the workings of the aura and the chakras before performing spiritual healing, otherwise they could risk having an adverse effect on their clients as well as themselves. Where possible, individuals who wish to learn spiritual healing should apprentice themselves to someone who can. Many covens and pagan groups have individuals who teach spiritual healing, but if they are unable to find someone within the pagan movement locally, they could do worse than approach their local Spiritualist temple. Most of these temples are very open-minded to individuals of diverse paths, and would be happy to help sincere applicants.

Training as a spiritual healer can take several years, and should not be taken on lightly. It requires dedication and the willingness to study, and like most spiritual disciplines, its first effect is to change the student. It is possible to train yourself if you cannot find a teacher; with this in mind we have included a series of simple exercises to start the student on the path of the spiritual healer. It is also essential to study chapter 6, The Psychic and Spiritual Body, thoroughly. We have also included a list of essential reading within the bibliography.

Correct Frame of Mind

As with all types of healing, the healer must have the correct attitude for what he or she is doing. This is particularly true for spiritual healing. The healer must realize that he or she is a vehicle for healing energy, or to use the fashionable New Age term, channeling energy. Being a healer is not something you do, rather it is something you learn to become. Good healers do not need to try to heal, they just allow the healing energy to flow. This takes practice as the ego fights to maintain control in such situations.

It is important that healers develop the attitude that they are not performing healing, but sharing healing energy with the clients. It is a two-way process which involves two parties who are equally responsible for the outcome of the healing session. This attitude helps to increase the connection psychically between healer and client, and therefore increases the flow of energy during healing. Failure to view the individual as an equal in the task of healing blocks the flow of energy, and prevents the person being healed from continuing the healing process once the session is over. It is important that the healer realizes that people cannot be healed unless they want to be. Ultimately it is the individuals who are being healed who are responsible for their own health.

To allow healing energy to flow, healers must develop the ability to connect with those they are healing. Quite simply this is done by having compassion for the human race as a whole, and therefore the individual you are healing (see page 26, chapter 2). This is referred to as unconditional love by some healers, and often arises spontaneously once individuals have decided to dedicate themselves to the healing path, and have developed some of the attitudes we have already mentioned. We are all ultimately related to each other, so feeling that the individual being healed is family helps considerably in the healing process.

It is also important to be able to connect with where the energy ultimately flows from. As pagans we view this as the god and goddess, but we can help further in the process of healing by invoking our own particular healing deity before starting. The choice of the deity to be invoked is the decision of the individual healer, but it should be one that he or she has developed a relationship with over a period of time (see page 126, chapter 8).

As we have previously mentioned (see page 42, chapter 3) there is always the danger of the healer going on a power trip. This is prevented from happening if the healer develops the correct attitudes to what he or she is doing. The correct frame of mind is probably one of the most important things to learn if you are going to heal, so we have included below several practical exercises to develop it, as well as some of the other skills that a spiritual healer needs.

Opening and Closing the Chakras

It is essential to open the chakras before any form of psychic healing involving direct contact. Many pagans who work magic in a Circle, particularly raising the Cone of Power, find this quite easy because activity such as dancing within the Magic Circle has the effect of opening them naturally. Shamans may use herbal preparations as well as dancing and drumming, but this can be potentially dangerous unless you know what you are doing.

We recommend that the student of spiritual healing use the following opening and closing exercise on a daily basis until they are adept at the processes involved. It takes about 20 to 30 minutes to do this exercise. We recommend having somebody present who is sensitive and able to see the chakras the first couple of times you do it; your helper can confirm when the centers are open. With practice it takes less and less time to open your centers, and you will eventually find you can discard this exercise completely and open them with willpower alone.

The first stage is to find somewhere quiet and comfortable to sit. The best position to sit in is the well-known lotus position, used in

Eastern yoga, because it has the effect of bringing the Muladhara, or root center, into line with the other chakras. If you are not supple enough to use this position, sitting cross-legged or kneeling will have the same effect; the important thing is to stay comfortable for a reasonable period.

The next stage is to breathe regularly. There are various breathing patterns used, but we have found that breathing out for seven seconds, holding for two seconds, breathing in for seven seconds and finally holding for two seconds is the most effective. It is important when breathing in to breathe from the base of the lungs, by expanding the stomach first, and then the ribs. It will take awhile to get used to this, so give yourself time to master it. The next stage is to visualize that you are breathing in light. Initially this should be white light, before going on to the next stage.

Energizing the chakras, one by one, is the third stage. Continue the breathing pattern that you began with; by now it should be natural and rhythmic. Visualize the root center at the base of the spine as a red, glowing, spinning ball. As you breathe in, visualize the color of that breath as the same, in this case red. This should have the effect, after several minutes, of making the chakra expand while spinning faster and brighter.

Finally, imagine the energy from the center you have just energized moving up to the next chakra (in this case the sacral center), but changing the color of the light you are breathing in to that of the new chakra (in this case yellow). Again it should take several minutes to energize the chakra, which should behave in the same way as the first center. You then simply repeat the process until you reach and energize the third eye or brow center. Then visualize all the colors from each of the energized chakras moving swiftly up to the crown center at the top of the head. Allow the energy to leave the top of the head like a fountain and bathe your aura.

It is important to close your chakras immediately after you have finished healing. Leaving them open can result in a loss of vitality, higher risk of disease, and mental stress. The easiest way to close them down is to eat. Most pagans have a good "cakes and wine" session after having their chakras open in Circle which closes them in minutes.

Another way, for people who are first learning to open their centers, is an equally simple visualization technique. Visualize the energy draining back down from one chakra to another. Once you have drained the energy from each chakra to the one below it, visualize a shutter closing it from vision. Repeat this center by center. When you reach the root center, remember that it is the only one you leave open all the time, because it acts as the body's grounding point and helps to prevent mental and psychic overload.

Practical Exercise

The following exercise is designed to help the student healer feel the flow of energy needed for healing purposes. Two people are required for this exercise, just as there are two participants in the process of healing. You also need to be aware of which is your primary healing hand----the one which gives positive healing energy; the other removes negative, diseased energy. One easy way to find out which is which is to clasp your hands together and then to see which thumb is on top. Normally this is the primary healing hand. Some healers find that if they repeat this exercise several times the thumb changes; this is not unusual, and means they can use either hand.

The first stage is for both of you to open your centers (see page 153) and sit comfortably facing each other. You can be sitting on chairs or cross-legged on the floor. The important thing is that you are both of roughly equal height. You should place the palms of each of your hands facing each other at chest height, and about 12 inches apart. It is important that your hands do not touch at this stage, as the object is for each of you to feel for the other's aura. After a period of time sitting in this position you should both begin to feel the energy emitting from the minor chakra centers which exist in the palms of your hands. This normally feels like heat to most people, but some individuals may perceive it differently.

Once both of you have felt the flow of energy you should signal to each other and simultaneously close your eyes. Very slowly you should move the palms of your hands together, slowly entering each other's auras, and then touch fingertips to fingertips. You should then visualize the energy flowing from your heart centers in a circuit going clockwise, from your left hand to your partner's right hand, through your partner's heart center and back, through your partner's left hand, to your right hand.

After a period of time visualizing and sitting in this position you may begin to get the sensation that your partner's hands are moving ever so slightly in a circular motion. You should try to follow these movements, but on no account should either of you try consciously to lead these movements. What is actually happening is that you are feeling the flow of energy within your partner's aura as it emerges from their chakric centers.

At this point you and your partner should try to see what effect concentrating on various significant words, colors, and concepts have on the flow of energy. For example, concentrating on the word "love" will probably increase the flow of energy because of its associations with the heart center which is being used in this exercise. This is the perfect opportunity for you, and your partner, to find what triggers the flow of energy for you personally (see The Healing Centers below), and for you to develop the correct frame of mind for healing. Developing this will enable you to flow with the energy that is in your client's aura. This is essential if you are going to heal, and when healing, you should try to repeat the feeling that you experienced when using this exercise. You should repeat this exercise using the crown and the root chakra (the two other healing centers), but remember to pass this energy through the heart center.

The Healing Centers

Healers primarily work with the three main chakras, but an experienced healer can use all of the centers. The three main chakras are the heart center, the crown center, and the root center.

The Heart Center

The primary healing center is the heart chakra as the healing energy from both other centers must pass through it. All energy must pass through it before flowing down the arms to the minor centers in the palms of the hands, so all energy passing through it is transformed by its actions. This is why it is important to foster the ideals of love and compassion if you are going to heal successfully, as the heart chakra opens and allows energy to flow in such conditions.

To use the heart center you should visualize some of the happiest moments of your life, moments of love and tenderness, and of the greatest joy. The object is to feel that you are sharing these experiences with the person that is the object of the healing. This will start energy flowing from the heart center, which is normally visualized as green/turquoise, although some healers use healthy rose-pink. Childhood memories seem to have the strongest effect, possibly because of the innocence attached to them.

The healing energy that comes from the heart center is the softest, yet strongest form. When channeled by the healer into the mental/emotional aura, it can release deeply hidden trauma. Applied to the etheric aura and the physical body, it is useful in removing muscle tension, and in repairing damaged organ tissue. Because of its primary action of relaxing the client, it should always be the first center to be used when healing begins.

It is the first center that the student of healing must learn to use as it helps to promote spiritual growth within the healer. If a healer is damaged emotionally, he or she will be unable to heal, as the heart center will have become blocked by negative emotion. It is therefore important that the healer realizes that "physician heal thyself" is one of the first actions that students of the healing path must take if they are to heal successfully.

The Crown Center

As pagans, it is the crown chakra which links us to our concept of the god and goddess, and to the realm of spirit. It produces an energy which is purifying and cleansing; therefore, it is of great use in cleansing the areas of the mental/emotional aura which have built up negative thought forms or have been damaged. Within the etheric aura, it is often used to combat malignant diseases such as cancerous tumors for the same reason.

To use the crown center requires a developed spirituality, and as pagans this means a belief in the god and goddess. As a healer priest or priestess you may have built up a relationship with one of the many healing deities (see page 126, chapter 8) whom you can call upon. This may take the form of an invocation, verbally or mentally, when you feel it is time to open this center to heal. When you do this you should visualize the energy of that deity pouring as silver-white light into your crown center from a shaft of light above your head. You should maintain this vision until the light forms a halo around your head. It can then be channeled through your heart center, and down your arms, to your client.

One important point——always allow the energy to flow down, rather than allowing your consciousness to go up to meet the energy. Otherwise you will end up having an out of body experience due to the astral component of your aura leaving your physical body. If you do begin to feel light headed or airy while using this center, allow some of the energy to pass down through all your centers until it reaches the root chakra. This should have the effect of grounding you.

The Root Center

The primary use of the energy that emerges from the root chakra, when healing, is for grounding any negative energy which is loosened by the use of the other two centers. Its energy can also be used to heal bones and regenerate damaged tissues when used within the etheric aura. The Earth-mother quality of this energy can be used within the mental/emotional aura to soothe individuals and make them feel more secure.

To use this center, you should visualize the earth beneath your feet, and feel the pulsating energy of Gaia, the living planet, under you. You should imagine this energy coming up through the minor chakra centers in the soles of your feet (see page 99, chapter 6) and up to your heart chakra. If this energy is used for healing, soothing and regenerating, it should be visualized as green, but if it is used for grounding it should be visualized as turning to red after the energy has left the root chakra.

Not all healers can use all of the centers. Normally, a healer finds he or she has a preference for using either the crown chakra or the root chakra. An airy person may have a natural aptitude for using the crown chakra, and find it difficult to relate to the earthy nature of the root chakra. The reverse, of course, applies to the earthy person who may have problems channeling the light and airy energy of the crown chakra. Healers tend to find that they have a natural gift for healing particular ailments. This phenomenon is well known in traditional Irish folklore, where there is reference to "bone menders" and other specializations. As a healer, you should never feel uncomfortable with the energies you are using, and you should not have to force yourself to use certain energies. If you find that you have a natural gift, stick with it, but never feel afraid of experimenting with the other centers.

Colors within the Aura

Colors within the astral, mental/emotional and etheric bodies can be useful for diagnosing illness and disease on a physical, mental, emotional and spiritual level. These colors are generated by the appropriate chakras; hence the appearance of a violent red in the root chakra will also be seen in the aura. If this color is positioned over another chakra, for example the heart center, it indicates aggressive emotions; if it is lower, over the sacral center, it indicates sexual aggression. These colors can also be seen in the individual's chakras.

It is not essential for the healer to see these colors, and often they can only be seen by those with psychic ability. Many healers find that after a period of time they can feel the colors rather than physically see them. This is a common experience, and student healers should not be afraid to go with their instinct on what color is present in the chakra or aura.

The healer should also remember that the perception of these colors and their associations with particular functions and disease is subjective. One healer may perceive a disease as one color, and another may see it as a color belonging to the other end of the spectrum (all the colors listed below and in Figure 20 are only guides----they do not replace personal experience). This is often due to the personal associations of the healers concerned; for example, the healing energy from the heart chakra may be seen as either green or rose-pink, but some healers may perceive it as the color yellow if, say, they have received yellow roses as a token of love.

The only rule that does seem to apply to colors in healing is that muddy, dirty and dark colors are always associated with illness. Also, dullness within the normal coloration of the auras and chakras indicates that the center or auric body is being run down in some way, and vividness in color always indicates over-activity----such as in the solar plexus during periods of stress.

Below we have listed the colors that appear most in the aura, and have outlined their use in visual healing techniques.

Red: Associated with strength, energy and passion. Bright scarlet can indicate pride, greed and selfishness; if it is flashing, anger; if positioned in the aura around the root center, nervous disorders. It will indicate inflammatory disorders if in the etheric body. Intense red shows that the individual has been bending the rules magically, while rose-pink indicates somebody seriously smitten with love!

Orange: Relates to self-control, intellectual development and consideration for others. It can also indicate pride and ambition. Dirty orange can mean selfish motives. A healthy shade can show that the person is fit and full of vitality. A good color to use if an individual is physically run down.

Yellow: Like orange, related to intellect, but ability rather than development. A fresh yellow can show optimism and emotional well-being. A strong yellow can mean self-sufficiency, but a pale shade can mean the opposite as well as a weak will. In the spiritually well developed, it can appear as gold, particularly around the head. Yellow in healing helps to invigorate the patient physically, emotionally and mentally. Dirty yellows are common in the etheric body when cancerous tumors are present.

Green: A sign of good health when around the lower chakras. Vibrant pale greens around the brow and crown centers show that a person has natural healing abilities. Emerald shows versatility and easy adaptation to new situations, but gray and browny greens can show deceit and cunning. In healing, luminous blue/green is probably one of the most widely used colors because of its broad range of healing abilities.

Blue: Dark and clear blue indicates a high-minded and religious person. In the spiritually devoted it appears as a cobalt blue. Pale blue can show that the individual has not yet reached full potential spiritually. Blue combined with black appears in the aura of the religious fanatic; however, when combined with violet, it shows affection and devotion. An excellent color to use in healing depression.

Violet: Relates to the individual's spirituality and psychic abilities, and normally shows wisdom. Ultraviolet appears when someone is highly developed psychically and spiritually. Within the etheric body, violets and purples combined with red can be indicative of circulatory disorders.

Black, Brown and **Gray**: Generally these are all negative, as are colors which are dirty or muddy in appearance. These often appear combined with other colors. Black suggests hate and malice; and when combined with scarlet, anger. With any of the other colors it can indicate negativity in the meaning. Brown is associated with avarice, but appearing with green it can mean that the person is in love; if scarlet is also present it can indicate jealous love. Gray is normally predominant in those with depression; with green present, it shows deceit.

Damage to the Aura and Chakras

Apart from colors being present to indicate illness and disease, both the chakric centers and the auric bodies may be damaged. It is harder to perceive damage to these areas than it is to feel the colors of a dysfunctional or diseased area, and it may take quite awhile for the healer to start feeling any damage. Student healers should be patient with themselves and allow this perceptive ability to grow naturally, rather than try to force the inner vision which is required by the healer. As with healing in general, it is a matter of simply allowing it to happen.

Usually the etheric body is the first area where damage is discovered. This is normally due to illness of a particular organ or area of the body, and manifests in the etheric body as breaks above the area of physical damage. This is useful to know, even if you are still unable to feel any damage, as knowledge of any illness given to you by your client will enable you to feel for any breaks, and will indicate the necessity to heal that area of the etheric body even if you are unable to perceive anything.

The same process can also be applied to the mental/emotional body. If you discover by assessment before healing that a client has emotional trauma, breaks in the aura may be present above the associated chakra. For example, if there is repressed anger contained for a long period, there will very likely be breaks in the aura around that center.

Damage to both the etheric and the mental/emotional bodies is common in alcohol and drug abuse, and is normally prevalent around the area of the head and the crown center. Particular colors will also be seen if the abuser has been using psychedelic drugs, such as LSD, for prolonged periods.

Generally auric cleansing (see below) will heal any minor damage to the aura, but deeper damage will require the healer to concentrate on that area. The client may require several healing sessions with the etheric body to fully repair the damage. To repair such damage will first require the removal of the cause: this is done by using the heart center, in the case of damage to the mental/emo-

Root Center	
Healthy Color	Red
Physical Disorders	Anemia, skin, and nervous system. Urinary disorders.
Mental Disorders	Depression, impatience, and anger.
Colors related to Disorders	Scarlet (all disorders except depression). Muddy brown/gray (depression).
Chakra Used by Healer	Use Heart (blue/green), and Brow (indigo).

Sacral Center	
Healthy Color	Orange
Physical Disorders	Impotence, lack of energy. Irritable disorders of lower intestine.
Mental Disorders	Nervousness, repressed desires.
Colors related to Disorders	Dull orange (lack of energy), Red (nervousness/lower intestine).
Chakra Used by Healer	Use Heart (blue/green), Crown (silver/ white), and Sacral (vibrant orange). Root (green).

Solar Plexus Center	
Healthy Color	Yellow
Physical Disorders	Fatigue, digestive problems. Recurring infections.
Mental Disorders	Mental exhaustion.
Colors related to Disorders	Dull yellow, muddy brown/gray. Red (stomach/intestines).
Chakra Used by Healer	Use Brow (indigo), Solar plexus (yellow). Heart (blue/green).

Figure 20: Chakric Color Chart

162

Heart Center	
Healthy Color	Green
Physical Disorders	Circulatory disorders, hypertension, heart failure, coronary heart disease.
Mental Disorders	Negativity, repressed emotional trauma, jealousy.
Colors related to Disorders	Red/purple (circulatory disorders). Dirty/dark green (mental disorders). Red (repressed anger)
Chakra Used by Healer	Use Heart (vibrant green). Crown (silver/gold). Root (green).
Throat Center	
Healthy Color	Blue
Physical Disorders	Bronchitis, asthma, throat infections. Metabolic disorders.
Mental Disorders	Withdrawal, poor self image.
Colors related to Disorders	Dull blue (mental and metabolic disorders). Dirty blue (infections), reds (bronchitis/asthma).
Chakra Used by Healer	Use Heart (green/blues), Throat (soft blues), and Crown (gold/silver).
Brow Center	
Healthy Color	Indigo
Physical Disorders	Migraines/headache, sinusitis. 'flu, upper respiratory and ear infections.
Mental Disorders	Irritability, egotism, conceited and intolerant behavior.
Colors related to Disorders	Gray/brown and black (headaches/migraines), red (mental disorders).
Chakra Used by Healer	Use Crown (gold/silver), Brow (indigo) and Throat (soft blues).

Figure 20: Chakric Color Chart

163

Crown Center	
Healthy Color	Silver/gold/white
Physical Disorders	Poor resistance to illness, insomnia, migraines.
Mental Disorders	Depression, hyperactivity, and creative exhaustion.
Colors related to Disorders	Gray/brown (depression), with black (migraines). Dull colors (insomnia and low resistance to disease).
Chakra Used by Healer	Use Heart (green/blue), Crown (gold/silver), and Brow (indigo).

Figure 20: Chakric Color Chart

tional body, and by the root center in the case of physical maladies.

Damage to the chakric centers normally occurs after, and during, periods of chronic conditions, which result in the blockage of energy between the centers and subsequent damage and disfigurement. A good example of such an illness where this happens is cancer. Detecting such damage is an advanced skill, but like damage to the aura, if someone has a chronic illness, the healer can deduce that the appropriate chakra is also damaged and requires prolonged exposure to healing energy. For example, a chronic disorder of the upper digestive tract would indicate the need to repair damage to the solar plexus center by using the healer's own root center initially to repair, and solar plexus center to recharge.

Healing Techniques

Forms of healing using color visualization on the chakric centers and aura are generally referred to as "the laying on of hands." Here we give directions for two techniques: chakric balancing and auric cleansing. These are the commonest forms in use by pagans and spiritual healers. For both techniques, it is important to enter the patient's aura slowly for your own protection. If you enter it too fast you will not give your own aura time to prevent discharge of energy from your open chakric centers.

The first stage in any form of healing is assessment (see page 169). People seeking healing may be well aware of their infirmity, but many individuals come forward because they feel run down or low. Before starting the healing process it is important to prepare properly. The first requirement is a warm, quiet room where neither you nor the patient will be disturbed. Many healers like to play appropriate music, which helps to relax both of the participants and to block out the noise of everyday life. The patient can either sit in a comfortable chair, or lie down. Many pagans like to perform healing in Circle, perhaps with incense; this is not essential, but does give a feeling of security to aid the healer in his work. Invoking the elements at the four quarters can also help to boost the energy produced by the healer.

Auric Cleansing

Dirty energy which collects in the aura needs to be removed (see Fig. 21). Normally the dirty energy is manifested as black, browns or grays. Auric cleansing, which can be combined with chakric balancing, is particularly suitable for healing individuals under mental or emotional stress.

The best chakra to use is the heart center, visualizing green/blue light coming from it and down your primary healing hand. If you detect specific damage to an organ or chakra, you may of course wish to switch to using another chakra and color.

Very slowly, move your hands into the patient's aura around the head, keeping your hands within the field of the mental/emotional body (normally at rest it projects about 8 to 12 inches from the body), and slowly move to the edge of the etheric body (approximately 3 inches from the body), but do not touch the patient. Start the flow of visualized light from your heart center into your primary healing hand, while at the same time remove any negative energy you feel with your other hand. Use the technique that you developed for yourself during the practical exercise (see above).

Negative energy should be collected within your right (taking) hand, and should be shaken of at regular intervals. With practice this energy can also be grounded through your root center, but you must ensure that it is removed completely from your energy system after healing. It is not unusual during healing to develop some of the patient's symptoms yourself; this indicates that you are not grounding the energy correctly. Some healers also ground the energy by holding their hands under flowing water, or shaking the energy off during the healing process.

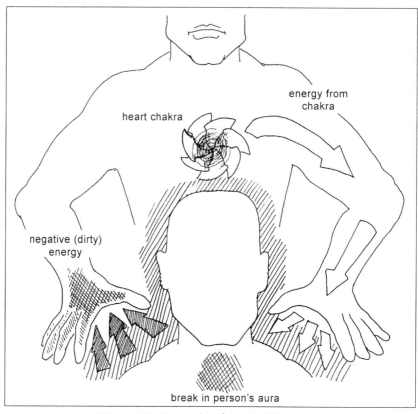

Figure 21: Example of Auric Cleansing

After some time you may actually wish to touch the patient, particularly if you can sense deep-rooted negative energy and damage around the areas of specific organs or chakric centers; this is specially beneficial around an individual's forehead when helping to remove stress. Continue this, moving slowly down and using the same technique as for the head, until you reach the patient's feet. Covering the whole area of the body, feel for breaks in the aura and heal them with the green/blue light that you were visualizing.

Chakric Balancing

Chakric balancing consists of visualizing the appropriate colored energy and transferring it to the appropriate chakra (see Fig. 22). You start by deciding which center needs to be worked on, and which color you need to use. For example, if an individual comes to you complaining of problems with indigestion, the appropriate

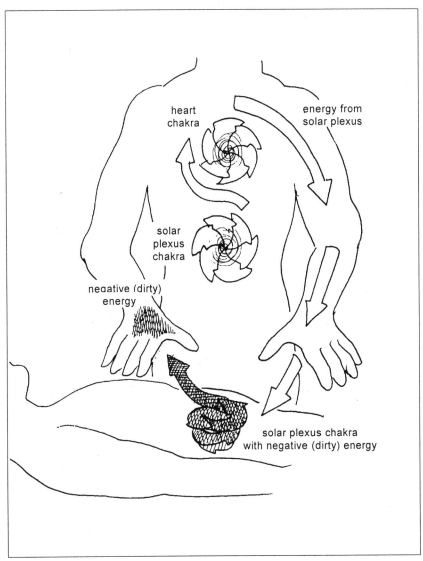

Figure 22: Example of Chakra Balancing

chakra to work on will be the sacral center. The normal color of this chakra is orange, but with digestive problems it will have faded or become dirty in appearance.

The first objective, in this case, will be to clear the center of its dirty appearance by placing both hands over the chakra and then visualizing clear light coming from the crown center, down through your heart center, along your arm to your primary healing hand, and into the patient's sacral center. At the same time you should visualize that you are removing the dirty energy and repairing the damage that is there. Remember to shake the negative energy off your hand or send it down your body to be grounded in your own root chakra. Continue this until you can visualize the center being a clear color, and repaired of any damage.

The second stage is to restore the chakra to its normal healthy color. Visualize vibrant orange coming up from your own sacral center, and as before, bring it down your primary healing hand into the patient's sacral center. Continue this until you can visualize it as a healthy orange.

It is advisable after any chakric balancing to check and balance the patient's other centers.

Suggested Healing Routine

There are several possible routines using the techniques that we have suggested. Normally, based on experience, a healer develops several healing routines to suit particular situations. These may be unique to that healer's form of practice; healing is an art as well as a science. Below we have given a simple but effective routine for use by the student healer:

1. **Assessment** (see page 35, chapter 2): Assessment is the first stage of all forms of healing, spiritual or otherwise. If you are lucky enough to have clairvoyant ability, use this as an opportunity to scan your client's chakras and aura for apparent damage, or colors indicating damage or dysfunction. If you do not have this ability, make a note of recent illnesses or emotional problems, and apply this information (see Damage to the Aura and Chakras earlier in this chapter).

2. **Auric cleansing**: Use your heart center (green/blue light) to relax your patient, starting at the head and working down. Feel for any damage or dysfunction within each chakra center, as well as the mental/emotional and etheric bodies, while applying this energy. Work your way down your client's whole body until you reach the feet.

3. **Heal damaged chakras**: Return to the chakras where there was specific damage, and use your appropriate chakric center and color to heal it.

4. **Balance the chakras**: Transfuse energy from each of your own centers to ensure that each of your client's centers is spinning brightly, with vibrant energy. If they are too bright, ground off some of this energy through your hands.

5. **Energize the chakras**: Starting with your client's root center, move up the body to each of the centers in turn and apply energy from your crown center.

6. **Heal and seal the aura**: Go back to the areas of your client's aura which are damaged, and apply healing energy of the appropriate color to that aura, and to the organ covered by the damaged area in the case of the etheric body. Seal the aura with energy from your crown center, in the same way that you cleansed the aura with your heart center. Ensure that you cover all areas of the body with the sweeping movements of your hands.

7. **Grounding**: Check that you have grounded all negative energies that you may have picked up. During the early stages of learning to heal, it is best to get another healer to check your aura for you, until you have enough experience to recognize the presence of negative energy.

8. **Evaluation** (see page 36, chapter 2): Discuss with your client how he or she felt about the success of the healing session and whether a further session is necessary. Evaluate your own performance and apply any changes that are required to your healing techniques.

11

Holistic Massage

Massage developed from the basic instinct to rub an area when it hurt, or to provide consolation and support to people by touching them during periods of stress (the word "massage" comes from the Greek word meaning "to knead"). This final action has, in recent years, become more important as society depersonalizes the individual. We all develop our own body space, an area around the body which is a no-go area for strangers and people we feel ill at ease with.

This can be seen in body language when individuals cross their arms in a form of protection when they feel they are standing too close to someone. In towns and cities where everybody has more anonymity, this is more pronounced, developing a social trend to avoid touch instinctively. Not surprisingly, encounter and support groups now incorporate touch exercises as an important part of their process of getting to know each other. It is unfortunate that the act of touching is becoming a taboo, as our forefathers knew that it was an important part of healing, not only individually but also socially. This realization is one of the fundamental principles of holistic massage.

The use of massage can be traced back to the ancient Greeks; in fact it was a prerequisite before entering the Temple of Aesculapius at Pergamus. Massage was probably introduced to the Greeks by the Egyptians. By the time Rome conquered Greece, massage had developed into a skilled art form far surpassing what had been learned from the Egyptians. This was mostly due to the introduction of many more strokes.

The Romans adopted massage from the Greeks, as they did with many aspects of their culture. Whereas massage was essentially a healing practice among the Greeks, to the Romans it developed into a social practice; having a massage became a daily custom of the upper classes when they visited the baths. Schools of massage existed within Rome where slaves were sent for training and then for service within the households of the wealthy. Also, like the Greeks, massage was used to tone the bodies of athletes, and every gladiator school had its trained masseurs. As Roman culture spread throughout Europe so did the practice of massage, and most of the massage techniques which exist today have changed very little since then.

During the 1960s there was a revival of interest in massage, particularly of the form known as Swedish massage. From this form, which consisted of light, invigorating strokes used to stimulate the body, developed deep tissue massage, which as its name suggests uses penetrating strokes designed to release tension from the muscles. This form releases tension and is more relaxing.

All forms of massage stimulate both blood and lymph flow through the muscles and the body as a whole. This increases the oxygen reaching the body's organs helping them to function better. Also, the increased flow of lymph helps eliminate waste products from the body. Combined with the effect it has on reducing stress and relieving anxiety, massage also helps boost the body's immune system preventing infections from taking hold.

Masseurs soon noticed that both forms of massage not only had physical effects on their clients, but also had a beneficial effect on their mental, emotional and spiritual well-being—something, no doubt, that the pagan ancient Egyptians, Greeks and Romans had always been well aware of. Modern practitioners began to realize that the real benefit of massage came in a truly holistic sense. It was from this realization that holistic massage developed within the hippie counterculture of the late 1960s and early 1970s; it became commonplace to see holistic massage being performed at open-air festivals.

The use of holistic massage has gained in popularity since this period, both within the pagan and New Age communities. In some American pagan groups, it has become commonplace for holistic massage to be used on new members immediately before their initiation. This is because of its ability to encourage trust and comradeship, while relaxing the receiver. This is a development that we feel should be encouraged as most new members are nervous, resulting in doubts about whether they should be initiated. A massage helps to clear the mind and relax the individuals, allowing them to think more clearly about the step they are taking and giving them the opportunity to make a clearer decision.

Like all holistic therapies, massage is about helping the body heal itself, but unlike other therapies it has one other benefit: because of the intimacy of touch involved, it helps to break down the barriers between masseur and client, or as most holistic masseurs like to say, between the giver and the receiver. This makes it useful in building trust, particularly before counseling, or any other form of therapy where a personal relationship is required. It is a two-way process, involving active participation of both individuals concerned, and ultimately benefits both the giver and the receiver. The receiver gets attention, care and healing from the giver; and in return, the giver feels a personal, fulfilling closeness to the receiver.

Within holistic massage it is the closeness and intimacy----the merging of spiritual, and mental/emotional auras----which triggers the healing process in both individuals. (An understanding of the body's energy systems is very useful within holistic massage----see page 88, chapter 6). Because of this two-way flow of energy, many who use holistic massage choose to refer to it as helping rather than healing----it reduces the division between healer and client. The giver may, though, decide to define his or her role as healer by using the knowledge of spiritual healing techniques during the massage.

Holistic massage is based on the use of intuition on the part of the giver who may decide to spend more time using a particular stroke over a particular area, just because it feels right. Nine times out of ten, the giver finds out later that this is an area of particular tension in the receiver. The giver may decide on no particular time limit to the massage (the average massage lasts twenty minutes) or may decide to pause the massage because the receiver is releasing deep emotional trauma and it is an appropriate moment to counsel on what he or she is feeling.

Even though holistic massage is intuition based, techniques should not be used which endanger the receiver just because they feel appropriate at the time. There are several safety rules that need to be followed by all who perform any type of massage, or use essential oils for massage:

1. Always wash your hands before and after a massage session.

2. If you are massaging individuals of the opposite sex with whom

you are unfamiliar, have a chaperon present with whom they are comfortable; this is for your own protection as well as theirs.

3. Do not massage somebody who has a viral infection, such as a cold, or if you have a contagious infection yourself.

4. Do not massage somebody with an infectious skin condition; you may spread the infection not only to yourself, but also to other parts of his or her body.

5. Avoid massaging over scar tissue, recently healed wounds, open wounds, unknitted bone fracture sites, and burns.

6. Do not massage somebody with circulatory problems, such as high or low blood pressure, angina or other heart problems. Avoid varicose veins when massaging.

7. Do not massage somebody with visible malignant growths such as melanoma (skin cancer).

8. Only massage lightly around the abdomen during pregnancy.

9. Do not massage over the vertebrae; use light strokes around them instead.

10. Always massage the abdomen in a clockwise direction, following the flow of the intestines; avoid massaging a person who has just eaten.

11. Always use firm strokes upwards toward the heart, and light pressure when moving away from the heart; this assists the venous return to the heart.

12. If using base oils and essential oils, check that the receiver is not allergic to them, or that there are no contraindications to them being used. It is always good practice to place a small amount of oil on the inside of the receiver's elbow to test for allergic reaction.

13. Avoid using essential oils around the eyes.

Basic Massage Strokes

Every massage should begin with effleurage----superficial stroking along the length of the body (see Fig. 23). This normally begins at the buttocks and proceeds up to the neck, then to the arms and legs. It is normally followed by the strokes known as petrissage----kneading and friction. These strokes are repeated in a similar fashion to effleurage; starting at the buttocks and moving slowly up the back to the neck.

The pressure should initially be very light, and should slowly increase with each upward stroke of the hands. It is important that the pressure is increased only on the upward strokes, with the return strokes being as light as possible. This buildup of pressure should be done so slowly and so lightly that it is not obvious to the person receiving the massage. If the masseur progresses too fast, the massage will become uncomfortable; the receiver will tense up with each stroke rather than be taken into a deeper state of relaxation. The masseur must therefore watch the receiver for any such reactions and change the pressure and speed of strokes accordingly.

A slow, relaxed pace during massage helps to build up a rapport between the receiver and the masseur. It is important therefore that the speed of the massage is consistent throughout; this gives the effect of a flowing, holistic experience, with the change in strokes being undetectable to the receiver. The building up of pressure on each stroke should last for the first two-thirds (10 to 15 minutes) of the massage. After this the pressure should gradually be decreased, until the final light strokes of effleurage are hardly discernible to the receiver.

The use of breathing is also an important part of the holistic massage experience; it helps to build up rhythm and the flow of natural healing energy. The receiver should be encouraged to regulate his or her breathing, inhaling and expiring rhythmically. Breathing from the bottom of the lungs----diaphragmatic breathing as opposed to chest breathing----helps to relax rather than stimulate the receiver, thus enhancing the massage.

As we have said, holistic massage is a two-way process, so the giver should also regulate his or her breathing pattern in the same way, and should also try to shadow the receiver's breathing pattern, breathing in time with the receiver whenever possible. This has several beneficial affects: it allows the giver to link emotionally and spiritually with the receiver, to flow with the massage, enabling him or her to get into a rhythm with the massage strokes being used, and to block out the everyday world and stresses and focus completely on the receiver while bringing the intuitive processes to the forefront.

The use of the body is another important factor in defining holistic massage, as compared with other forms. The whole body is used during the massage itself, rather than just using the arms and hands as in conventional massage. The giver's body moves with the strokes being used; this can be perceived as a rhythmic rocking motion of the torso. It encourages the flow of energy, and also prevents the giver from tiring quickly from over use of the hand and arm muscles. The receiver benefits from this motion by receiving a more rhythmic and relaxed massage.

The positions of the giver and the receiver are therefore also important. The giver must be comfortable so as to focus completely on the receiver. For this reason, most holistic masseurs prefer to place their clients on a mattress on the floor, ensuring that they are comfortable in this position. This enables the giver to kneel alongside, and to move with the massage strokes in comfort without tiring easily.

There are many different types of massage stokes, but it is only necessary to learn four basic strokes to have a satisfactory effect. They are as follows:

1. **Effleurage** (Fig. 23): As the first stroke that needs to be mastered, effleurage is the basis for what is often referred to as Swedish massage. It is a light stroking of moderate pressure, normally performed along the full length of the trunk of the body, legs and arms, using the whole surface of the hand. It helps to increase blood flow around the tissues, and has a calming effect on the person being massaged. For these two reasons it is always performed at the beginning and end of all massage sessions. One other beneficial effect is that it allows the masseur to get in touch with the body of the person he or she is massaging, allowing the massage to develop rhythm and flow.

2. **Petrissage** (Fig. 24): Unlike effleurage, which has a longitudinal motion, petrissage normally has a circular or transverse motion. This is a moderate-to-deep stroke to the muscles and tissues using the whole of the hands, allowing the masseur to find areas knotted from tension and stress. It can be performed with both hands making circular motions at the same time; or if there are particular knotted areas, by reinforcing the circular action of one hand by placing the other on top of it.

3. **Kneading** (Fig. 25): This deep manipulation is often incorporated into petrissage movements. The motion is similar to that used in kneading bread, using the thumb and fingers of your

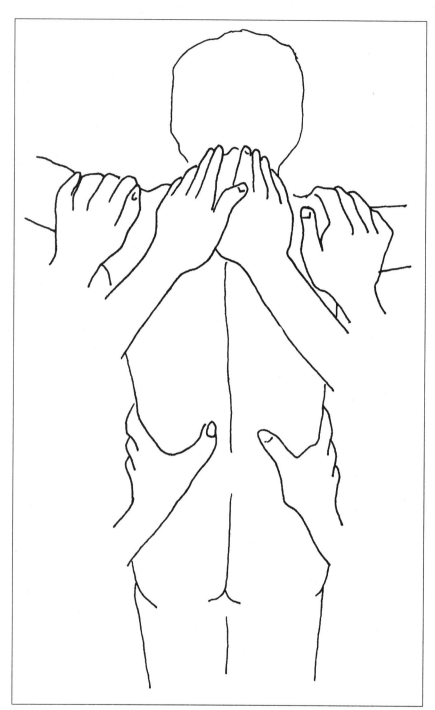

Figure 23: Effleurage

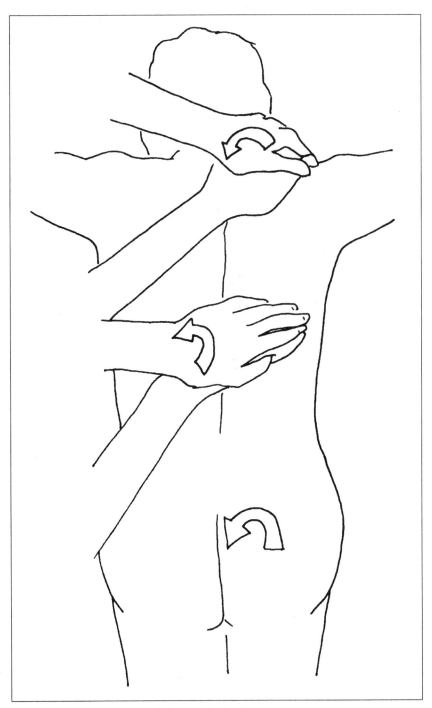

Figure 24: Petrissage

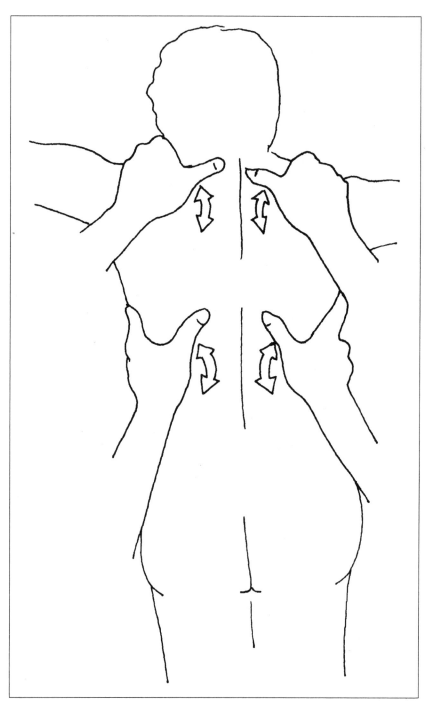

Figure 25: Kneading

178

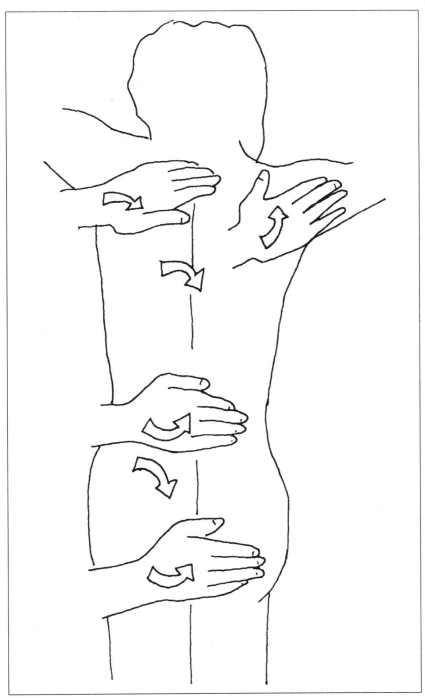

Figure 26: Friction

hands. This stroke is normally used to break down knotted areas after they have been found spontaneously during the massage (but never during effleurage).

4. **Friction** (Fig. 26): Pressure is concentrated on an area of the tissue by using circular motions of the thumbs, knuckles or the ends of fingers. Normally friction is applied up the spine, using both hands and incorporating deep circular motions of the thumbs about one and a half inches across. It is also used in other areas of the body, similar to petrissage.

Using Oils

Base oils are commonly used in massage to prevent friction, and therefore help the natural flow of the massage as it progresses. Commonly used base oils include wheat germ, mineral, and coconut oil, but plain baby oil will suffice for a basic massage. However, when using essential oils it is necessary to have the correct base oil, otherwise the oils will not mix evenly and will not penetrate the skin. Base oils suitable for mixing with essential oils include wheat germ, avocado, sweet almond, apricot and grape seed. Most light vegetable oils are suitable if they are as close as possible to 100 percent pure.

Aromatherapy----the use of aromatic essential oils during massage----can be traced back to ancient Egypt. It would have been inseparable from the art of massage; in fact, it is highly unlikely that they would have differentiated between the two, as we do today. The extensive Greek knowledge of herbalism would have no doubt been applied to the use of oils during massage.

The interest in aromatherapy has increased in recent years to the point where most doctors accept that the use of essential oils does have a beneficial physical effect on the body. It is becoming commonplace to find aromatherapy in use in hospitals and other medical establishments. Gavin used both lavender oil and tea tree oil regularly when he worked as a staff nurse. Essential oils work by penetrating the skin, thereby being absorbed into the lymph system (see page 63, chapter 4); hence, massage using essential oils should put emphasis on using light effleurage strokes around the area of the thighs, groin, arms and armpits, where the lymph system is closest to the surface.

Essential oils are generally mixed in quantities of 15 to 30 drops to a 50 milliliter (2 ounce) bottle of base oil, depending on what strength and effect is required. For example, 30 drops of ylang-ylang in a 50 milliliter bottle may be suitable for depression, but used on someone who is just run down will induce drowsiness. (Only 2 to 3 drops of the essential oil will actually enter the body during the massage.) Premixed base and essential oils are available from most stores specializing in holistic health, and we recommend these for the casual user.

Towels are essential whenever massage is performed. They are not only used to wipe off excess oil, but also to cover receivers during the massage to prevent them from getting cold.

Here is a selection of oils commonly used in aromatherapy. We feel that these are essentials in any healer's cabinet:

Camomile, German and **Roman**: Both share most of the same qualities, although German camomile is more effective in dealing with inflammatory and immune problems. They both have antibacterial, antidepressant, antiseptic and antispasmodic properties. Because of these properties, camomile is used in aromatherapy for gastrointestinal complaints, for promoting menstruation (it should therefore be avoided in early pregnancy), and for reducing fever. It is also a diuretic (increasing urination), and, an added bonus, it has a sedative effect. Camomile blends well with geranium, patchouli, lavender and rose.

Camphor: Effective in treating many disorders of the gastrointestinal system, camphor oil helps relieve constipation and flatulence. Like camomile, it also has a diuretic effect and is effective as a sedative, particularly in cases of insomnia and depression. Its commonest use, though, is for treating respiratory problems, particularly those resulting in shortness of breath. Other uses include the treatment of mild burns, bruises, ulcers and other skin conditions. It blends well with frankincense.

Eucalyptus: Most commonly used in breathing disorders, eucalyptus helps clear the bronchioles, sinuses and nasal passages. It has antibacterial, antiviral and antiseptic properties; it also acts as an expectorant, and it reduces fever, making it particularly useful in respiratory tract infections such as influenza. Other beneficial qualities include its ability to heal wounds, boost the immune system, and act as a diuretic. It mixes well with lavender, sandalwood and tea tree.

Frankincense: Frankincense is the primary oil for use in all problems related to mental stress. It helps to calm the whole nervous system by reducing nervous tension, calming breathing and generally uplifting the spirit. It is favored as an incense for meditation purposes for this reason. It is also excellent for treating weathered and damaged skin, as well as sores and wounds. Other benefits include its astringent qualities, which help with heavy menstrual flow and related hormonal problems, such as premenstrual symptoms. It blends well with camphor, geranium, lavender and rose.

Geranium: In the past this plant was highly treasured for its abilities to heal fractures, internal bleeding and even cancer. It helps to stimulate new cell growth and stop bleeding, the main reasons for its reputation. As an oil, it is prized for its antidepressant, anti-inflammatory, antiseptic and astringent qualities. It is most commonly used to treat circulatory, skin and gastrointestinal problems. It blends well with most essential oils which, with its good all-round healing properties, makes it one of the aromatherapist's most prized oils.

Jasmine: Apart from being a good base oil for massage (it mixes well with most commonly used oils), jasmine has very beneficial effects on the emotions and the mental state. This makes it particularly useful in the treatment of depression, anxiety, and all stress-related illnesses. It also benefits the gastrointestinal system, being an antiseptic, antispasmodic and anti-inflammatory; as well, it is a traditional cure for impotence. It should not be used on children or babies. Care should be taken in its use during pregnancy; it should only be used after the first 20 weeks. Some people also find that they develop an allergic reaction to it, so test the oil first.

Lavender: Although it is one of the most commonly used oils due to its all-round healing abilities, lavender is most commonly known as a sedative. It has antibacterial, antiviral, antiseptic, antifungal and anti-inflammatory properties, and to list its use in specific disorders would take a whole page. Quite simply, in case of doubt, use lavender! It mixes well with most oils, and its use should only be avoided in pregnancy if there is a history or a serious risk of miscarriage.

Rose: Two types of rose oil are commonly in use: damask rose and cabbage rose. Damask rose is widely considered to be the more superior in therapeutic use. Although regarded as one of the mildest oils to use, it has several very powerful healing qualities, particularly its ability to detoxify the body, while reducing blood pressure and the effects of stress. This makes it an excellent oil to use in cases of depression or mental overload. It is also valued for its anti-inflammatory qualities, which, combined with its other abilities, makes it useful in the treatment of heavy menstruation (menhorragia), headaches due to nervous tension, and other uterine and premenstrual problems. Because of its ability to promote menstruation, rose oil should be avoided in the early stages of pregnancy (up to 20 weeks). It blends well with most oils, but is particularly beneficial when mixed with jasmine.

Sandalwood: The best sandalwood oil comes from the Mysore in India; avoid if possible Australian sandalwood. Sandalwood is very therapeutic in the treatment of upper respiratory tract problems such as coughs and colds, due to its astringent, anti-inflammatory, antibacterial and antiseptic qualities. It is also an antispasmodic, which makes it useful in first aid treatment for asthma and bronchitis. It is also considered to be a sedative and a diuretic. It blends well with most oils.

Tea Tree: Tea tree oil is an excellent antibiotic, antifungal and antiviral agent. It is therefore the most popular oil for use on infection, and it also helps to reduce fever. During the autumn and winter months, regular use helps to boost the individual's immune system, therefore preventing the usual seasonal colds and flu. Like lavender, it is another essential for the aromatherapist's collection. Its antifungal qualities make it a favored oil in the treatment of athlete's foot and *Candida albicans*. In some sensitive individuals tea tree oil can cause irritation; test the oil on a small area of the person's skin before using.

Ylang-ylang: The primary use of ylang-ylang oil is in the treatment of depression due to its emotionally uplifting effect and its sedative properties; it also helps lower blood pressure. These properties also make it useful in premenstrual situations, as well as in general nervous tension, anger, and anxiety. It also has a beneficial effect on sexual dysfunction such as frigidity and impotence; it is one of the few true aphrodisiacs. It mixes well with most oils.

Suggested Plan for your Holistic Massage

1. **Preparation**: You may wish to use suitable soothing music, incense and candlelight to make your working space more relaxing. Ensure you have towels and appropriate oils, and that you are not going to be disturbed. Sit with your receiver and discuss his or her particular problems; apply the safety rules mentioned in this chapter, and the methods of practice mentioned on page 44 of chapter 3.

2. **Focusing**: Get the receiver of the massage comfortable. You should also relax, taking deep breaths while encouraging the receiver to do likewise. Concentrate on what you wish to achieve by doing this massage while clearing your mind of everyday thoughts. You may wish to do this for several minutes before starting the massage.

3. **Start the massage** (effleurage): Apply the appropriate base oil and/or essential oil mix to your hands; rub them lightly, ensuring that the oils are evenly distributed across your hands and that your hands are warm. Start the effleurage strokes using superficial pressure and then slowly increase.

4. **Use deeper strokes** (petrissage): After several minutes of using effleurage and feeling the rhythm build up, change your stroke to a circular and deeper transverse movement. Use alternate circles on both sides of the torso, arms and legs, and then use hand on hand on each side.

5. **Use your intuition** (kneading and friction): Start to go with the flow of the massage; let the massage take on a life of its own, let your hands go to where it feels right. Use kneading and friction strokes when and where you feel it is appropriate. Take as much time as feels right.

6. **Finish the massage** (effleurage): Slowly decrease your strokes, making them smoother each time until the massage finishes naturally and rhythmically of its own accord.

7. **Grounding**: Ground yourself (see page 169, chapter 10). Allow the receiver to take the time to get up of his or her own accord. Take time to talk about the experience.

12

Counseling: Divination and Past-life Regression

Counseling as a form of therapy has only really developed in the past fifty years. Up until then counseling fell under the domain of the organized religions; in fact, it has always been a role which has fallen upon the priesthoods of all religions. Not surprisingly, the decline in popularity, and some say the control, of the Christian religion has left a void in society which needed to be filled. Thus counseling has developed as an organized therapeutic practice. It has become an essential skill for any high priest or priestess who is running a coven----not only for counseling members of the general public using divination and regression techniques, but also members of his or her own group.

Before the introduction of Christianity into Europe, counseling was as a matter of course the role of the Druid, the Godi (Norse priest) or the Egyptian, Greek and Roman priesthoods. Even with the suppression of pagan religion, the village witch continued the practice of being the friendly ear for her neighbors as the village wisewoman. She had one advantage over the Christian priesthood; she was able, using divination, to show the possible trends that might appear in the future.

This pagan tradition of fortune telling (an unfortunate term which misleads the public about the true nature of divination) using tarot cards, runes, astrology and other similar oracles was impossible for the Church to stamp out completely; many of the royal households of Europe throughout the Middle Ages continued to employ a royal astrologer, and the pagan tradition of using tarot cards for divination and counseling has continued unbroken since that time.

The Art of Counseling

We feel it is important to point out that the training of a counselor, like that of a nurse or doctor, takes many years of hard work and dedication. All we intend to do in this chapter is give some indication of the counseling skills required by anyone who uses divination and past-life regression for therapeutic purposes, which of course is the only good reason for their use in the first place. It is not our intention to create instant counselors. We have used the term "counselor" below to define a role, rather than in a professional sense.

Who needs counseling?

Counseling is not just for the mentally imbalanced or the abused. Everybody at some point in life reaches an impasse where the way out of a situation is difficult to see. Sometimes one may just lack the courage to make that all-important decision, but on other occasions there may be no apparent solution to the problem. All of us hold items deep within our own subconscious. Situations from the past which we have repressed, and which prevent us from making the decisions that will give us a healthy, creative life. If unchecked, such repressed feelings can have an adverse effect on us, not only mentally but also physically and spiritually.

Esoterically speaking, such an impasse, and the ability to pass through it, is a form of initiation----the start of a change which will profoundly affect the individual spiritually. To pass through life's initiations sometimes requires help. No man is an island, entire of itself----and we all need each other's help. This is well expressed by the Nordic rune *Mannaz*, which translates into English as "man," and stands for cooperation. It symbolizes the act of counseling, the help which all of us need at some point in our lives.

First of all it is important to define how counseling differs from giving advice. Counseling is not telling somebody what to do; it is not taking charge and dealing with the problem for them; it is not telling the person you are counseling what their personal problems are; and it is not telling somebody to "sort yourself out!"

Counseling is about helping individuals explore problems so

that they can decide what to do about them while maintaining control of their own lives. The task of the counselor, in whatever form the counseling takes (tarot reading for example), is to give the client the opportunity to explore, discover and clarify ways of living more resourcefully and toward greater well-being. This is normally achieved by the counselor making the client aware of possible constructive alternatives. During this process, the individual doing the counseling helps the client to redirect suffering into one of these constructive channels. Hence, by its very nature, counseling takes a holistic approach (see page 29, chapter 2).

There are many different styles and approaches to counseling, but generally those who define counseling using the above criteria are using the client centered approach, even though they may not be aware of it (in fact all who have a spiritual and holistic base use this approach). This is sometimes referred to as "Rogerian" after Carl Rogers who was the first to define it as such. He believed that:

> The human being is basically a trustworthy organism capable of self-understanding... of making constructive choices and of acting on these choices.

It is the client who interprets and explains his or her attitude and behavior, helped by the counselor, who should be neither judgmental nor critical while clarifying the issues. The direction of the session, be it tarot reading, regression or whatever, should be in the hands of the person doing it. It is important that when counseling takes place that it remains directed by the client.

There are four principles to counseling which involve the freedom of individuals, individuality, the ability to integrate socially, and the spiritual tensions which exist within an individual:

First Principle: Freedom

It is the function of the counselor to lead the client to an acceptance of responsibility for the conduct and outcome of his or her life. It is important that the counselor is able to show how deep the client's ability to make decisions lies and how tensions from past experiences and within the personal unconscious must be dealt with, particularly those aspects that have been repressed within the shadow (see page 82, chapter 5).

These repressed traumas, emotions and aspects restrict the client's freedom by preventing the free flow of creative thought, thus restricting him or her to the choices that the shadow dictates through the ego. Recognition of these aspects will aid clients in using their own freedom by releasing their creativity and allowing them to make constructive decisions for themselves.

Second Principle: Individuality

It is the function of the counselor to help the client both to find his or her own true self and to have the courage to be this self. It is very important that the counselor is nonjudgmental in his or her approach. There is always the danger that the counselor will try to direct the client; this goes against the very nature of both the first and second principles. The counselor's function is to help people accept themselves as they truly are, not as they think they are.

Finding oneself----recognizing one's own individuality and uniqueness within the cosmos----is by its very nature a spiritual quest. One finds oneself by linking the conscious self with the elements of the unconscious self. This is a solitary process, all of us being on our own unique and individual paths. But what happens if we come to a junction, or wander off our path and get lost in the woods? This is when we need help to return to the path, and find which direction we are heading in. This is the role of both the priest or priestess and the counselor----to help clients return to their own individual paths and find their own true selves.

Third Principle: Social Integration

The counselor functions to help the client toward a positive acceptance of social responsibility, to give courage which will release the client from the compulsion of feeling inferior, and to help the client direct his or her own striving toward socially constructive ends. We live in a society where everybody is dependent on everybody else, where there is an ever-present danger of our own unique individuality being lost.

This tension between individuality and social integration is one of the chief causes of anxiety within modern society, and results in feelings of inferiority within individuals because they feel the constant need to gain a position of superiority within society to maintain their uniqueness. This social striving can result in antisocial behavior (a good example is the gangster phenomenon of the 1920s), but if utilized correctly it can be a source of personal power for the good of all society. According to the psychologist Alfred Adler, the two highest virtues are social interest and cooperation. He believed that these two qualities mark healthy individuals who happily accept social responsibility.

Fourth Principle: Spiritual Tension

It is the role of the counselor, while helping the client to free himself or herself from morbid guilt feelings, also to help the client accept courageously and affirm the spiritual tensions inherent in all of us. The counselor aims to transform destructive conflicts into constructive ones. Feelings of guilt can never be wiped away entirely, nor would it be desirable to do so; sometimes they are the reverse side of our own sense of spirit----they make us who we are.

What is important is that the counselor is able to help the client remove the morbid nature of his or her guilt (the Christian Church has not only ignored, but actually encouraged, this morbid aspect of guilt) and accept that it is part of his or her nature. If harnessed constructively, feelings of guilt can be used to cause positive personal and social change, and this is what the counselor should be trying to achieve with the client's own feelings of guilt. A healthy individual sees spirituality as inherently creative and this is essential if a healthy personality is to be maintained.

Developing Counseling Skills

Counseling is the domain of the crone and the sage, the archetypes of wisdom brought about by the fusion of experience and intellect. Obviously, anyone in a role involving the use of counseling techniques needs to have well developed skills. One or two of these skills may be inherent within the personality of the counselor, but even if they are not, it is possible to develop them with practice.

Good communication skills and understanding the theories behind them are essential (we have covered these on page 33, chapter 2), but many other skills are also needed. These skills are also useful when applying the other healing methods mentioned in this book, so even if the reader does not intend to practice the healing techniques in this chapter, we recommend these skills be developed as a matter of course.

Self-awareness

The first process that counselor trainees go through is a regular period of counseling themselves to develop their own self-awareness. It is not possible to develop the other skills of genuiness, unconditional positive regard, and empathy without it.

The constant element within all counseling is the person performing it. Clients will change, all bringing with them their own unique personalities, problems and solutions; no single counseling session is ever the same. So it makes sense to concentrate on the only constant factor----the personality of the counselor. Self-awareness allows us to be aware of our own strengths and weaknesses, which allows us to tell how well we are able to assist someone, and if we need to redirect our client to someone who can help if we can't (this is an ethical necessity for a healer----see page 44, chapter 3).

Self-awareness encourages maturity and enables us to be at ease with ourselves. Only when we have this can we be at ease with our clients during the counseling process. If we do not have this, we will be unsure of our abilities and competence as a counselor and unable to use the skills we have learned. Anyone who wants to use counseling skills must therefore be committed to his or her own holistic growth----physical, mental, social and spiritual. Not surprisingly, this growth is encouraged within the esoteric paths which exist within paganism (such as Wicca) and is encouraged within paganism as a whole.

Genuiness

The development of genuiness within counselors is very much linked to their own self-development. Only when they have self-knowledge----when they can understand their own emotions and are aware of their own reactions to situations----will they be able to concentrate on the feelings of others.

Genuineness comes from the ability to drop the concerns of our ego, to be able to drop any artificial image we project for defensive purposes, and to be who we really are, not who we think we should be. This allows us to admit our mistakes, to have the courage of imperfection: the ability to accept failure, not only to ourselves but also to our clients when appropriate. Within counseling, this allows the counselor to be open and receptive, allowing the client to know that we are what we seem and mean what we say. Genuiness results in the development of trust between counselor and client, which is essential in any therapeutic relationship.

Unconditional Positive Regard

In spiritual healing unconditional positive regard is referred to as "unconditional love" and is an essential requirement in any form of auric or chakric healing (see page 152, chapter 10). It is the ability to respect people for what they are, for their essential humanity, and to understand their worth and value as human beings, without any preconditions. It is therefore necessary to develop the ability to remain unprejudiced by somebody's class, sex, appearance, ethnic background, and most important of all, actions. Objectivity and the ability to be detached are essential, while at the same time showing warmth and concern for the client.

Empathy

Empathy----an essential requirement within spiritual healing----is the ability to place oneself in the position of the client, to try to understand what another person is feeling due to his or her unique situation. It is not feeling sorry for that person (sympathy), nor seeing how we would feel in that situation because as individuals we would undoubtedly feel differently.

It is, in essence, the ability to sense the private world of a person's feelings, and from an esoteric viewpoint is very much a psychic skill. In order to be effective within counseling, empathy must be conveyed to the clients so that they know that the counselor accurately understands them. Of course, this also requires effective communications skills, both verbally and with body language (see page 33, chapter 2). Imagination and creativity on the part of the counselor are essential for the process of empathy; they also allow the counselor to offer clients new perspectives on their situations, and on the alternative actions open to them.

Other Skills

We have covered the main skills required by practicing counselors but there are several other characteristics that good counselors have. Patience is essential, as the pace of any form of counseling must always remain in the hands of the client. If the counselor tries to hurry a session, the client may regard it as pressure to behave in a particular fashion, and vital insight may be missed by the counselor. It is therefore important that the client is always aware of the time allotted for any session.

A sense of humor and the ability to use simple language are both important for good communication. The ability to lighten the atmosphere at an appropriate moment can break a deadlock and make the client feel more comfortable. It also helps if counselors are able to laugh at their own mistakes. They should never take themselves too seriously, or use technical psychobabble. Both do very little to encourage a trust relationship between the counselor and the client.

Divination

The use of archetypal symbols (see page 77, chapter 5) to divine future events has always been a traditional counseling tool used by the priesthoods of the premonotheistic religions. The Northern Europeans used runes; the Greeks and the Romans, pyromancy (staring into a naked flame looking for symbols); and the Chinese used the I Ching. During the Middle Ages both the tarot and astrology came into vogue and have remained in favor ever since.

Although using chance may seem to be an unreliable counseling tool, the psychologist Carl Gustav Jung believed differently. He developed the theory of synchronicity as an acausal connecting principle. He is known to have used both astrology and the I Ching (even forewording a book, *I Ching or Book of Changes* by Richard Wilhelm) in diagnosis and treatment of his patients. Jung defines synchronicity as:

> ...the occurrence of a meaningful coincidence in time. It can take three forms.... The coincidence of a certain psychic content with a corresponding objective process which is perceived to take place simultaneously.... The coincidence of a subjective psychic state with a phantasm (dream or vision) which turns out to be a more of less faithful reflection of a "synchronistic," objective event that took place more or less simultaneously, but at a distance.... The same, except that the event perceived takes place in the future and is represented in the present only by a phantasm that corresponds to it.

Divination in all its forms comes under Jung's first category; the objective process being the use of the tool of divination, such as tarot cards, rune stones or yarrow sticks of the I Ching.

It is not possible in a work of this size to go into every form of divination used (we estimate there are several dozen forms currently in use worldwide), so we have decide to highlight one traditional form: the tarot. It is not possible to go into any great depth on the subject; it takes an entire volume to cover it, and that would not be exhaustive. We have chosen the tarot to show how counseling skills can be applied to all forms of divination. Anyone who intends to use them for counseling purposes should study them deeply for a long period before using them.

The Tarot

Tarot cards first appeared within Europe during the latter half of the Middle Ages. Nobody knows where they really came from, but there is a definite Semitic influence (tarot comes from the Hebraic word "tora" meaning "law"). They are the most well-known form of divination, having remained in the public's imagination since their introduction into Europe.

At the end of the nineteenth century there were less than a dozen different packs, the most popular being the Rider-Waite pack and the Swiss (Müller) pack. By the end of the twentieth century we estimate there probably are well over a hundred which range from the serious packs such as Aleister Crowley's *Book Of Thoth* (Thoth deck) to the slightly less than serious Morgan's tarot. Regardless of the change of symbolism within the packs, the meanings tend to be the same, as do the number of cards within each pack and the division between the major and minor arcana (22 and 56 cards respectively).

Why have tarot cards remained so popular? Probably due to their accuracy which in turn has resulted from the strong archetypes used within the images; these archetypes have defied the passage of time, and remain as relevant today as they did in the Middle Ages. This is the secret to their use as a counseling tool. The 22 cards of the major arcana show images which apply to our spiritual growth, images which show internal change, conflict and methods of resolving them. They show the options open to the client which may not be immediately obvious either to the client or the reader as counselor. This is the advantage they have over more conventional counseling methods—but they must be used with care, and the same principles for any other form of counseling should apply where appropriate. In Figure 27 we have listed the 22 cards of the major arcana, their meanings, and how they relate to counseling.

0 Fool	
Divinatory Meaning	New beginnings and opportunities. Energy, optimism and happiness. Unexpected occurrences.
Counseling Meaning	Clients may have unrealistic goals. They should think carefully about any decisions they are planning to make.

1 Magician	
Divinatory Meaning	Will, mastery, creative talents. The ability to perceive and utilize one's own potential.
Counseling Meaning	Clients have the ability to solve any problems they face if they trust their own judgement and have confidence in themselves.

2 High Priestess	
Divinatory Meaning	Unrevealed future; hidden influences at work. Hidden influences from the psyche which affect personal circumstances.
Counseling Meaning	Clients should trust their own intuition—they should learn to listen to the hidden voice within and be guided by it.

3 Empress	
Divinatory Meaning	Fertility, abundance and material wealth. Domestic stability. Creativity, security and growth.
Counseling Meaning	A good foundation is essential for the clients' growth. This lies in their home life, which should be nurtured for this reason.

4 Emperor	
Divinatory Meaning	Leadership, authority, mental activity and willpower. Self control.
Counseling Meaning	Clients can afford to take positive control of their situations; this may be the only way of solving their dilemmas.

5 Pope	
Divinatory Meaning	Good counsel, advice and teaching. A preference for the orthodox; conformity.
Counseling Meaning	Clients should listen carefully to any advice they are given; they should not ignore any unorthodox solutions.

6 Lovers	
Divinatory Meaning	Choice, temptation, attraction. Internal harmony.
Counseling Meaning	There are two options open to the clients; one material, the other spiritual. Choice between the two is inevitable.

Figure 27: The Major Arcana of the Tarot

7 CHARIOT	
Divinatory Meaning	Self control, confidence. Triumph, success due to effort. Self-limitation.
Counseling Meaning	Any process of counseling and decision making the clients are involved in must be given time to succeed. Much effort may be needed by the clients to succeed in their goals

8 STRENGTH	
Divinatory Meaning	Spiritual power overcoming the material. Courage, strength.
Counseling Meaning	Clients should base any decisions on the spiritual rather than the material—this is their greatest strength.

9 HERMIT	
Divinatory Meaning	Silent counsel, prudence, discretion. Counsel sought and taken.
Counseling Meaning	The answer to the clients' problems are within themselves, but they are as yet unaware of it. They may need a period of serious contemplation on the matter at hand.

10 WHEEL OF FORTUNE	
Divinatory Meaning	Success due to unexpected turn of luck. The beginning of a new cycle; karmic change.
Counseling Meaning	The clients can afford to sit back and wait; the situation is ongoing and may change unexpectedly. They should allow the current situation to develop fully before taking hasty action.

11 JUSTICE	
Divinatory Meaning	Legal action, litigation. Contracts and agreements. Justice—balance is required.
Counseling Meaning	The clients need to think carefully about all their intended actions. They should be careful not to make any spur-of-the-moment decisions.

12 HANGED MAN	
Divinatory Meaning	Sacrifice of material to achieve spiritual. A pause in one's life. The ability to adapt to changing circumstances.
Counseling Meaning	The solution to the clients' problems may be that they must adapt to any change, even though this may mean sacrificing an important part of their life.

Figure 27: The Major Arcana of the Tarot

13 DEATH	
Divinatory Meaning	Transformation, change, destruction followed by renewal. Can include new ideas, lifestyle and opportunities.
Counseling Meaning	If the clients have the opportunity for positive change regarding their lifestyle, they should take it.

14 TEMPERANCE	
Divinatory Meaning	Ability to adapt to circumstances. Coordination and cooperation. A well-balanced temperament.
Counseling Meaning	The clients are very capable of solving their own problems when they occur. This is very much due to the nature of their personalities.

15 DEVIL	
Divinatory Meaning	Desire for material or physical things and effort to obtain these things. Wrong use of force.
Counseling Meaning	The clients have neglected their spiritual and emotional needs. They must recognize this if they are to correct the problems in their lives.

16 TOWER	
Divinatory Meaning	Change, conflict and destruction, which alters the existing way of life and brings enlightenment. Selfish ambition fails.
Counseling Meaning	Major changes are unavoidable for the clients; they should not fight against them, however painful.

17 STAR	
Divinatory Meaning	Insight, inspiration and hope. A widening of mental and physical horizons.
Counseling Meaning	The clients need to seek help from many sources. It is through these that they will find their own unique ways of solving their own problems.

18 MOON	
Divinatory Meaning	Psychism, imagination and intuition. Deception and unforeseen perils.
Counseling Meaning	Before making any decisions or taking any action the clients should make sure they are aware of all the factors involved.

Figure 27: The Major Arcana of the Tarot

19 SUN	
Divinatory Meaning	Material happiness. Good health. Pleasure in simple things. Academic or artistic success.
Counseling Meaning	The answers to the clients' problems are rooted in their past. They need to examine their past, particularly their triumphs and successes.
20 JUDGEMENT	
Divinatory Meaning	Awakening, renewal. Pleasure in achievement. Renewed health and vitality.
Counseling Meaning	The clients should be encouraged to make a positive decision now rather than later.
21 WORLD	
Divinatory Meaning	Completion, success and fulfillment. The end of a personal cycle, project or series of events.
Counseling Meaning	The clients should relax; the problem is not as bad as it may seem. They should have faith that the Universe will always unfold as it should.

Figure 27: The Major Arcana of the Tarot

Many people go to tarot readers to find answers to problems within their lives. As a result, responsible tarot readers have had to develop counseling skills; this has led to the popularity of the name "tarot counselor."

Janet can testify to this; the majority of her clients are looking for help, either to make decisions or to find a solution to problems within their lives. Very few come along for a laugh, and most who do tend to leave in a state of shock. One woman that regularly comes to Janet sits for three-quarters of an hour talking solidly, ignoring what Janet sees in the cards. She then walks away telling everyone what a good tarot reader Janet is! She comes just to talk and let out all her problems and then goes home feeling much better for it. For her, a tarot reading is no different from going to confession.

So how are counseling skills applied to a tarot consultation? First of all, some adaption of the basic counseling guidelines may be necessary. In a tarot counseling session, the first difference is that the reader can make suggestions to the client with regard to solutions the reader sees in the cards. This is avoided in normal counseling sessions unless clients make the suggestion themselves. What must be remembered is that clients are making the tarot suggestion psychically via synchronicity and the archetypes of the cards. Apart from this, the same principles apply (see Counseling page 186).

If the tarot reader senses a possible development which may be dangerous or harmful to the client, the reader should not alarm the client by stating it baldly. Rather, the reader should give constructive advice which will result in the client navigating past the danger by some alternative positive action. For example, if the reader feels strongly that there will be a death in the client's family, rather than saying so, he or she should advise the client that it is necessary for the family to strengthen its unity by sharing problems and pulling together.

Clients should be told that tarot advice is not a command to be followed slavishly, or an excuse to avoid responsibility for one's own life. A tarot reading is a signpost, not a red or green traffic light. A reading can indicate potentials and risks, but it is always up to the individual concerned to take the information into consideration and then make up his or her own mind as to what action to take.

One tendency that many tarot readers have is the need to prove that they are good readers by not being told the clients' query and subsequently not questioning them about it as the reading progresses. This would in fact make true tarot counseling impossible; the reader must bear in mind that the objective of the reading is to help solve the client's problems, not prove how good the reader is!

It is essential that an ongoing dialogue continues during the reading. As each card is read aloud, the reader uses the opportunity to prompt a response from the client. Normally, it is the accuracy of the cards' meaning which will assist the reader in doing this, but if not, the reader may need to question the client to see how it applies to his or her life. The reader should not be afraid that this is cheating. This fear is due to the reader feeling the need to prove psychic skills; he or she should always remember the objective of the reading.

Past-Life Regression

The majority of the world's population believes in reincarnation—that we live many lifetimes. The soul transmigrates at the moment of death and passes in due course into the newly born.

Theories regarding reincarnation differ. The Hindus believe that it is possible to be reincarnated as an animal, whereas the Western Mystery Tradition believes that you remain within your species. One important theory is that memories of past lives are recorded within an area of the astral plane called the Akashic Records. This area is linked to the individual via his or her own spiritual aura (see page 91, chapter 6) and allows the individual, and some psychics, access to this information. This is the principal theory which allows past-life recall.

The fact is, whatever you particularly believe regarding reincarnation is irrelevant when it comes to using past-life regression as a counseling tool----you do not even have to believe in reincarnation itself (although it helps!). What is important about past-life regression is that it allows a counselor and client to recognize the causes of ill health in a controlled fashion, the hallmark of a true holistic therapy. A good example of this is given by our friend Lhianna Sidhé. She trained with Dick Sutphen, who we will talk about later.

> Many people today experience emotional and physical illness and disabilities which are connected to a past life. Using regression it is possible to identify specific causes for present health or emotional problems. For example, a woman who is overweight discovered that she lived a prior life where there was famine and she had starved to death. A man who had chronic neck pain for which doctors had no explanation or cure, discovered that he had been beheaded on the guillotine during the French Revolution. These people were able to "see" the cause of their illnesses and were able to overcome them. With a clear understanding of the cause, the effect can be removed. Healing can be achieved by suggestion directly to the subconscious mind.

The use of past-life regression became fashionable in the 1960s. The new consciousness which arose during that decade spawned an interest in alternative philosophy and many began to explore Eastern religion, particularly Hinduism. As a result, an interest developed in the West in reincarnation. At the same time, hypnosis began to be accepted as a real form of psychotherapeutic treatment.

It did not take long for some of the pioneer hypnotherapists who were regressing clients back to childhood to go that one step further. Some of them were surprised to discover, and to have to believe in, reincarnation when their clients unexpectedly recalled earlier lives.

One of the early pioneers was Dick Sutphen who published the now famous work on regression You Were Born Again to Be Together. He developed techniques for past-life regression which were revolutionary for their time; he also developed the theory that we come together countless times in different lifetimes to continue work on relationships. He considered this the key to understanding reincarnation.

Initially the work of such people as Dick Sutphen and other past-life therapists was treated with derision by the scientific lobby; they considered it a gimmick, refusing to treat it seriously. The fact that it had captured the public's imagination did not help. Suddenly it became trendy to have "come as you were parties" and it even spawned a Hollywood movie on the subject----On a Clear Day You Can See Forever, starring Barbara Streisand. Regardless of all the media attention, a small dedicated band realized that past-life regression had great possibilities as a counseling tool, and continued to develop it. By the mid-1970s it was beginning to be used by many serious psychotherapists; Alma Traub was one of these, and Janet and Stewart were lucky enough to work with her.

Regression Technique

The process of regression is simple; the regressor places the client in a relaxed state. If the counselor is able to use hypnosis this is even better, but hypnosis is not essential to regress someone. The same effect can be achieved through a deep state of relaxation and controlled visualization. After explaining the technique to the client, the regressor begins by getting the client comfortable and then taking the client through a series of relaxation and breathing exercises (these are the same as the ones used for shamanistic trance states----see page 212, chapter 13).

The next stage is to start the regression back through this life. This is done in a relaxed and unhurried manner, giving the client plenty of time to answer the questions. The regressor should be careful in the use of wording and try to avoid leading questions and placing suggestions into the client's mind.

If necessary the regressor may need to ponder on an area and alter his or her standard techniques during the regression. The regressor should encourage the client to answer questions in the present tense, rather than the past. This helps the client to regress effectively. An example of a regression technique, and the questions and directions of the regressor, are given below. The client's answers to the questions are of course fictional.

Regressor: "I want you to tell me what you were doing this time yesterday?"

Client: "I'm at home watching television."

Regressor: "What are you watching?"

Client: "A documentary on African wildlife."

Regressor: "Is there anyone else there?"

Notice that this question isn't worded as "Who is there with you?" which is a leading question which might suggest an answer. This is particularly important during the actual past-life recall stage.

The regressor repeats this line of questioning in a similar fashion, but changes the time span to week, then month and finally year. After each question the regressor should encourage the client to relax. The questioning then moves on to important life events. (It is useful to question the client, before the regression session, about important events in his or her life.)

Regressor: "Now we're going to go back further; much further. It's your wedding day; what is happening around you?"

Client: "I'm in my bedroom at my parents' home; I'm getting changed. My mother has just entered the room; she's crying."

Regressor: "Why is she crying?"

Client: "I have just asked her that. She is emotional about the whole day."

If possible, the regressor follows a line of questioning until it reaches a natural end. They then move on to other important life experiences in a similar fashion: the client meeting his or her spouse for the first time; twenty-first, eighteenth and sixteenth birthdays; first day at college and school; and other such experiences. Once the regressor has reached back past the obvious memorable events, the line of the questioning changes.

Regressor: "Now we're going to go back, even further back. I want you to go back to the first Christmas or birthday you can remember. Where are you? Is there anyone else there with you?"

Again, the regressor allows the questioning to flow naturally. At this point it is important for the regressor to bring the other senses

201

into play; what can the client smell? or hear? It is easy to forget that the recordings of our other senses are also stored within our memories. Remembering a smell, for example, can trigger off memories of events which have been stored deep within the subconscious mind.

The next question is one of the most important, and the regressor should try to use memories of all the senses in his or her questioning. The client should be given plenty of time to answer.

Regressor: "I want you to go back. Further back into the past, as far back as you can remember. Where are you?" ("What can you see/smell?" etc.)

After the client recalls his or her earliest memory, it is time to actually take him or her back beyond the birth experience.

It is important to point out that the client may have already started recalling traumatic events during this lifetime. If so, the regressor may wish to halt the regression and focus on resolving these rather than taking the client any further. This leads us an important rule: if the client becomes seriously distressed or the regressor becomes unhappy at any stage with the client's reactions, the regressor should return them to the present immediately (see below).

The next stage is for the regressor to help the client relive the moment of his or her birth, in reverse! This is a visualization technique based on the tunnel experience, that of moving down the mother's vagina during birth. A similar process is used in shamanism for power animal retrieval (see page 212, chapter 13). It culminates in the client relaxing within the womb.

Regressor: "I want you to relax. Breath deeply and relax. As you relax you become aware that you are surrounded by light——bright light. Very slowly you can see a dark spot, and you begin to move toward it. As you do so, the spot becomes bigger and the light begins to fade around you. I want you to push yourself into the darkness, push yourself with all your might further and further into the tunnel, into the darkness. Now I want you to relax again. The darkness is still around you but you feel relaxed, as if you are floating. Just relax and float."

The regressor now moves the client back to his or her first actual recall experience:

Regressor: "I want you to move back to the place where you are, back into the past. Back and back beyond your birth. What can you see?"

Client: "I'm in a room."

Regressor: "What can you smell (or hear)?"

The regressor continues the questioning: What are you wearing? What sex are you? What is your name? Where do you think you are (country or town)? After establishing the time period and who the client was then, the next questions should be about the lifestyle: Are you married? What is happening in your life? etc. This will help to establish causes of any problems in the client's current life. Sometimes a person being regressed may only get impressions----the odd image and smell, not necessarily a full-blown recall experience. The regressor should always bear this in mind.

After noting the recall experience (a cassette recorder is very useful) the regressor returns the client back to the womb, encouraging him or her to relax, particularly if any memories are disturbing. We recommend that the client only be taken back to three recalls at most during regression, as the experience can be very tiring.

The process for returning the client to the present is basically a reversal of the regression technique. The client is slowly brought forward to the present via the womb, birth experience, and any of the memories which were of significance. This reversal process should be done slowly and methodically. If hurried, it may result in the client not feeling completely returned to the present, with resulting uneasiness.

The Four Types of Regression Experience

Generally regression experiences can be classified into four types. The first two----fantasy and historical----are closely linked and sometimes overlap. In many cases they are expressions of the imagination of the individual being used to express past traumas. The second two----hereditary/genetic and realistic----are very likely actual past-life experiences.

Fantasy: "In a past life I was a high priest/ess of Atlantis!"

During both Gavin's and Janet's use of regression techniques they have both heard this phrase used several times. In the majority of cases it has come from practicing occultists who have in fact gained access to the astral plane. Gavin's particular theory on Atlantis is that it has become the Western Magical Traditions equivalent to the aboriginal dream time which has clothed the astral plane.

(Many historians and archeologists believe that the Atlantis referred to by Plato was in fact the Minoan Empire before it was decimated by the volcanic destruction of the island of Santorini.)

The fantasy regression is used to clothe the repressed traumas, desires and aspects of an individual's persona. One woman that Janet met, while working alongside a psychologist, actually transferred all of her early life experiences into the fantasy as a way of coming to terms with them. She would state during her regressions, "I was sent away from home to train as a priestess in Atlantis." Under later psychotherapy it came to light that she had seen a fantasy film about Atlantis several years earlier, and had in fact been sent to boarding school at a very young age! Her way of coping with the still present trauma of this separation from her family and home was to transfer it onto the plot of the film.

Atlantis, although common, is of course not the only fantasy which may come to light. It is just as likely to be a life as a Venusian princess (don't forget the Edgar Rice Burroughs books) or something else from science fiction literature. Although fantasy, it is a real experience for the client undergoing the regression and an expression of real traumas which have occurred in this lifetime. The fantastic details of the story may be unreal, but the general story line will be true. Anyway, who are we to say that someone can't have a real past life as a Venusian princess----though Venus's atmosphere hardly supports the idea.

Historical: "In a past life I was Cleopatra!"

This has become a cliché. In fact, genuine experiences of being famous historical people are very uncommon. If a client being regressed does experience that they are a historical figure, it is very likely that his or her ego is seeking protection from revealing repressed trauma. Another more common experience is that of being Cleopatra's much-loved handmaiden or slave. Again, this is basically fantasy and a way of expressing repressed traumas, desires, and parts of the individual's personality. In the case of Cleopatra's handmaiden there is a repressed desire bubbling up from the person's shadow. The actual desire is to be subservient to a glamorous personality which has been clothed by the ego allowing the person to consciously cope with it. Such a person is probably normally very much in control or dominant. He or she probably does not express this subservient side too easily, possibly feeling that it is a weakness of character.

Gavin once counseled someone who, following a regression, began to experience recall of being a Nazi death camp guard. It turned out to be a form of historical fantasy. Gavin deduced there were two possible reasons. The regressed person had just started seriously studying runes; Gavin believed he was in fact coming up against a wall of guilt which had formed around the racial consciousness of the Nordic/Germanic racial group (the individual was of a Nordic family background).

Another possibility is that he had developed a guilt complex from being in an age group that had been bombarded with the horrors of Aushwitz and Dachau during childhood. Interestingly, he was antiracist to the point of being involved in an active anti-neo-Nazi organization when he was a teenager. His esoteric study of runes had forced him to confront his repressed guilt. (One of the primary laws of magic at work: the first thing magic changes is oneself).

It is noticeable that particular historical past-life trends can be fashionable, dictated by media influences on the individual. For example, there has been a noticeable increase in past-life experiences as Native Americans since the release of several films on the subject (including *Pocahontas* and *Dances With Wolves*). This leaves several questions for the regressor to think about from an esoteric viewpoint, such as: do modern mass media methods affect the astral realm, with individuals being regressed picking up on the created thought forms?

A similar phenomenon occurs with Spiritualists and their spirit guides; from the 1920s Egyptian guides seemed to be in vogue----the time of increased interest in Howard Carter and the Egyptian excavations, which culminated in the Tutankhamen exhibitions of the early 1970s. Not surprisingly Egyptian past-life experiences followed the same trend. During the late 1970s and early 1980s Aztec and Toltec spirit guides and past-life experiences began to appear; the same time as the news media began to show increasing interest in Central America and the Nicaraguan conflict. Even Central American music became in vogue, with one group (Chachypya) hitting the top ten in Britain.

Of course some historical experiences may be genuine past-life encounters. If a person has a string of past lives, the laws of probability dictate that at some point he or she has been involved in a historically recorded event.

Realistic: "I'm in a room; it's covered in tiles, and I can smell blood.... I'm chopping meat with a large cleaver."

The first giveaway that a past-life experience is genuine is that the person is doing something very ordinary; in the example given above the person had been a pork butcher from Bradford, England. Rather than actually saying who they are and what position they hold socially, people are more likely to describe what they are doing. Description of their occupation normally comes from piecing together their actions during their experience. They may describe particular locations, and if lucky, actual place names and/or possible dates.

Such information provides the opportunity to research into records for evidence and proof of the existence of that particular incarnation, but this is not essential for counseling; the object of regression is to deal with the person's trauma rather than prove the existence of reincarnation.

Just because someone has a real past-life experience, this does not mean that it is not possible to use that experience for counseling. Many realistic past-life recall experiences will be of very ordinary everyday activities: shopping, cleaning and the general day-to-day acts of human existence. Sometimes the regression experience may be of another type: a person may experience a violent and traumatic event which not only shaped that particular incarnation, but has continued to shape other lives after it.

This is explained by one theory of reincarnation—that we pass the effects of repressed trauma down from one incarnation to the next. In some cases, a past-life trauma is unconsciously staged again in this lifetime to validate repressed past-life experiences. The result is a continual cycle from lifetime to lifetime, which prevents the growth of the soul. In the case of this form of recall, the object is to counsel the client to break the cycle.

Hereditary/Genetic: "I have researched my past life, and discovered I am my own ancestor!"

This is a theoretically fascinating area. Do our past incarnations go back through our own blood line, or is it possible that historical information can be passed on in a hereditary fashion? During a realistic regression experience a person may not necessarily realize that he or she is actually genetically related to the past incarnation until follow-up research at a later date.

From an esoteric viewpoint, it is highly plausible that the soul may seek to remain within a family group because it has developed an area of its own within the collective unconscious. In the case of race, it is generally accepted by Jungian psychology that the area of racial consciousness exists, so why not the family area? This may be a learned response to the ideas of family loyalty or blood being thicker than water (to quote a cliché) being deeply instilled; the soul may seek to incarnate within the same family because of unresolved difficulties within it, and strong feelings of kinship.

Genetic scientists are investigating the theory that it is possible for DNA (Deoxyribo-Nucleic-Acid) to be encoded during an organism's lifetime. If this is so, it means that many past-life experiences may in fact be memories handed down from generation to generation. One interesting example was witnessed by Janet, who was responsible for helping regress someone who claimed to be a Roundhead soldier (Parliamentarian during the English Civil War). His experience seemed to be of the realistic type, until he came back to Janet and the psychologist she was working with several days later.

The name he had remembered seemed familiar, so he asked several members of his family if they had heard of it. His mother was stunned when she heard the name; it belonged to one of his ancestors, someone he had no knowledge of and who was a Parliamentarian cavalry officer. But the most interesting part was this: his mother only knew the name because she had researched the family history while she was pregnant with her son! This leaves the question: was this information passed down his family line for several generations, was it originated with the mother's research of the family history, or was it an instance of genuine past-life recall?

Applying Counseling to Recall Experiences

When regression was first experimented with, the participating individuals were allowed to leave immediately after the recall session. This resulted in several side effects over the next few days as the individuals tried to deal with what they had released from their unconscious minds. They almost always returned to their regressor within 48 hours asking for help in dealing with the emotions that had been released by the process. This is how counseling became linked to past-life regression; past-life recall cannot be performed without counseling being required after it.

The first stage of this counseling is to go through the past-life recalls one by one. Then the client should be encouraged to examine the events to see how they relate to the present-life situation and to see if there are any similarities with events within the current lifetime. The client should also be encouraged to look at the recall for answers to any current problems. The principles of counseling (see page 187) will of course apply.

Hopefully, if the counseling session is fruitful, the client will be able to recognize similarities between past and present lives and be able to use these to his or her benefit. The client may be able to recognize problems that have recurred through many incarnations, and may be able to learn how to avoid that situation from occurring again. In unavoidable situations, the client may be able to recognize a way of lessening trauma and to realize why a specific happening is necessary. The client may also recognize individuals within the recall that are still around in this lifetime; this may help the client to understand these people better and avoid conflict and misunderstanding.

As we said at the beginning of this section, it does not matter if you believe in reincarnation and past-life recall. If the experiences expressed during the regression are not from a past life, they will of course be from the client's own unconscious mind which is seeking a way to express itself through the imagination. If this is so, whatever you believe, the regression technique and subsequent counseling will yield the same results.

13

Shamanistic Forms of Healing

The terms "shaman" and "shamanistic" have become buzz words in both the New Age and the pagan communities. This revival in interest can be attributed to the work of the French anthropologist Mircea Éliade whose book, *Shamanism: Archaic Techniques of Ecstasy*, is still considered one of the finest works on the subject, and to Michael Harner who is regarded by some as the father of modern neo-shamanistic practice. Harner was the first proponent of shamanism as a valid magical path, and the first in the West to publish usable rituals which included healing techniques.

Because of the primal nature of shamanism, healing has always been an integral part of its practices. The ancient Greeks combined the visionary nature of shamanism in the form of dreams (*incubatio*) and divination (see page 13, chapter 1) with their healing practices in the temples to Aesculapius. Whether they held the same animistic beliefs as the Native Americans, the Celts or the Lapps is debatable.

According to shamanistic philosophy we live alongside a spirit world inhabited by both benevolent and malevolent entities, the latter being responsible for disease and illness. The belief in a spirit world has survived in Celtic legend as the realm of the Sidhe or fairy folk, and in Norse/Saxon tradition as Alfheim––the realm of the elves. In the Middle Ages this belief became trivialized to the point where we now have the archetypal gossamer-winged fairies of Arthur Rackham's illustrations and Sir Arthur Conan Doyles notorious photographs.

Dealing with the malevolent spirits that cause disease is the basic tenet of all true shamanistic forms of healing. In its simplest form the healing may consist of the shaman, medicine man, or spirit man going into trance and traveling the underworld looking for the bad spirit that caused the illness and then combating it. This is why shamans are often referred to as "spiritual warriors."

Unlike many modern occult practices, shamanism not only divides the cosmos elementally, into upper, lower and middle worlds, but also into animal, plant and mineral realms. To aid him in his quest, the shaman may have a number of allies from the realms of the plant, mineral and the animal worlds. The plant ally can sometimes be a hallucinogenic plant or fungus which allows him to travel to the spirit world; the animal ally is first found during such a trance, and the shaman takes its form during the battle with the malevolent spirit.

In psychological terms, particularly those of Jung (see page 82, chapter 5), shamanism works in the realms of the shadow and the collective unconscious. The battle with a malevolent spirit can be seen as a battle with the person's shadow and repressed desires which have gained a foothold within the individual's aura as thought forms. Initially these exist within his or her mental/emotional aura, but if untreated descend into the etheric aura and cause disease within the physical body. These may manifest to the shaman-healer as insect-like entities. An understanding of psychology is important for anyone who is going to study shamanism seriously, as is an understanding of the spiritual and etheric makeup of the body.

The taking of an animal ally or power animal is the first stage in all shamanistic practice, as is the use of meditation and the study of trance techniques. These techniques do not suit everybody. Within a tribal context, shamanism is considered to be a vocation and is not practiced by all the tribe. It involves someone with latent gifts which can be exploited for the benefit and survival of a tribal family. Some of the techniques----such as the sweat lodge----can be used by anyone without prior commitment.

It is the use of trance which separates shamanism from other forms of pagan magical practice. Generally, trance can be induced by four methods:

1. The use of a visualization technique, often referred to as "path working."

2. The use of white noise, such as rhythmic drumming or rattling.

3. The use of a breathing technique which mildly decreases oxygenation of the brain tissues (pranic breathing).
4. The use of a plant or fungal substance (natural hallucinogens such as peyote).

Methods 3 and 4 cause the sublimation of the ego and allow the practitioner to let go of conscious control.

Trance states induced in this manner are often referred to as shamanic states of consciousness (SSC), a term coined by Michael Harner to separate them from the ordinary everyday state and from other forms of trance used by mediums and clairvoyants. Shamanistic trance differs from the latter in that it is active rather than passive in its approach to the astral and spiritual realms. Whereas mediums expect a spirit guide or guardian to come to them on the physical realm, a shaman travels into that realm with the help of a guardian, normally a power animal.

Preparation for Shamanistic Healing

The first exercise in the exploration of shamanistic practice is the finding of one's power animal. This is important, as the power animal not only acts as guide to the astral realms, but also protects the individual from attack from less benevolent entities during journeying and healing.

Most people who have experienced the finding of a power animal are quick to state that their animal guide finds them. The power animal arises from the collective unconscious just as a medium's spirit guide does, the main difference being that the power animal comes from the collective unconsciousness of the animal concerned. Just as humans have their own areas within the collective unconsciousness, so do our animal cousins. This area is actually far stronger than the human one, as most animals' conscious thought is housed here. It is debatable whether it is possible for human consciousness to enter this area, but the animal collective unconscious does recognize kindred spirits within the human realm, hence the power animal will be a reflection of the soul of the individual. Personality traits between the power animal and the individual will also be noticeable.

One often-used term which can cause confusion is "totem animal." This term was originally used in the Native American traditions. It has become interchangeable with the term "power animal," but may also mean something different. Sometimes a tribe, coven or similar group may have a group totem representing their purpose or group characteristics, such as an owl for a Wiccan teaching coven. Unlike power animals, mythical beasts such as dragons, unicorns or phoenix may also be used. Totemic group animals are the root source of modern heraldic beasts, incorporated in coats of arms. Because of its sustained use, a thought form of that beast may develop (intentionally or otherwise) within the collective unconscious; it is therefore not unusual for a magical worker to have both power and totemic animals.

Journey to Find a Power Animal

The journey to find a power animal can be done by yourself or with others. Preferably, somebody should read the journey out to you after you have finished the breathing exercises.

Find a place for this exercise where you feel comfortable and safe. If this is outside or somewhere you are unfamiliar with, we suggest you cast a protective Circle (see page 110, chapter 7). A student of Gavin's once did such an exercise outside and came up with a power animal which resembled a cross between an elephant and a giraffe. The exercise was interfered with by various local (but benign) nature spirits who wanted to play!

You may wish to use soft background music, but make sure you are not going to be disturbed during the journey---and don't forget to take the phone off the hook.

Once you are lying or sitting comfortably, relax and start to breathe using the following pattern: exhale for seven seconds, hold for three, inhale for seven seconds, and hold for three again. Repeat this pattern---don't force it---just relax into it.

Starting from your toes, tense and relax the muscles of the feet. Repeat the process of tensing and relaxing up the whole of your body: your buttock, spine, stomach, arm, shoulder and neck muscles. Finish by tightening and then loosening the muscles of your face, paying attention to the mouth, eyelids and brow. Once you have finished, confirm that your entire body is relaxed then pause for two minutes before moving on to the next stage.

Now try to clear your mind of your everyday thoughts. This can be difficult, and different techniques work well for different people. You may find it useful to visualize a rose and imagine it slowly opening, or to follow the flow of a river (if so, use suitable, watery music). Don't be afraid to experiment and find what works for you.

Now it is time to start the journey into the underworld to find your animal of power. Get your partner to read out the following or memorize it yourself----whichever strengthens your ability to visualize using your imagination. Do not force your imagination---- if other relevant images come into your mind, accept them too.

The Journey

Imagine you are standing in a forest. The air is cold, and a mist hangs above the leaves which litter the floor of the forest. You can hear a soft breeze through the leaves of the trees. As your eyes explore the thick forest which surrounds you, you can see that the shadows cast from the trees are big and long. And you become aware of the sun setting, large and red, through the branches to the left of you.

(Pause)

Before you, half covered by the mist, you can see a path. It is worn into the earth from the passage of many feet, and curves through the trees to the right, disappearing finally into the darkness of the woods.

You become aware that the mist is thickening around you, and that the path may be the only way out of the woods. You decide to follow it, and as you start your journey the woods appear to become darker, and darker.

As you follow the path, curving always to the right, you feel the earth beneath your feet, and the mist seems to have grown thicker, making it more difficult for you to see the path. You can hear the small animals of the forest foraging in the under-growth and a fox cry in the distance.

Undeterred by the darkness, and the strange sounds, you continue to follow the path----always to the right.

(Pause)

It is now dark; the sun has set, and ahead of you a full moon is riding in the sky, illuminating the path. As your eyes adjust to the light you can see the silhouette of a tree, a large oak tree, probably the largest you have ever seen.

The path you are on slowly winds its way toward this tree, and as you come closer to it, you become aware of its enormous size; it seems to tower high into the sky, and the buttresses of its large roots plunge deep into the soil of the woods around it.

Slowly, as you approach the base of the tree, you become aware of a dark patch between two of the larger roots. This circle of darkness grows as you get nearer to the tree and seems to suck in the light around it.

You can now make out that it is a hole, a large animal burrow. You crouch in front of it and peer into its darkness. You realize that, with a bit of effort, it is large enough for you to enter.

You push your head into the hole, then your shoulders, wriggling to get them in completely. The hole is tight, but not so tight as to prevent you moving your body and pushing yourself into it.

You begin to push more of your body into the hole; now your hips are in, and with a bit more effort your knees, and finally your feet leave the outside world.

You are in darkness, complete darkness. You feel the earthy smell of the soil around you, and feel the tendrils of small roots touching your head.

You push yourself down the hole, wriggling like a snake.

Down and down you descend, down and down. Pushing with your shoulders, your hips and your feet, down and down into the unknown.

You descend further down into the darkness, down and down, down and down.

You feel a root brushing your shoulder, but continue to descend, down and down, down and down, into the blackness.

The tunnel you are in begins to feel tighter as you go deeper, but undeterred you descend further, pushing with all your strength. Down and down, down and down you go.

The tunnel is now becoming so tight that you have to squeeze all of your effort out of your muscles to move. Down and down, down and down you go.

Very slowly you begin to make out a faint point of light, a grayness within the absolute blackness of the tunnel. You continue to head down, down and down, and nearer and nearer to this point of light.

The tunnel is now tighter, but the light has become nearer, and you push yourself toward it.

You become aware that it is an opening to a dimly lit cavern, and you finally push your head through and the whole of your body tumbles into the dimness that is beyond.

(Pause)

You look around and become aware that the light you could see was the phosphorescence of the cave walls. There is enough light just to see the ends of your arms and no more.

Suddenly you become aware of a presence apart from yourself, the noise of movement but nothing else.

You feel something brush past part of your body, and then a second later it happens again.

Slowly, as your eyes adjust to the light, a shape begins to take form in front of you, and then it disappears into the dark shadows of the cave.

Suddenly it is in front of you again, and you can make out the eyes of a living creature staring back at you.

Then it is gone again into the shadows, but it returns. This time you can see not only its eyes, but also its shape----and you recognize what kind of creature it is.

(Pause)

This happens several more times; the creature passing you, brushing against you, staring at you, and then finally it disappears into the shadows. You become aware that it does not intend to return.

(Pause)

You decide it is time to return with this experience. You find the entrance that brought you into the cave and push yourself up into it.

The tunnel is tight, but you push yourself up with your shoulders, hips and feet. Up and up, up and up.

Up and up, up and up you go, retracing your journey.

The tunnel does not appear as tight as it was, and you push yourself up. Up and up, up and up.

The smell of the woods wafts down the tunnel, but you can see nothing but darkness. Up and up, up and up you go.

It has now become much easier to move in the tunnel, and you can see a bright point ahead of you. You push yourself up toward the light, up and up, up and up.

The daylight is now much brighter and you can see the tunnel's entrance hole. You push yourself up and up, up and up, toward it.

Up and up, up and up you go.

Finally you push your head out of the tunnel. You can see nothing, your eyes being unaccustomed to the sudden experience of sunlight, but you can hear the birds singing in the trees and smell the sweet perfume of flowers.

Your eyes slowly become accustomed to the light, and you see the trees towering above you and the sunlight filtering through the topmost branches. You see the path that brought you to this place stretching ahead of you. You slowly begin to retrace you steps, walking on the path, which curves always to the left.

You finally reach the place where the path originally started and your journey began.

(Pause)

When you are ready, slowly return to this world by opening your eyes, and return to it with the experience of meeting your kindred animal spirit for the first time.

Once you have found your power animal it is important to exercise it----to reinforce your connection with it. The commonest form is known as dancing your animal; this is done by invoking the bird or animal and assuming its form and behavior (this can be seen in traditional Native American dancing). This should be done immediately after the above exercise and on a regular basis afterwards.

You may also wish to collect fetish items related to your ally. These will come naturally to you with time, and very soon you will find yourself with a collection of statues of the animal or bird, fur, feathers, claws and similar items. These are referred to as "power objects" and help to increase your rapport with the animal or bird spirit.

Some Common Power and Totem Animals Related to Healing

All power and totem animals have some healing attributes, but it is interesting to note that the most powerful are predators. This is hardly surprising, as the healer has to hunt down and kill the cause of the disease. Shamans are often referred to as warriors for this reason. A few examples of power animals commonly associated with healing are listed below.

Badger: The badger not only walks on the surface of the earth but also digs beneath it, among the roots of trees and plants. It is therefore said that the badger has a deep knowledge of the underworld, as well as natural skills in herbalism from living among the roots. Those with a badger are able to see beneath the surface of a situation, as well as having natural skills in trance. It has always been regarded as a creature of wisdom, and it should be listened to by the healer when it speaks. The badger, incidentally, is *not* a predator, whatever those who make a sport of hunting it may pretend; it harms no other animals.

Bear: Within some Native American mythology it is the bear which calls all the other animal to counsel. It is also the only animal which is said to heal its own wounds (Chippewa tradition). If the bear appears to people during their journey, it indicates that they may best use their skills in the field of counseling; this of course indicates a predisposition to using divination as a tool. The bear is not only a ferocious and indomitable spirit, but also gives the gift of rapid healing—ideal attributes for a healer dealing with intrusive spirits.

Dolphin: The dolphin is unique among animals in that it was an animal of earth which decided, very early in its evolution, to return to the water. It is also highly intelligent and has become known for its compassionate behavior. Those with the dolphin as a power animal have the necessary empathy to be spiritual healers, working with the aura and the chakras. They also enjoy the experience of healing, and see this as their vocation.

Owl: While some consider this a bird of ill omen, the Chumash Indians see the owl as the medicine bird. The same seems to apply in the West, where some consider it a bird of darkness, but to others it is a symbol of wisdom----the wise old owl. The owl flies from darkness into light, symbolically bringing the end of disease. On a psychological level it brings the death of egotism, renewal and rebirth----possibly why it has developed a reputation for being an ill omen. The owl brings change, which makes it a potent bird of power for the healer.

Plant and Mineral Allies

While the power animal acts as a protector for the healer, it is also important for him or her to recruit the spirits of plants and minerals to act as allies. This is particularly important in the act of extracting intruding spirits from the ill person's aura (see etheric sucking, page 221).

It is important for the shaman to collect as many of these allies as possible, because in the shaman's world they relate to the different types of malignant entities which exist. The first stage is to go out and explore the local countryside for wild plants and herbs. Use your instinct to find plants or collections of minerals which seem to be particularly special to you, then carefully remove some of your chosen plant's leaves and stems.

Do not use iron on a plant, as this is believed to bleed off the plant's power. Remember to say "thank you" to the spirit of the plant or mineral by leaving an offering for it. In European shamanism it was traditional to use a couple of spots of your own blood, but colored stones will suffice if you are averse to this!

The next stage begins when you return home. Find out about the plant or mineral; study books on botany, herbalism and mineralogy. Once you are happy that you have enough knowledge about the plant or mineral you have collected, it is time to think about collecting the spirit of the plant or mineral.

The journey to collect the spirit of such allies is identical to that for finding a power animal. The shaman explores the cavern looking for an entrance other than the one he entered through, and exploring beyond that. While in the state of SSC, he should search for the types of plants or minerals that he found in a normal conscious state. On finding the plant or mineral it should change into an insect or similar creature. This is an indication of its power (which is why insects can never be power animals; they are associated with the power of the plant and mineral worlds). The shaman should grasp the form that the plant or mineral has transformed into and eat it, then return to his ordinary state of consciousness.

Power Songs

Power songs are used to call to all the spirit allies that the shaman has in the animal, mineral and plant realms. Sometimes a song or tune may come to people while they are in trance, normally while retrieving their power animal or other ally. Sometimes it may be necessary for them to write their own, but always it should come from the individuals themselves. Here is an example (repeated continuously):

Spirits, spirits, come to me,
Over water, through the trees.

Spirits, spirits, be with me,
Give me power, set my soul free.

Spirits, spirits, help me feel,
Give me bird's wings, let me heal.

Normally a rattle or a drum is used during the recitation of the song. These both help to induce the SSC, with the drum being beaten at about three beats a second and the rattle shaken to create white noise. It is from these power songs, particularly those associated with a plant ally, that many healing charms develop.

Healing Techniques

Retrieving An Individual's Power Animal

The power animal represents, on a symbolic level, the individual's personal power. In the shaman's cosmology everybody has a power animal, therefore a person who is ill or without power is believed to have lost contact with this guardian spirit.

It is the power animal which fills an individual with strength, making it impossible for external forces to intrude physically or spiritually within the body of that person. It helps prevent or fight disease, as well as maintaining psychological health by increasing mental agility and self-confidence. From the viewpoint of spiritual healing (see chapter 10), the retrieval of a person's power animal boosts the protective abilities of the etheric, mental/emotional, and spiritual auras.

The journey to retrieve a person's power animal should be done in a dim, candle-lit room, preferably in sacred space (see page 107, chapter 7). Intoxicants, such as alcohol, should be avoided, as should food, for four to six hours before the ceremony. A person other than the shaman and the patient is needed for drumming.

Start by shaking the rattle at each quarter—north, east, south and west. (You may wish to invoke according to your tradition.) Then shake the rattle above your head to invoke the spirits of the upper worlds, and below your waist to invoke those of the underworld.

Have your patient lie quietly in the center of the circle, and start to circle around him or her shaking your rattle and singing your power song. The drummer should start drumming, holding a steady beat. Continue to circle around the patient until you begin to feel the change in consciousness within yourself. You may notice that your singing or rattling has changed in tempo, or that you are beginning to tremble—recall your experience from your own power animal journey.

Kneel at the head of your patient, lay one hand within his or her aura (see page 88, chapter 6) while you continue rattling and singing your power song. Visualize your descent into the underworld as you did for the journey. Once you have started to descend you should stop shaking the rattle, but the drummer should continue with a steady beat.

You are now descending into your patient's underworld. You may see insects in the tunnel which appear malign and dangerous. Avoid these, but make a mental note of them; they are intruders within the etheric aura of the individual, which can be dealt with later (see Etheric Sucking).

Once you have entered the cavern, search for your patient's power animal. It will appear just as yours did to you. Once it has manifested several times, grasp it in your hand and bring it to your chest (in physical reality remove your hand from your patient's aura). Signal to the drummer in a predetermined way, that you intend to return. On this signal the drummer should increase the tempo, and you should visualize ascending the tunnel rapidly and returning to a normal state of consciousness.

Immediately cup both of your hands over the patient's heart chakra, and blow into it, visualizing the power animal entering into the person's body. Repeat this procedure with the crown chakra (for chakras see page 91, chapter 6). Shake the rattle three times around the person's body—this closes the aura, which has been opened during the previous actions.

Now sit down with the person and say what his or her animal is, and discuss the experience you have had. If you have seen any intrusions within the person, you may wish to finish by etheric sucking.

Etheric Sucking: Removing Harmful Intrusions

Etheric sucking removes entities which have entered the person's etheric aura and have proceeded to cause disease (see above). Indications of such intruding entities include all the symptoms of any other illness—in fact the entity can be seen as a hidden spiritual aspect of disease in the physical realm. Symptoms will therefore include high temperatures, pain and discomfort.

During trance the disease and entities will manifest to the shaman as an insect form, similar to those seen during the hunt for plant and mineral allies. The procedure for removing these intruders starts with the healer singing his or her power song to call upon the power animal and other spiritual allies. The procedure is identical to the method for retrieving an individual's power animal, the only differences being that a drummer is not necessary, and that the healer should be leaning over the body of the patient.

The shaman begins the descent into the tunnel leading to the underworld. It is within this tunnel that the shaman should see the entity or entities already described. On seeing such an entity, he or she should stop within the tunnel to deal with it. The malign entity should be similar to at least two of the plant or mineral allies that he or she has already collected. If not, the shaman should ascend the tunnel to collect these allies before returning back to heal the patient. One other option if this is the case (often used by Gavin) is to use a piece of obsidian as an ally.

It is then important that the shaman finds where in the body the entity is lodged. This is similar to feeling for damage during auric cleansing (see page 165, chapter 10). If the healer is without an ally, the piece of obsidian should be placed in his or her mouth and the healer should lean over the patient, cupping the hands or using a tube, and visualize sucking the entity out of the person's etheric aura, while actually physically sucking. A tube is often used in this process, but it is important that the healer does not swallow—the healer should visualize the entity entering the obsidian, or being

221

absorbed by the appropriate plant or mineral allies. This should be repeated as the healer descends the tunnel in trance. The healer should then blow the entity (including the piece of obsidian if used) into a bowl, bottle or jar containing salted water. This vessel should then be sealed and its contents disposed of later.

Because of the danger of actually taking such an entity into yourself, it is important to ensure that you are properly grounded and that you have cleared your aura (see page 169, chapter 10). Traditionally, shamans who employ this technique work in pairs, so that should an entity enter during the technique, the partner can remove it in the same fashion.

The Power of Naming

The power of naming is very suitable for use by any group of people. It is very simple and does not require the preparation that is needed for the other techniques mentioned, but familiarity with chakras and basic spiritual healing may be useful. In many respects this method of healing is no different from the raising of the cone of power performed in many Wiccan covens.

Those involved in the healing sit cross-legged, surrounding the patient who sits cross-legged in the middle. Very slowly the group doing the healing begin to chant the person's name, while using rattles or drums. This will be either his or her given name or Craft or magical name if he or she has one.

The group should visualize that they are transferring energy from themselves to the patient, normally in the form of light. They may wish to put their hands out in front for this reason. The tempo of the chanting, drumming and rattling should slowly increase, until at a given signal all stop. The group should then ensure that they are adequately grounded, and that the aura of the patient is sealed.

Sweat Lodges and the Teach Alluis

The sweat lodge has traditionally been associated with Native American ritual practice, and this has meant that some pagans have felt reticent about using it, feeling that it does not belong within the sphere of Western occultism. However, there is plenty of evidence that such practices were widespread within Europe, and not just within Scandinavia, where the preoccupation with saunas is a remnant.

The Native American sweat lodge is traditionally a domed structure, either woven from willow like a basket or made from a
framework of saplings and covered with skins (many modern practitioners of shamanism have replaced the skins with canvas or blan-
kets covered with plastic sheeting to retain the moisture). A deep
fire pit is always dug centrally within this structure. This is to hold
the rocks heated on the fire. The size of the lodge varies, depending
on the number of users, but approximately seven feet in diameter
seems to be the norm. Its orientation may vary according to tribal
tradition, but generally the entrance faces south, with an altar in
front of the door or a spirit trail leading to the entrance from the
fire.

Each participant in the ceremony is expected to bring a stone
for the fire and tobacco as a gift of thanks to the individual responsible for holding the ceremony. Normally, there are no more than
eight people involved in the ceremony itself, plus one person who
is responsible for keeping the lodge supplied with red-hot stones
from the fire. He is often referred to as "the fireman" as his duties
include building the fire before the ritual. The stones are normally
placed on platforms within the fire while it is built, and it can take
several hours to heat them to the right temperature. It is also
important to have the right type of stones. Some stone contains
flint, which can explode within the lodge when dowsed with water
resulting in injury.

The fireman is also responsible for ensuring an adequate supply
of water. For this reason the lodge is normally built near a water
source such as a lake or river. Water is required within the lodge for
the ceremony and for drinking. After the ceremony, it is important
that the participants bathe in cold water----apart from being very
invigorating, it also closes the skin pores and prevents skin infections.

The sweat lodge ceremony varies from tribe to tribe, but the
commonest comes from the Lakota, where it is referred to as the
Inipi ceremony. Several stones are placed in the lodge prior to the
ceremony beginning and, after praying at the altar, the participants
are smudged----wafted with sage incense using a feather----before
entering the lodge.

To enter the lodge, it is necessary to crouch down on all fours
and crawl in. Some see this as an important act of humility before
the spirits of the lodge, and a return to the womb, which the round,

warm and dark structure of the lodge surely symbolizes. The participants move round the lodge clockwise until all taking part have entered. The lodge master is the last to enter; he is responsible for conducting the ceremony and therefore sits next to the entrance so that he can call for more stones. He normally takes into the lodge a rattle, a ladle, some sage (or other herbs), a pair of forked sticks for positioning the hot stones and a container of water for dousing them.

The ritual within the lodge is normally divided by the lodge master into four quarters or rounds, each lasting approximately fifteen to twenty minutes. These all start in the same way: the lodge master calls for stones from the fireman outside the lodge; the fireman places them into the lodge's fire pit with a shovel. The lodge master sprinkles them with sage, while using the rattle to call for the spirits of the lodge. He then douses the stones with water using a ladle. This increases the humidity within the lodge quite rapidly.

The next stage within each round is the calling of prayers. These are called out by the lodge master, one for each round. They differ according to the purpose of the ceremony, but are typically as follows:

"Our first prayer is that the spirits will accept us giving something away."

Normally this is something negative within the participants such as anger or greed.

"Our second prayer is that the spirits will give us something we each need."

Peace of mind for example.

"Our third prayer is that the spirits will give to a friend something they need."

"Our fourth prayer is for Mother Earth and all her children."

At the end of each prayer the rattle is passed clockwise around the lodge, and as each person receives it, he or she rattles it and says what the purpose of their prayer is----for example, in the case of the first prayer: "I give away my anger." Between the prayers, the lodge master is responsible for maintaining the energy within the lodge by leading chanting, singing, and of course ensuring the humidity within the lodge is maintained.

When leaving the lodge, normally at the end of the fourth round or between rounds, it is traditional to offer a prayer: "To all my relations" is probably the most commonly used, as a recognition of the part that the trees, rocks, and so on have played in creating the lodge. This helps individuals connect with nature on a personal level and recognize its importance in their lives. After bathing in the nearest water source, they may join the others in chanting, drumming, and dancing their power animals around the fire.

On many occasions when Gavin has participated in a lodge, although some have left between the rounds because of the humidity, many have gone on past the normal four rounds when the supply of hot stones has permitted. This is not unusual, and it is important to remember that the decision is made by the lodge master, as is the nature of the prayers and the ceremony itself. The sweat lodge ceremony is far from dogmatic, even though its ritual structure tends to differ very little.

Within Ireland, remnants of the 'Teach Alluis' or sweat house, have been found in the counties of Derry, Cavan, Tyrone, Fermanagh, Donegal and Leitrim. All the descriptions of them are the same: oval or circular structures, about seven feet in diameter and five feet high. They were generally built entirely of stone, with a hole cut into the flagstones of the roof to act as a chimney. The floors were generally of beaten clay, although in several examples flagstones have been laid. The door was often small, so it was necessary to crawl inside in the same manner as you do when entering a Native American lodge. They tended to be located near a water source, often a well or a stream. In one archeological study of an example in County Leitrim, there is a description of its purpose, as well as its structure:

> ...a small rude structure built of stones and clay and resembling a beehive in shape. It is used for the cures of certain diseases, principally rheumatism, by means of artificial heat to induce excessive perspiration. The building is heated inside by peat fires which are then removed and the patient goes in by a small opening or doorway, and remains until the cure is supposed to have taken effect.

The turf fire normally burned for several days before the patient was admitted to the house. ("Turf" in Ireland does not mean grass; it means peat dug up and used as fuel.) He would then crawl through the entrance taking with him a bundle of rushes to sit on and to protect his feet. He would plug up the doorway with his clothing to prevent the heat escaping. Water was often sprinkled on the hot flagstones in the same fashion as in a sweat lodge. When leaving the Teach Alluis the patient would plunge into the nearby well or stream to close the pores.

It was traditional to use these sweat houses during the summer or autumn. This was probably due to the weather rather than any magical or spiritual significance. Winter in Ireland is usually cold and wet, and the rain doesn't stop until after the spring.

The similarities between the Teach Alluis and the Native American sweat lodge are striking, but there are no surviving indications of the ceremonies performed with the Teach Alluis, although there is little doubt among Irish archeologists and anthropologists that some type of ritual was performed and that the purpose was healing.

Both the Teach Alluis and the Native American sweat lodge heal in the same holistic fashion. Primarily they cause the participant to sweat profusely, with the result that toxins are excreted from the body within the sweat. On an auric level, this same action helps to cleanse both the etheric and mental/emotional auras----it should be remembered that sweat contains both water and salt, which have traditionally been cleansing agents within occult practice.

The high humidity has another effect, more specifically associated with shamanistic practice----that of trance. Trance is commonly induced by the use of breathing techniques which increase the carbon dioxide content of the blood, while decreasing the oxygen supply to the brain. The sweat lodge has a similar effect, the humidity within the lodge decreasing the passage of oxygen across the membranes of the lungs.

People who participate in a sweat lodge often describe the feeling of entering a light trance. This has the effect of releasing emotions and anxieties which have been suppressed, which not only has a beneficial effect on them mentally, but also helps to clear blockages within the associated chakras, particularly the heart and solar plexus centers. It is therefore not unusual for participants to break down in tears while in the ceremony, and to enter a fetal position on the floor of the lodge (Gavin has witnessed this on several occasions). On leaving the lodge, the individuals who have gone through this process normally feel as euphoric as the rest of the ceremony's participants----cleansed, fresh and alive.

14

Herbalism

The use of herbs is one of the oldest forms of healing known to man and is therefore common to all pagan traditions. Traditionally, it has been associated with the practice of witchcraft, but it can be found in all of the ancient cultures of the world: from China to America and Africa to Europe. In China, herbalists can trace their unbroken methods of practice back past the Ming dynasty. In Europe unfortunately, the more traditional hedge witch form of herbalism, or "wort cunning" as it was known, went underground with the coming of Christianity. Although some families continued to pass the lore down it became heavily Christianized and its original pagan heritage was forgotten.

Many of the drugs commonly prescribed by doctors originated in the herbal preparations of the village witch: aspirin was discovered by the Druids, who scraped willow bark for its pain-killing salicylic acid; both foxglove and belladonna were prescribed by the village witch for heart complaints. Foxglove, more precisely known as Digitalis, is still used by doctors as the drug Digoxin, which slows and strengthens the heart's pumping action.

In Europe, herbalism was traditionally in the hands of women, and its secrets were passed from mother to daughter. Two aspects were taught----the medicinal properties of herbs and the occult use of herbs. Witchcraft has traditionally used both aspects, and even when suppressed they have remained with us in folklore and myth. Not surprisingly, many of the herbs used have retained names associated with the occult and witchcraft.

To the Church, this occult knowledge of healing herbs gave

women power, something which it wished to suppress due to its own misogynistic belief that women with power were the servants of the Devil. The Church tried to take over this power by employing monks to wander the countryside and collect information on herbal preparations. Many of the beautifully illuminated manuscripts created by the monks can still be found today in European museums; one of the most famous is the *Lacnunga Script* in the British Museum (see page 18, chapter 1).

With the onslaught of the fourteenth-century witch hunts, women practicing the craft of herbalism and midwifery, even if they were devout Christians, found themselves under suspicion of witchcraft. Herbalism under the influence of Christianity became a male domain, particularly that of the monks who brought the influences of Greek herbalists such as Galen, Discorides and Pliny into Western herbal practice. These influences actually enriched the knowledge of herbalism which already existed, and paved the way for the creation of the modern medical profession. The monks introduced astrology as a theoretical principle, as well as the Greek influenced pharmacology of Paracelsus.

Astrological Herbalism

The practice of applying astrology to herbalism has early roots among both the Egyptians and the Mesopotamians. During the Middle Ages it would have been widely adopted by the village witch in Europe, who was already picking herbs according to the phase of the moon; the period between the waxing and the full moon would have been the time to pick herbs for constructive magical use, the full moon being the time when they reach their full vitality.

The theory of astrological herbalism is that each herb and medicinal plant comes under the influence of a planet or a sign of the zodiac (see Fig. 28); it is also important to know which parts of the body are influenced in a similar fashion (see page 104, chapter 6). In theory, a herb ruled by one particular sign of the zodiac should cure a diseased part of the body ruled by the same sign----for example, indigestion should be treated with a herb such as adder's tongue; the stomach and the herb are both ruled by Cancer. Similarly, herbs ruled by the Sun (and therefore Leo) would act as a general tonic, and so forth. In many cases, a herb's association with a planet or sign was based on its physical appearance----for example, the orange-

Planet	Herb
Sun	burnet, camomile, celandine, centaury, chicory, eyebright, heartsease, marigold, mistletoe, pimpernel, rosemary, saffron, Saint John's wort, sundew, viper's bugloss
Moon	adder's tongue, chickweed, goose-grass, loosestrife, privet, purslane, white rose, watercress, white poppy, willow
Mercury	dill, fennel, hazel, honeysuckle, lily-of-the-valley, maidenhair, marjoram, mulberry, parsley, vervain
Venus	alder, birch, blackberry, burdock, coltsfoot, cowslip, daisy, elder, fennel, foxglove, ground ivy, groundsel, marshmallow, meadowsweet, mint, mugwort, periwinkle, plantain, primrose, sanicle, sea holly, sorrel, tansy, thyme, valerian, vervain, violet and yarrow
Mars	basil, broom, hawthorn, lesser celandine, stonecrop, thistle, toadflax, wormwood
Jupiter	agrimony, balm, betony, borage, chervil, chestnut, cinquefoil, dandelion, dock, houseleek, hyssop, red rose, sage, thistle
Saturn	bistort, comfrey, hemlock, henbane, ivy, knapweed, moss, mullein, nightshade

Figure 28: Planetary Rulership of Herbs

colored Marigold was associated with the Sun.

Astrological herbalism was probably one of the commonest forms used by the medical profession up until the eighteenth century. Some of the most famous work on the subject was done by Nicholas Culpeper in the seventeenth century. He was originally attacked for his work, mainly because he had dared to publish the secrets of the medical establishment, but all he published was the common practice of the medical profession of his day. Although a shop called Culpeper's still exists today in London, England, the use of astrological herbalism has gone out of favor due to the advances of pharmacology. Whether astrological herbalism was ever the domain of the witch is uncertain, but it most certainly belonged to the court magician during the Middle Ages from which the modern medical profession can trace its roots. The approach used by the village wisewoman for herbal treatment was probably much closer to what is known as The Doctrine of Signatures.

229

The Doctrine of Signatures

The notion that herbs were put on this planet for our use was first put forward by Theophrastus, a Greek botanist and philosopher who lived in the third century B.C. His work became the basis for the development of the theory of the Doctrine of Signatures by Paraclesus in the fifteenth century. The theory is a simple one, that herbs and plants are shaped according to their use----liverwort, for example, which has liver-shaped leaves, is suitable for treating diseases of the liver.

Many of the herbs in use today still retain the names given to them because of the belief in their healing qualities: pilewort (European lesser celandine), fever few, all-heal, lungwort, heartsease and boneknit, among others. One other belief was that cure could be found near the cause. Herbs which grew near water, for example, were used as diuretics to remove water from the lungs. Although at first appearing illogical, it may be that early herbalists were instinctively guided to the herb that was needed, which is why it became associated with early magical practices. The philosophy of this practice was that of a holistic belief in the oneness of nature, that all things are created from a common substance----the *Prima Materia.*

Homeopathy

As a form of therapy, homeopathy is quite modern, only appearing during the late eighteenth century. Its origins, however, are far older; its major principle of "like curing like" being suggested by the Greek philosopher Hippocrates. Homeopathic medicine always strove to be accepted as a medical science, which led it into a period of disrepute during the Victorian era. It has regained its acceptability during the latter half of the twentieth century as scientists discovered that its medicines do appear to have an effect on the body in a similar way to a vaccine.

In homeopathy, the person is treated rather than the illness. This means that two persons having the same disease may take completely different remedies. At first this may seem odd, until you realize that the homeopath is actually treating the person's symptoms. The belief in homeopathy is that the symptoms of an illness are, in most cases, a healing response by the body, therefore the object should be to give a remedy that replicates these symptoms----

like cures like. (It is interesting to note that one side effect of many forms of holistic healing is a sudden flare-up of symptoms before positive results take place.)

What initially caused homeopathy to be ridiculed was that the amount of ingredients in a homeopathic remedy are so minuscule; in some cases as little as one molecule of an ingredient is diluted in several thousand of water. (Although herbs are one of the major ingredients used, homeopaths also use minerals and animal extracts). This is achieved by diluting and then shaking the solution vigorously, and repeating the process several times.

In many cases, this action seems to make the solution stronger in effect medicinally than an equal weight of the original ingredient. One current belief among scientists investigating homeopathy is that the process of diluting the remedy actually changes the structure of the water molecules, so that the water itself becomes the cure.

Modern Herbal Practice

Very few modern pagans practice astrological herbalism or use the doctrine of signatures as their main form of prescribing herbs, although they may still pick the herbs according to the moon's phase or position of the planets. One reason for this is that plant pharmacology developed considerably in the nineteenth century. These studies have proven that the village witch knew her herbs well; she also knew that if herbs were wrongly prescribed they created serious repercusions. Herbalism is now considered an effective alternative to modern drugs which often have undesirable side effects.

To be a good herbalist takes time and effort. It is not a skill that can be learned overnight and practiced by somebody without experience (see chapter 3). There are Wiccan covens and other pagan groups that teach the skills of herbalism, and as these groups move with the times, their herbal teacher often has recognized qualifications in the skill.

There are many excellent books that remove the dangers of dabbling by publishing known, safe recipes of herbal remedies (we have listed some such remedies later on in this chapter). These are of course only a short cut, and do not make the individual using them a herbalist, any more than putting a Band-Aid on a cut makes someone a nurse!

Many pagans have combined the modern practice of herbalism with traditional occult philosophy. Modern shamanistic practitioners and some witches still leave offerings to the spirit of the herb when collecting in the wild. This is considered good manners, ensuring the assistance of the herb spirit concerned. This offering may consist of anything from tobacco (traditional with Native Americans) to colored stones, or even to a small amount of the picker's blood left on a remaining leaf of the plant as an exchange of life energy.

One other piece of traditional lore which has come down is that herbs should not be cut with metal, particularly iron which is believed to leech off the power of the herb. This does have some scientific basis, the iron oxidizing with the chemicals within the herb cause the healing properties to change. Other metals are known to have a similar effect, particularly aluminum. Interestingly, silver----the metal of the moon and therefore of occult practice----does not. A silver herb knife will of course be expensive, but a good alternative is bronze which, like silver, causes no change. Knives made of bone and ivory, found at Iron Age archeological sites, are believed to have been used for herb gathering.

Identifying and Picking Herbs

Picking herbs can be fraught with dangers. It is important to know what you are looking for and where it will be found. If you intend to gather herbs from the wild, you should go with someone who has experience, or use a good guide to herbs which has photographs of the herbs you are looking for. Avoid older books on the subject with color illustrations; it is easy to mistake one herb for another, especially if they are from the same family.

One other problem is that many herbs growing near farmland may contain pesticides or fertilizers which affect their performance as healers (this is something our forefathers never needed to take into account). One easy solution to the problems of picking herbs is either to buy them from a reputable herbal dealer or to stick to growing your own in the traditional witch's kitchen garden. Growing your own herbs also helps to link you with nature, and encourages familiarity with the herb not only physically but also on an occult level.

One should also distinguish carefully between American and European sources—whether in books or by friendly advisers. It is unsafe to assume that the same name means the same plant in Britain and America (or even in different parts of America). The safe thing to do is to learn the Latin names, which can be relied upon as international. For example, pilewort in Britain and Ireland is a name for the lesser celandine, *Ranuculus ficaria,* an infusion of which is a very effective treatment for hemorrhoids. What America calls pilewort is fireweed (known in Britain as rose bay), *Epilobium anustfolium.* Moreover, America has only one celandine, *Cheliodonium majus L.,* which is Britain's greater celandine—and to use it as a cure for hemorrhoids would be disastrous.

Preparation of Herbs

There are many different methods of preparing herbs for medicinal use, so it is important to understand the terminology involved. Many herbs have a better effect if they are prepared using a specific method, and in some cases they may lose all their potency if prepared incorrectly. We have listed several of the main methods below with examples of recipes.

Infusions and Decoctions

Infusions and decoctions are made by dissolving herbs in water or milk. Normally one teaspoon of a herb is sufficient if dry, but two are normally used if the herb is fresh. Flowers and fleshy parts are normally bruised to help release the beneficial oils.

To make a cold infusion, a herb is normally soaked in cold water or milk for several hours and then strained. This is used when the active ingredient of the herb is likely to be damaged by heat. The herbs are consumed in the form of a cold drink, such as a cordial, punch or ale.

A hot infusion is the commonest form used, and is produced by hot water being poured over a herb and then being left to steep for 15 minutes to half an hour. Herbal teas are one of the most popular forms of hot infusions, being simple to make and palatable. They are left to steep for no longer than 15 minutes.

If tougher roots, bark and stems are being used they are normally prepared by decoction: boiling and simmering for a prolonged period to release the active ingredients.

Infusions and decoctions are normally preserved by straining when hot and then bottling, ensuring that no air is trapped in the bottle.

Gentian Root Tonic (decoction): The gentian root is particularly bitter, and is therefore normally prepared by decoction. Bitter substances are known to stimulate gastrically, and the tonic of this root works well as a digestive aid and an appetite stimulant. If the root is bought from a supplier, it is very likely to have come from the European *Gentiana lutea.* If picked fresh in America it may be substituted with Sampson's snakeroot (*Gentiana villosa*). The decoction is prepared using peppermint to lessen the bitterness and make the solution more palatable. A half cup to a cup should be taken half an hour before mealtime.

1 - 2 teaspoons chopped dried gentian root
1 teaspoon dried peppermint leaves
1 cup water

Place the root in a saucepan (never use aluminum in the preparation of herbs) with the water and bring to a boil. Reduce the heat and simmer for 15 minutes. Turn off the heat and add the dried peppermint. Cover the saucepan and let the contents steep for a further 5 minutes. Strain into a cup and leave to cool until lukewarm.

Raspberry Tea Leaf (infusion): The following is a well-known midwife's recipe; it not only aids labor during childbirth, but also acts as a general tonic.

1 teaspoon dried raspberry leaves (2 if fresh)
1 cup water

Boil the water and add the raspberry leaves. Let steep for 10 minutes. This tea should only be used in the latter stages of pregnancy (after six months), otherwise there is a risk of causing miscarriage. During those stages it helps to tone and strengthen the muscles of the womb and vagina.

Tinctures

Tinctures are herbal preparations similar to infusions or decoctions, but are prepared using alcohol or vinegar. There are three ways of preparing them: by steeping the herbs in the fluid, by heating the fluid and the herb together, or by filtering the fluid through the herb suspended in a cone paper filter (the type used for coffee). The alcohol used is of the consumable variety of high percentage proof; commercial vodka or gin is often chosen.

The alcohol dissolves all the active ingredients of the herb and acts as a preservative. This is the method's major advantage over infusions and decoctions. Also, because tinctures are very concentrated, very little is needed; the measurement for dosage is normally in drops (between 5 and 15 is normal). This also makes the preparations easy to store.

Tinctures can be taken in a number of different ways, which include being added to herbal teas, added to water for external compresses or baths, and added to oils and fats (see Ointments, page 237).

The technique for preparing a tincture is the same for all herbs. The alcohol used is normally a clear, strong spirit, such as 90 percent proof vodka. The herbs (approximately 1 to 4 ounces) are normally cut and allowed to steep in a pint of the spirit for two weeks. Stronger tinctures are made by filtering alcohol through the herbs using a paper coffee filter. This alcohol solution is passed repeatedly through the powdered or cut herbs, and the solution is allowed to drip into a glass jar or bottle. The more this process is repeated, the stronger the tincture will become. This method is particularly suitable for coarser plants.

Rosemary and Lavender Tincture: This tincture is particularly useful for stomach upsets, nausea and flatulence.

¼ fluid ounce lavender oil
¼ fluid ounce rosemary oil
½ ounce cinnamon powder
¼ ounce fine nutmeg powder
1½ pints alcohol
2 cups water
filter paper
bottle

Dissolve the oils of lavender and rosemary in the alcohol, and then add the water. Mix the nutmeg and cinnamon powders and moisten with a fluid ounce of the previously prepared alcohol solution. Put the damp powder into the filter paper, and slowly pour the remainder of the alcohol solution through and into a glass bottle or jar. Pour the resulting solution through the filter paper once more, then bottle.

The dosage is 30 drops on a lump of sugar, or the same dosage in a sugary beverage.

Fortified Wines

Wine has several qualities that make it particularly useful in medicinal herbalism. First of all, its low alcohol content means that it will dissolve the active ingredients in most herbs, even if they will not dissolve in water; secondly, it helps to resist any changes occurring within the chemical constituents of the plant; and thirdly, wine is less stimulating than the alcohol used in tinctures, but the affect of the grape acid within gives it the same preservative qualities. Most importantly, it is the most pleasurable way of taking a medicinal herb! Not surprisingly, this method was often used in traditional witchcraft. The liqueur *Strega* (Italian for witch) can still be found on sale today. Its main herbal ingredient is wormwood, and it is still manufactured in Benevento, the town mentioned in Charles Godfrey Leland's *Aradia*.

Camomile Wine: As well as working to settle the stomach, the camomile flowers help to alleviate body spasms and colic.

> 1 bottle white wine or madeira red wine
> 1 handful camomile flowers

The flowers are added to the wine, and the solution is allowed to steep of a week to ten days. It is then strained through fine gauze into a bottle. Use two tablespoons to settle the stomach. It may also serve as a compress, if a clean cloth is dipped in it and applied to the abdominal area.

French Aromatic Wine: As well as acting as a tonic and a digestive aid, if heated it can be used as an external compress for ulcers.

> 2 pints claret
> 2 tablespoons sage leaves
> 2 tablespoon thyme leaves
> 2 tablespoons hyssop leaves
> 2 tablespoons spearmint leaves
> 2 tablespoons wormwood leaves
> 2 tablespoons marjoram leaves

Chop the herbs as finely as possible. Moisten the resultant coarse powder with some of the claret. Place the damp powder into a paper coffee filter, and pour the claret through into a bottle beneath. Repeat for a more fortified wine.

Ointments and Balms

Applied externally, ointments and balms give relief to sores, painful skin irritations and wounds. They are made by dissolving the active ingredient of a herb in a base oil or other fatty substance. Traditionally, the base used was pork fat, but many herbalists now use lanolin, almond oil, cocoa butter, wheat germ or vitamin E cream.

The normal method of preparation is by heating the plant and the fatty substance together until the plant has lost its color and consistency, and the healing chemicals have been absorbed by the fat. The fatty solution is then strained and beeswax is added to harden it (this may be mixed with paraffin wax). Preservatives may also be added at this stage, such as glycerin or benzene. All ointments must also contain a thickener; both lanolin and cocoa butter are thickeners, which is why they are now the preferred base substance used by most herbalists. Other thickeners include glycerin (which is also a preservative), honey, and agar (seaweed extract).

Chickweed Ointment: This helps relieve the irritation of itchy skin rashes, psoriasis and similar complaints.

2 cups chopped chickweed
2 cups lanolin
2 - 3 tablespoons beeswax

Put the chickweed in a pan with the lanolin. Simmer for 10 minutes, stirring well. Strain through fine gauze into a glass jar. Heat the beeswax and add to the lanolin and chickweed. Apply generously when cool.

Juniper Berry Ointment: This ointment is helpful for relieving wounds, scratches, itching, burn scars, and sores. The berries should be collected wild just as they are ripening.

2 cups juniper berries
2 cups olive oil
2 - 3 tablespoons beeswax

Soak the berries overnight in water and strain in the morning. Simmer the berries in the oil, while heating the beeswax in a separate container. Strain out the berries and add the melted beeswax. If necessary, reheat and add extra wax. Apply generously to affected area when cool.

Syrups, Gargles and Lozenges

The only difference between syrups, gargles and lozenges is that a hardener is added to the recipe to make lozenges. All are used for easing the effects of a cold or sore throat. Gargles are sometimes made with herbs that have an astringent effect—they tighten the membranes of the air passages, relieving tickly coughs. All are made by mixing a herb or plant with a suitably thick solvent such as honey or sugar. The syrup which is formed helps to line the passages of the upper respiratory system allowing the active ingredient of the herb to take effect. Here are three examples:

Hyssop Cough Syrup

1 cup honey
¼ cup water
2 tablespoons flowering hyssop tops
1 tablespoon aniseeds

Pour the honey and water into a saucepan and stir thoroughly until a thick syrup is formed. Slowly bring the syrup to a boil over medium heat, and skim off any impurities that form on the surface. Dampen the dried hyssop with a tablespoon of water and crush the aniseeds with a spoon. Stir the hyssop and the crushed aniseeds into the syrup. Simmer for 30 minutes. Allow to cool, then strain into a jar or bottle. Give two teaspoons for an irritated throat.

Astringent Raspberry Leaf Gargle

1 tablespoon dried raspberry leaves
1 tablespoon powdered cankerrot
2 cups boiling water
1 - 3 teaspoons honey

Place the raspberry leaves and the powdered cankerrot in a teapot and pour the boiling water over them. Steep for 10 minutes, then strain into a container. Add the honey. Allow to cool to room temperature. Store in refrigerator, and use within three days of preparing. Gargle one cupful as required.

Horehound Cough Drops

1 cup boiling water
¾ cup dried horehound

2 cups refined sugar
½ teaspoon cream of tartar

Steep the horehound for 30 minutes in the boiling water. Strain the solution into a saucepan while pressing to extract all the liquid. Add the sugar and the cream of tartar and stir over low heat until the sugar is fully dissolved. Cover the pan and cool for 3 to 4 minutes until the steam has melted any sugar crystals clinging to the side of the pan. Remove the lid and cook the mixture, without stirring, over high heat. Skim off any scum. Test the mixture with a cold spoon—if it begins to harden on the spoon, remove immediately from the heat. Pour the mixture onto a buttered or oiled baking sheet. As it begins to set, cut into convenient-sized pieces. When cold store in a suitable container.

Poultices and Compresses

The tree moss poultice which historically was used on infected wounds for its antibiotic effect is now almost legendary. A poultice is a fresh herb which has been cut, crushed and then mashed so that the active healing ingredients seep out. Tinctures and infusions are sometimes used as a base for a poultice or compress.

Both are applied directly to the body with pressure, either dry or damp, surrounded by a clean cloth. They are normally used to heal bruises, reduce inflammation, heal infected wounds while removing pus and toxins, and to clear lung congestion. Cold poultices and compresses are used in inflamed areas, as they withdraw the heat that is present. Hot poultices and compresses relax muscles in spasm and ease pain.

Many poultices and compresses make use of items that are not necessarily associated with herbalism. These include: yeast, for boils; salt, to draw pain; wine vinegar, for sprains, strains and aching muscles; rice, for painful wounds. Here are two recipes for poultices and compresses:

Plantain Poultice: Plantain is an invaluable herb in first aid; it helps to ease the pain of an open wound, and accelerate the healing process.

Crush or mash the plantain and directly apply it to the wound site. Keep it in place with a bandage or clean cloth. Replace it with a fresh poultice after 5 minutes. Repeat until the pain and discomfort has eased.

Linseed Poultice: This is used to reduce inflammation and soreness, particularly around joints.

1 pint boiling water
¼ pound linseed
½ ounce olive oil

Pour the boiling water into a basin. Sprinkle in the linseed and the olive oil, making sure to stir constantly. Spread the mixture thickly on a piece of clean linen and fold over. Apply to the inflamed area.

Several Commonly Used Medicinal Herbs

It would be impossible in a chapter of this size to provide information on all the medicinal plants which are used within herbalism. We have therefore listed a small selection which are regularly used in herbal remedies, are historically associated with witchcraft, and may be used by the reader.

Angelica *(Angelica archangelica)*: During the Middle Ages this herb was believed to ward off evil spirits and protect from curses and was often worn as an amulet for this reason. It was also believed to protect from contagious diseases. Until the beginning of the twentieth century, people chewed on it in the belief that it would ward off illness. It has a stimulating effect on the digestive system, and helps to relieve coughs. It can be taken in the form of an infusion, tincture or medicinal wine.

Arnica *(Arnica montana)*: Traditionally, this herb was believed to ward off large predators, particularly big cats. It has acquired the name 'leopard's bane' for this reason. It has been used medicinally since the sixteenth century, being prescribed as a stimulant for the heart and circulation. In recent years it has become popular in health-food shops as a homeopathic remedy, and is used in pill form for healing wounds. If taken in large internal doses, it has a toxic effect, so we recommend that it only be used in poultices and compresses (to reduce inflammation) until the practitioner has gained experience.

Basil *(Ocimum basilicum)*: During the Middle Ages this herb became associated with the mythical basilisk----the dragonlike reptile that could kill with a glance. Some believed it was a cursed plant; the Romans even trod the ground underfoot with curses, asking the

240

gods to make sure it did not flourish. Others believed the reverse, and in the Middle Ages it was carried as a talisman against black magic and to attract love. It is used in the form of a tea (infusion) to relieve nausea and stomach pains. It has been shown scientifically to be a cure for dysentery—the herb inhibits the growth of the bacteria. It also relieves the pain of menstruation and reduces fever.

Deadly Nightshade *(Atropa belladonna)*: Its Latin name, *Atropa*, is the name of one of the three fates. She traditionally cut the thread of life, and the plant inherited the name due to the fact that it is highly toxic. The second name *belladonna* is Italian for "fair lady"; it was customary during the Renaissance for Italian women to use it in the form of eye drops to enlarge the pupils. Several chemicals which are derived from this plant are used medically. These include scopolamine, hyoscyamine and of course atropine. They are used as sedatives, muscle relaxants, and antispasmodics for a variety of conditions. Because of its toxicity it should only be used in herbalism as an ointment for the treatment of gout and rheumatism (and regardless of the Italian custom, never on the eyes).

Elder *(Sambucus nigra)*: The elder tree has been held in high esteem by witch and country folk alike. It was often (and still is) referred to as "the lady's tree," having strong associations with many of the pre-Christian goddesses of Europe.

> Elder is the Lady's tree;
> Burn it not, or cursed you'll be.

It was traditional up to the nineteenth century to bow and lift your hat as you passed it as a sign of respect. It was also said that it would only grow near a house if its inhabitants were happy, and that it would help to protect them from evil. Probably because of its associations with the Goddess, it was believed to have strong healing qualities. The flowers and berries make an excellent wound ointment for cuts, scalds and burns. The buds can be used in lozenges as a laxative, and an infusion of elder flowers helps to soothe the nerves and acts as a diuretic. It was also used in a traditional cure for epilepsy. The berries of the elder can help to soothe coughs in the form of a syrup, as well as relieving any difficulties in breathing. With so many healing qualities it is not surprising it was treated with so much respect! It is probably the only tree which gives an excellent red wine (from the berries) and an equally good white wine (from the flowers).

Mandrake *(Atropa mandragora)*: The mythology surrounding mandrake abounds, and no book on herbalism and witchcraft would be complete without mentioning it! It belongs to the *Solonaceae* family of herbs, which also include henbane, deadly nightshade (see above) and thornapple. (In America a medicinal plant called *Podophyllum peltatum* is known as American mandrake, but they are not the same plant.) The mandrake was believed to be half human and half vegetable, due to the root often taking the form of a homunculus or human-like figure. It was prized by witches and sorcerers as a familiar----a spirit willing to help the individual who possessed it.

Because it was so highly prized, several myths were developed to prevent it being taken by anyone who was not occult inclined. One such myth claims that when pulled from the earth it gives out a fearful scream which kills anyone who hears it. An ivory staff was said to be needed to loosen the earth around the root. A hungry dog should then be tied to the top of the root by its tail. The sorcerer collecting the root should protect himself within three magic circles, and make sure that he was downwind from the screams and that his ears were blocked with sealing wax. He should then entice the dog with fresh meat. The dog would leap at the meat, pulling the root from the ground, and then, no doubt, the poor dog would die from the screams! It was also said to give off a narcotic and stupefying scent. There is some truth in this, as it does have anesthetic qualities and was used in the early days of surgery for this reason. It is highly poisonous if used wrongly, so we recommend its use only as a magical amulet.

Mistletoe *(Viscum album)*: Mistletoe is a semiparasitic plant, well known for being the sacred plant of Druidism (the Golden Bough). Although this association attributes it to being found on oak trees, it is actually more common on apple and poplar. In early herbalism it was said to be a cure for epilepsy and dropsy. It is known to be good for the circulation, being an antisclerotic. In recent years medical science has also discovered that it has anticarcinogenic properties. In large amounts this herb is toxic and we recommend avoiding internal use until experience is gained. As a lotion, compress, or poultice, it has the effect of cleansing the skin and loosening stiff joints.

Mugwort *(Artemisia vulagaris)*: This herb was once referred to by herbalists as *Mater Herbarum* or "the Mother of Herbs." Because mugwort's leaves are silver on the underside it was associated with the Moon, as well as Venus, astrologically. This lunar association resulted in it being named *Artemisia* (Artemis is the Greek equivalent of the Roman Diana), but its link with the Goddess of the Witches probably has deeper roots than this. It was believed that a tea made of mugwort could instill psychic ability—a true witches brew—and that its leaves increased menstrual flow and aided childbirth. These qualities directly link it to the practice of witchcraft and midwifery, a role that the village witch once fulfilled.

Saint John's Wort *(Hypericum perforatum)*: Saint John's wort was once known as *fuga dedemonum*, the "devil's scourge," because it was believed to ward off evil spirits. It traditionally flowers on the Summer Solstice, and was gathered on Midsummer Eve as a charm against ill fortune. According to custom, Saint John's wort was suspended in the doorway of one's house to prevent evil from entering. As a traditional prescription for madness, many believed that if it was hung around the neck of a possessed person it would drive out or exorcise evil spirits. Superstition aside, as an ointment it is an excellent astringent for skin irritations, insect bites and other wounds. It also has anti-inflammatory and antibacterial properties, and was used by Native Americans to treat tuberculosis with remarkable success.

Yarrow *(Achillea milleofolium)*: During the Middle Ages yarrow was used as a love charm. A girl who wished to see her future love had to collect the herb when the new moon was in the sky. Then she would sew the herbs into a flannel bag. In order to dream of her future love, she would place the bag beneath her pillow while reciting the following verse:

> Thou pretty herb of Venus' tree
> Thy true name is yarrow;
> Now who my bosom friend may be
> Pray tell thou me tomorrow.

As a poultice, this herb was used by the ancient Greeks to treat cuts, burns, bruises and wounds, hence its name *Achillea*, referring to the hero Achilles of Homer's *Iliad,* who is said to have given the herb to his soldiers to stanch the flow of blood from their wounds. It is more commonly used by herbalists to reduce fever and encourage appetite in the form of an infusion, decoction or tincture. It also has anti-inflammatory and astringent properties.

Rue *(Ruta graveolens)*: Rue has strong associations with Italian witchcraft. It was worn as an amulet, the *cimaruta* or *cima di ruta* (Italian for "sprig of rue"). Jewelry made of silver was modeled after it, with occult symbolism often incorporated into the design. Rue was often referred to as "the herb of grace" and was believed to be pleasing to Diana, the queen of Italian witchcraft. The herb was worn to show you were a worshipper of that Goddess. Rue was believed to bring good luck and protect the wearer from the evil eye. Medicinally, this herb is an antispasmodic, and is also believed by some to be beneficial in suppressing coughs and encouraging menstruation, the last being the probable reason it was associated with a female lunar deity.

15

Last Rites

In this final chapter, we have decided to cover the subject of death----an area which has not only been neglected in western culture, but also in many pagan publications. We are not only going to cover the final passage rite of the soul, but also one other area that the healer as priest or priestess within the pagan community will have to be prepared for----the subject of bereavement counseling, both for friends and loved ones, and for those preparing for their death. In our travels to the United States, we have come across pagan priests and priestesses counseling the terminally ill, particularly victims of HIV.

It may seem strange to include the subject of death in a book on healing, but according to pagan philosophy (as with Buddhism) it is seen as the final act of healing----the unification of all aspects of the soul through self-reconciliation. In pagan myth this is continually shown as an act of judgment, just as it is in the Christian Bible. The main difference is that the pagans view the afterlife as a self-judgment----a learning from past mistakes in preparation for the next reincarnation of the soul.

Our ancestors indisputably considered last rites as their most important rite of passage. Most of the paleolithic sites which have been discovered were once used for death rites. Such sites include the Valley of the Kings and the Pyramids in Egypt, Newgrange in Ireland, and the numerous dolmen, tumuli and burial mounds of western Europe. Death rites and the customs pertaining to them appear in all the world's cultures, as death is an essential part of the human experience. It is not surprising that most of these rites are similar.

Such rites have remained intact within much of the world. They are still an important part of Islamic, Hindu, Shinto and Buddhist culture, but within the Western world their use has declined. Only in Roman Catholicism and Judaism has some sort of spiritual care for the dead survived. Protestantism seems to have abandoned it almost completely. Society in the West has become afraid of death. This is best summed up by Sogyal Rinpoche, a Tibetan Buddhist who first came to the West in the 1970s:

> ...What disturbed me deeply, and has continued to disturb me, is the almost complete lack of spiritual help for the dying that exists in modern culture.... I have been told of many stories of people dying alone and in great distress and disillusion in the West without any spiritual help.... Wherever I go in the West, I am struck by the great mental suffering that arises from the fear of dying, whether or not this fear is acknowledged. In Tibet it was a natural response to pray for the dying and to give them spiritual care; in the West, the only spiritual attention that the majority pay to the dying is to go to their funeral.

This may be due to the Christian church's past theology of the afterlife being a place of eternal damnation if you sin, rather than a place of love, joy and reconciliation. This has resulted in society trying to ignore the subject altogether because of fear of what will come after death. It is not just the failure of orthodox Western religion which is to blame, but also the mechanistic view of the universe which developed after the industrial revolution. Under this view, spiritual belief was relegated to the realm of superstition—the philosophy being that there is no proof of a spiritual afterlife, therefore it does not exist.

This viewpoint has instilled even more fear, and has resulted in a society which not only inadequately expresses death within its culture, but also encourages people to avoid contact with those who are grieving or who are close to death, for fear of having to face unanswered questions.

Pagans themselves are only just beginning to realize the importance of the spiritual preparation for death; it has taken so long because the Wiccan (and then pagan) revival developed within declining Protestant cultures. Pagans realize that such rites perform a role socially, helping those who grieve to come to terms with their loss. Janet and Stewart realized the importance of such rites when writing *Eight Sabbats For Witches,* and included a pagan requiem; and Raymond Buckland included a rite called 'crossing the bridge' (at death) within *The Tree: The Complete Book of Saxon Witchcraft.* Buckland introduces the rite as follows:

> Since the Seax-Wica, in company with other traditions, believe in reincarnation, death is a time for celebration rather than grief. Death signifies the completion of a learning period----the individual has "graduated" and will be going on to other things. This they feel, should be celebrated. Sorrow, then, is a sign of selfishness. We are sorry for ourselves, that we have been left behind without the love and company of one dear to us.

But these requiems are not last rite rituals; they are centered purely around the act of saying farewell to a friend. What is equally important is the act of performing a rite on someone close to death, or immediately after death, so that he or she is made aware of the need to pass over to the other side. If this ritual is not performed, the personality embodied in the lower mental/emotional aspects of the astral body (spiritual and mental/emotional auras, see page 90, chapter 6) may remain on the physical plane, which causes the person confusion and results in psychic disturbance around the area of death; the place becomes haunted by the restless spirit of that person who is desperately trying to seek the attention of the living.

What actually happens at the moment of death is unproven, and it will probably remain so. But we do know what is reported back to us from those who have undergone near-death experiences---- those who have actually died and been revived. The description seems to be the same among all cultures. Such people describe retaining what appears to be their physical body, even though their actual lifeless body may be seen in front of them. What they are actually describing as their body is the lower mental aspect of their spirit----their perception of what their body looks like and feels like.

They often also describe a "silver cord" or "cord of light" connecting the components of their astral body to their physical body. This cord is often seen during the more pronounced forms of out-of-body experiences. It normally breaks at the moment of death (although there is one theory that it is part of the etheric body). The etheric body is the last part of the astral body to break down; the energy from it dissipates as the physical body cools down and starts to deteriorate. Theoretically, this may explain why it is not safe to revive someone who has been dead more than three minutes. Brain damage normally sets in after the brain is deprived of oxygen for this long. There may be a relationship between this and the break-down of the etheric aura. However, this process appears to be slowed if the physical body is cooled down suddenly----in drowning, for example, people have been successfully revived after 15 to 20 minutes.

People who go through near-death experiences almost always described a light----a brightly lit circular tunnel, which is the journey from this world to the next. Some describe it as spiraling; others say that it is full of mist. One particular theory formulated by Gavin is that the tunnel is actually the person's crown chakra center (see page 98, chapter 6), and that the journey along it is the ascent and absorption of the rest of the chakra system into it. Those that have returned from death describe traveling up it, being beckoned on by loved ones standing at the other side. They describe a feeling of total tranquillity and peace on completing the journey, before abruptly being told they have to go back because it isn't their time yet. Those that wake up after having such a complete experience are often annoyed at being brought back to the physical realm, much to the confusion of the medical team that has resuscitated them. As Gavin can vouch for, most doctors and nurses can recount such stories.

Most hauntings where the ghost is of the nature we have already mentioned, are in places where a violent or sudden death has taken place. Typical of these in modern times are car accidents, places where someone has died suddenly of a heart attack without prior warning, or violent deaths such as shootings or stabbings. The death happens so fast that the person is unaware of what has happened, and therefore is unaware of what to do next; he or she does not go toward the light and does not realize the need to travel up it. Passage rites which inform the newly dead of their situation, and what they are to do next, are therefore of vital importance in cases of violent death.

There are of course other reasons why individuals do not pass over. One of these is the belief that the afterlife is a place of punishment rather than of joy and forgiveness. Unfortunately, it is enforced Christian dogma that is to blame in these cases; the discarnate people genuinely believe that they will go to Hell if they pass into the light.

One other reason for a person's spirit remaining materially bound is a feeling of obligation to protect loved ones for some reason (a good example of this was shown in the film *Ghost*). The spirit will not go over until sure that the family or loved one is safe. One frequent instance of this is where a recently dead elderly person may remain earthbound waiting for his or her partner to die, but this will only normally happen if the deaths are close together; which is not unusual among devoted elderly couples.

One other occurrence which confirms the need for last rites is the number of individuals who go through a particular form of traumatic event during past-life regression (see page 200, chapter 12). A number of clients recount postmortem examinations. These memories distress the clients during regression and disrupt what should otherwise be a comfortable experience. In some cases the clients are able to describe the whole procedure vividly, which has a marked effect on their psychological well-being. There are a number of reasons why this is happening. First of all, the number of post-death examinations has increased since the end of the Second World War because the medical profession is seeking more and more knowledge about disease and illness and such examinations are required in cases of violent death. Relatives are also more likely to agree to such examinations.

Second, from a psychic viewpoint, the normal occurrence at death is for the etheric body to break down and the cord to be released, allowing the spirit of the person to go to the other side. But prior to postmortem examinations it is normal procedure for the physical body to be kept either frozen or at least well below body temperature to preserve it. This may well have the effect of causing both the etheric body and the cord to remain intact and keep the person's spirit earthbound until the natural course of events is resumed.

As postmortems are normal for violent deaths, there is also the possibility that the spirit accompanies the body, due to its state of confusion, and witnesses the examinations that take place. We would like to point out that this is all theory on Gavin's part; we do not want to alarm people. Such cases occurring in regression are rare. With correct preparation, both before and after death, such experiences can be avoided completely. We would also like to point out that postmortem examinations are an important part of medical research, and have been responsible for breakthroughs in medical knowledge.

Pagan Last Rites Ritual

The ritual we have created is for use immediately after death, or at any time after. The words and phrases of this ritual are written for the death of a practicing pagan; it is not intended for use with individuals of other spiritual beliefs. We strongly recommend, whether they are pagan or not, that the wishes of the individual, and the family, regarding last rites should be discussed at some time prior to death. This should be incorporated where possible into the final stages of bereavement counseling (see page 254). Where necessary the rites should be altered to suit their wishes, but the actions regarding the cutting of the cord and the auras should be retained (these are in fact the major actions of the rite, and the words of the ritual are not actually necessary after the death).

It is necessary for the priest or priestess to have some experience in using body energy. Therefore, this rite should only be carried out by those with some experience of working with the chakras and the aura, such as a spiritual healer.

Items Required:
approximately a yard of silver/white embroidery thread
small pair of scissors or small, sharp ritual knife (such as a Wiccan white-handled knife)
a small bowl of water
anointing oil (frankincense, myrrh or rose)
white virgin candle, lit and placed in the south

The priest or priestess stands on the south side of the body facing north. He or she places one end of the silver/white embroidery thread on the body's solar plexus, and the other end on the crown of the head. He or she then places hands into the etheric aura of the body and says the following:

> I ask the Guardians of the North to relinquish the earthly ties that bind the soul of (name of person) to this world, and to the lower planes of existence.

The priest or priestess then cuts the embroidery thread, and puts the scissors/small knife down. He or she then moves hands over the body's solar plexus (still within the etheric aura), and visualizes the silver cord breaking. From this point on, he or she is talking to the soul of the person who has just died who will be present in the room:

> (Name of person), it is time to leave this earthly plane, so I ask you to turn to the west, the place of death and initiation, the home of your ancestral spirits. Look for the light which is your passage from this world to the next, and those spirits which are waiting to guide you.

The priest or priestess then moves around the body, moving their hands up into the person's mental/emotional aura, and facing west over the body:

> I ask the Guardians of the West to open the doors between this world and the world beyond so that the ancestors, friends and loved ones may be welcome in this place of passing to guide the soul of (name of person) toward the light that he (she) seeks.

The priest or priestess takes the bowl of water and anoints the lips of the deceased. He or she then waves their hands within the body's mental/emotional aura and visualizes it parting from the physical body. Then addressing the soul of the person again:

> (Name of person), as you leave this earthly realm let those who have loved you guide you toward the lesser light that shall lead to the greater, for toward the south lies the dawning of the greater light and the extinguishing of the lesser. May you never thirst upon the journey that shall lead to your rebirth.

The priest or priestess moves around the body so that he or she is facing the south and can easily blow out the candle:

> I ask the Guardians of the South to assist (name of person) in extinguishing the lesser light that holds all ties to this earthly plane, that he/she may see the greater light that calls from the realm of peace that is truly the dwelling place of the gods.

The priest or priestess blows out the candle, and addresses the soul of the deceased:

> (Name of person), as together we have extinguished the lesser light, perceive now the greater light of the eastern

sunrise that calls to you. Let all fear and regrets be left in this place and move toward the joy and happiness that await you. Let those who are with you embrace you with their love, and lead you to the home of the shining ones.

The priest or priestess moves around the body and faces the east:

I ask the Guardians of the East to show forth the glory of the light of rebirth that is between the realms of this world and the world of rest and renewal.

The priest or priestess anoints the body with oil on the third eye, and addresses the soul of the person:

(Name of person), go forward now, free of all earthly ties into the embrace of the light that calls you, free spirit that you are. Fear not, for those you are leaving will be with you in spirit, as you will always be with them. For you shall meet, know, remember, and love them again, in future lives to come.

The priest or priestess pulls the sheet or shroud, which is on the body, over the head, and says:

Farewell, dear friend. This rite is ended.

It is not necessary to banish the guardians of the quarters. They should be left to depart as and when they are ready.

Passing Over and Exorcism

The only difference between a last rite and a rite of passing over is the time that elapses between death and the rite of passage involved. A passing over is the assisting of a long-dead individual or spirit to leave the physical world and pass on to the next incarnation. Exorcism is quite different from passing over as it banishes a spirit or demon rather than assisting it.

Exorcism originates from the Roman Catholic Church, which has its own officially appointed exorcists, as do the Episcopalean Churches. Initially, the term "exorcism" was related to possession---the intrusion of the mental/emotional body of a dead person into a living physical body. The Catholic Church also believed that such possessions could be caused by demons and devils; this was in fact a useful explanation of mental illness when knowledge of the human mind and its workings was limited.

Since then, exorcism has come to mean any procedure which involves the removal of a ghost or spirit from a physical area. It is based on the principle that all earthbound spirits are either of demonic origin, or are the souls of the dead who are tormented by the evil they have committed in life. The principle aim of exorcism is to rid the living of the inconvenience of dealing with troublesome psychic disturbances, rather than helping disturbed spirits pass over; this form of exorcism can hardly be regarded as an act of spiritual healing.

Many appointed exorcists within the Roman Catholic Church now have a modern viewpoint on the subject, and realize that the discarnate spirit of a person is neither evil nor demonic, but they do understand that the spirit is in turmoil. They tend to use the Roman Catholic last-rites rituals, rather than the banishments the Church used during the Middle Ages. They also realize that many possessions are nothing more than mental illness; Gavin has actually witnessed a priest bringing a possessed person to the local psychiatric hospital.

The only time the use of exorcism is valid is when the psychic disturbance is of elemental origin. Generally, these disturbances result when uncontrolled thought forms cause telekinetic disturbances—poltergeist activity. This type of phenomenon normally occurs in an area where there is emotional stress between several individuals. Usually, one of the individuals concerned is psychically gifted in some way without knowing it. This person acts as the psychic amplifier for the situation and will be the focus for all the unusual occurrences.

There are groups of would-be ghost hunters and exorcists who dabble in this area with little knowledge, or compassion for those souls earthbound and in turmoil. Unfortunately, they occasionally appear in the pagan community, believing that casting a circle and telling the spirit "to be gone!" is enough. One example is provided by a woman in Ireland, a self-styled exorcist, who casts a large circle around a haunted house to protect herself. This action unfortunately prevents the spirit from departing. She also on one occasion appeared on the radio, giving details of a poltergeist haunting. This could in fact have the effect of increasing the disturbances; sometimes a haunted house becomes haunted because of the psychic energy people give to it. People who dabble in this area should be discouraged, just as dabblers should be in any other area of the occult. To quote the old maxim: "A little knowledge is a dangerous thing!"

We recommend that pagans adapt the last-rites ritual we have written in this chapter if they have to deal with a displaced soul. They may consecrate a poppet (see page 143, chapter 9) and use this as a surrogate body to perform the actions regarding the cord cutting and the auras.

Bereavement Counseling

The counseling procedures for bereaved relatives or for people who are terminally ill or close to death are the same as for any other form of counseling (see chapter 12). However, the psychological processes involved are different. Those dealing with death----either their own or that of someone close to them----go through several emotional stages, which often include periods of denial, anger, bargaining, depression, and the final acceptance of the situation. As individuals, they may miss any of these emotional stages or go through one of them earlier than the others.

The main role of the counselor in the bereavement process is to aid the individual through the transition from one stage of grief to the next. This should be done so that the transition is as smooth and painless as possible up to the final stage----acceptance.

The Five Stages of the Grieving Process

1. **Denial**: In its lesser form, denial may be the refusal to accept that the individual is affected emotionally by the situation; in its more extreme form, may mean the complete denial of the situation----a withdrawal from the outside world, and the creation of a fantasy that life has not changed in any way. A good example of this is a bereaved partner who continues to prepare meals or wash clothes for the dead partner. A common denial is for the terminally ill not to accept the diagnosis and continually question its validity. Denial normally passes very quickly, with the sudden realization by the bereaved that his or her life has changed forever.

2. **Anger**: Anger develops as a response to the feeling of helplessness caused by bereavement, and the inability to cope emotionally with the loss. It may develop slowly alongside the period of denial, and explode when realization finally comes. This anger

can be quite irrational, and the bereaved person is very likely to lash out at anyone who tries to help, particularly if he or she is still denying that there is a problem. This is something important to take into account if you intend to counsel a bereaved person. Anger can be directed at the self, at other members of the family, at the cause of the bereavement, at life and the gods in general, or at all of these at different times.

3. **Bargaining**: When the bereaved start to come to terms with what has happened, they typically blame themselves with questions such as, "If only I had done this," or "Why does this have to happen to me?" or "What have I done to deserve this?" At this stage counseling becomes important, by helping the individual come to terms with what has happened, without guilt or recrimination. With the terminally ill, this is the time when the counselor should be helping them come to terms with their immanent death, while making them realize that pondering on past possibilities will not help the situation. It is not unusual, if the bargaining process is not resolved, for the bereaved to return to the anger stage, which will prolong the grieving process.

4. **Depression**: Depression comes from the realization, after the bargaining process, that there is nothing that can be done to change the situation. It is during this period that the counselor brings the spirituality of the bereaved into the healing process. Traditionally, within most cultures, this is the time when the funeral or requiem should take place to aid the process for the bereaved relatives.

5. **Acceptance**: After all of the above stages have been dealt with, emotionally and spiritually, the individual is ready for acceptance. Sometimes, those who are approaching death who have come to terms with their mortality enter a period of elation, describing a feeling that they are living more now than they had previously. Many who are bereaved by the death of relatives or loved ones describe a similar experience, but this seems to center on a feeling of relief rather than elation.

Somebody approaching death over a period of time may go through these stages gently. In fact, the elderly normally enter a stage where they prepare for death several years before the actual event, and in such cases, counseling is obviously not needed. It is only when a person is emotionally distressed for a prolonged period resulting in the inability to move on to the final stage of acceptance, that counseling is called for. If a person dies feeling angry, this may result in what we have already mentioned above----the ghost, the lower mental/emotional element of the astral body, becomes earth-bound. Such people, because of their anger, quite simply refuse to accept that they are dead .

Bibliography

Balkam, Jan. *Aromatherapy: A Practical Guide to Essential Oils and Aromassage.* Leicester, England: Blitz Editions, 1994.

Bates, Brian. *The Way of Wyrd.* London: Arrow Books, 1987.

Battersby, William. *The Three Sisters at the Well.* Kells, Co. Meath: William Battersby, 1991.

Blades, Dudley. *Spiritual Healing.* Wellingborough, England: Aquarian Press, 1979.

Blatavsky, H.P. *The Secret Doctrine.* Los Angeles: The Theosophy Company, 1964.

Bord, Janet and Colin. *Earth Rites.* London: Granada Publishing Ltd., 1982.

Brennan, B.A. *Hands of Light.* New York: Bantam Books, 1987.

Buchman, D. *Herbal Medicine.* London: Rider and Company, 1983.

Buckland, R. *The Tree: The Complete Book of Saxon Witchcraft.* York Beach, Maine: Samuel Weiser, 1974.

Burland, C.A. *The Magical Arts.* London: Arthur Barkland Ltd., 1966.

Cahill, S, & Halpern, J. *The Ceremonial Circle.* London: Harper-Collins, 1991.

Capra, Fritjof. *The Tao of Physics.* London: Wildwood House, 1976.

Cavendish, Richard. *A History of Magic.* London: Sphere Books Ltd., 1978.

Coddington, Robert. *Death Brings Many Surprises.* New York: Ballantine Books, 1987.

Conway, David. *The Magic of Herbs*. London: Jonathan Cape Ltd., 1973.

Crowley, Aleister. *777*. York Beach, Maine: Samuel Weiser, 1970.

Culpeper, Nicholas. *Culpeper's Complete Herbal*. London: Foulsham, 1652.

Curries, Ian. *You Cannot Die*. Shaftesbury, England: Element Books Ltd., 1978.

Drury, Nevill. *The Elements of Shamanism*. Shaftesbury, England: Element Books Ltd., 1989.

Eliade, Mircea. *Shamanism: Archaic Techniques of Ecstasy*. New Jersey: Princeton University Press, 1972.

Ennemoser, Joseph. *The History of Magic, Vol. One*. New York: University Books Inc., 1970.

Farrar, Janet and Stewart. *Eight Sabbats for Witches*. London: Robert Hale, 1981.

---------. *The Witches Way*. London: Robert Hale, 1984.

---------. *The Witches' Goddess*. London: Robert Hale, 1987.

---------. *The Witches' God*. London: Robert Hale, 1989.

---------. *Spells and How They Work*. London: Robert Hale, 1990.

---------. *Dictionary of World Deities*. Unpublished manuscript.

Farrar, J & S, and Bone, G. *The Pagan Path*. Blaine, Washington: Phoenix Publishing, 1995.

Fortune, Dion. *Psychic Self Defence*. York Beach, Maine: Samuel Weiser, 1982.

---------. *The Mystical Qabalah*. London: Ernest Benn Ltd., 1972.

Frazer, J.G. *The Golden Bough*. London: MacMillan Press Ltd., 1974.

Gauqelin, Michel. *Astrology and Science*. London: Granada Publishing Ltd., 1972.

Gladstar, Rosemary. *Herbal Healing for Women*. London: Bantam Books, 1994.

Gray, Eden. *A Complete Guide to the Tarot*. London: Studio Vista, 1970.

Halevi, Z'ev ben Shimon. *Tree of Life, an Introduction to the Cabala*. London: Rider and Company, 1972.

Hall, C.S, and Nordby, V.J. *A Primer of Jungian Psychology*. New York: Mentor Books, 1973.

Hampden-Turner, Charles. *Maps of the Mind*. London: Mitchell Beazley, 1981.

Harner, Michael. *The Way of the Shaman*. New York: Harper and Row, 1980.

Hartley, Christine. *A Case for Reincarnation*. London: Robert Hale, 1972.

Jackson, Richard. *Massage Therapy*. Wellingborough, England: Thorsons Publishers Ltd., 1977.

Jacobi, Jolande. *The Psychology Of C. G. Jung*. London: Routledge and Kegan Paul, 1962.

Judith, Anodea. *The Truth about Chakras*. Saint Paul, Minnesota: Llewellyn Publications, 1994.

---------. *Wheels Of Life*. Saint Paul, Minnesota: Llewellyn Publications, 1994.

Jung, Carl Gustav. *Four Archetypes*. London: Routledge and Kegan Paul, 1972.

Larousse. *Larousse World Mythology*. Secaucus, New Jersey: Chartwell Books Inc., 1973.

Leadbetter C.W. *The Chakras, a Monograph*. Eighth reprint. Adyar: The Theosphical Publishing House, 1969.

Lethbridge, T. C. *Ghost and Divining Rod*. London: Routledge and Kegan Paul, 1963.

Lissner, Ivar. *The Living Past*. London: The Reprint Society, 1960.

Logan, Patrick. *Making the Cure*. Dublin: Talbot Press, 1972.

Lovelock, J.E. *GAIA: A New Look at Life on Earth*. London: Oxford University Press, 1979.

Lumley, Craven and Aitken. *Essential Anatomy*. London: Churchill Livingstone, 1973.

May, Rollo. *The Art of Counselling*. New York: Gardner Press, 1989.

McNaught and Callandar. *Nurses' Illustrated Physiology*. London: Churchill Livingstone, 1983.

Mellor, Constance. *Natural Remedies for Common Ailments*. London: C.W. Daniel Company, 1973.

Moss, P. and Heeton, J. *Encounters with the Past*. London: Sidgwick and Jackson, 1979.

Murray, Margaret. *The Witch Cult in Western Europe*. Oxford: Oxford University Press, 1921.

Neumann, Erich. *The Great Mother*. London: Routledge and Kegan Paul, 1963.

Oesterreich, T.K. *Possession and Exorcism*. New York: Causeway Books, 1974.

O'Farrell, Ursula. *First Steps in Counselling*. Dublin: Veritas Publications, 1990.

Patrick, Richard. *All Colour Book of Greek Mythology*. London: Octopus Books, 1972.

Perowne, Stewart. *Roman Mythology*. London: Hamlyn, 1969.

Pinsent, John. *Greek Mythology*. London: Hamlyn, 1969.

Powell, A.E. *The Astral Body*. London: The Theosophical Publishing House, 1927.

--------. *The Mental Body*. London: The Theosophical Publishing House, 1927.

--------. *The Etheric Double*. London: The Theosophical Publishing House, 1925.

Price, Shirley. *Practical Aromatherapy*. London: HarperCollins, 1983.

Reader's Digest Magic and Medicine of Plants. New York: The Reader's Digest Association, 1989.

Rodrigues, L.J. *Anglo-Saxon Verse Charms, Maxims, and Heroic Legends*. Pinner, England: Anglo-Saxon Books, 1993.

Roose-Evans, J. *Passages of the Soul*. Shaftesbury, England: Element Books Ltd., 1994.

Roper, Nancy. *Using a Model for Nursing*. London: Churchill Livingston, 1983.

Sutphen, Dick. *You Were Born Again to Be Together*. New York: Pocket Books, 1976.

Sun Bear, and Wabun. *The Medicine Wheel*. New York: Prentice Hall Press, 1986.

Valiente, Doreen. *An ABC of Witchcraft Past and Present*. London: Robert Hale, 1973.

--------. *Witchcraft for Tomorrow*. London: Robert Hale, 1978.

Weinman, R.A. *Your Hands Can Heal*. Wellingborough, England: Aquarian Press, 1988.

Whitton, Dr. J., and Fisher, J. *Life Between Life*. London: Grafton Books, 1986.

Witt, R.E. *Isis in the Graeco-Roman World*. London: Thames and Hudson, 1971.

Wolfe, Amber. *In The Shadow of the Shaman*. Saint Paul, Minnesota: Llewellyn Publications, 1988.

Wren, R. C. *Potter's New Cyclopaedia of Botanical Drugs and Preparations*. Rustington, England: Health Science Press, 1970.

Index